North Carolina

Unforgettable Vintage Images of the Tar Heel State

Note from the Publisher

Royalties from the sale of this book and the others in the Best of Series will be donated to the National Trust for Historic Preservation. These funds will be used to further their work and provide support to the preservation movement nationwide.

NORTH CAROLINA

Unforgettable Vintage Images of the Tar Heel State

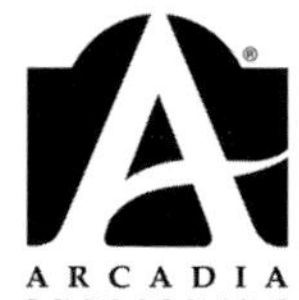

ISBN 978-0-7385-9712-6

Published by Arcadia Publishing
Charleston, South Carolina

Printed in the United States of America

Library of Congress Catalog Card Number: 00-104646

For all general information contact Arcadia Publishing at:
Telephone 843-853-2070
Fax 843-853-0044
E-mail sales@arcadiapublishing.com
For customer service and orders:
Toll-Free 1-888-313-2665

Visit us on the Internet at www.arcadiapublishing.com

Contents

INTRODUCTION

From Nags Head and Kill Devil Hills in the east, to the Great Smoky Mountains and the Cherokee National Forest in the west, from Mount Airy up north to Cape Fear in the south, North Carolina is a place of unparalleled beauty and uniquely rich in character.

Every schoolboy and girl learns early on about Virginia Dare, the first child born to English-speaking parents in the New World. Unfortunately, far fewer of us know the names of the Native American nations and tribes that called North Carolina home long before Sir Walter Raleigh sponsored the settlers at Roanoke Island in the 1580s. There were the Cheraw, the Eno, Chowan, and Moratok—and more familiar names like Cherokee, Waccamaw, and Hatteras.

Perhaps more familiar are the names of those native sons who reached the nation's highest office—Presidents Andrew Jackson, James K. Polk, and Andrew Johnson, who oversaw Reconstruction of the South after the Civil War. At the outset of that war, North Carolinians were greatly divided over the question of secession, although they finally voted to secede from the union on May 20, 1861. To its credit, the state supplied more men and material to the war effort than any other, but also suffered the greatest losses during the war. Popular sentiment attributes the coining of the state's nickname, "The Tar Heel State," to the Civil War period, referring to the state's soldiers as standing firm in battle, as if their heels were stuck in tar.

Perhaps the most significant event in the state's history came on December 17, 1903 at Kill Devil Hills near Kitty Hawk, when Orville and Wilbur Wright completed the first powered flight by man.

Today, we know North Carolina for its production of tobacco, and as the leading manufacturer of furniture and textiles. With its unique Research Triangle Park, the state is also a center for educational, institutional, governmental, and industrial research. But the richness of its people, and the grand beauty of its natural resources stand out as the most memorable aspect of North Carolina. Take a drive along the Blue Ridge Parkway, or sail the challenging waters off Cape Hatteras, to appreciate North Carolina for yourself.

Tom Rakness
Editor
Arcadia Publishing

Acknowledgments

Arcadia Publishing would like to thank the following authors and historical organizations. Your words and images have truly captured our hearts.

Authors

Piper Aheron	*From Avalon to Eden, A Postcard Tour of Rockingham County*
Norman D. Anderson	*Raleigh: North Carolina's Capital City in Postcards*
Durwood Barbour	*Johnston County*
Susan Taylor Block	*Along the Cape Fear*
	Cape Fear Lost
Mary Boccaccio	*Pitt County: Eastern Reflections*
J. Stephen Catlett	*Martin's and Miller's Greensboro*
Frances Eubanks	*Carteret County*
Monika S. Fleming	*Rocky Mount and Nash County*
	Echoes of Edgecombe County 1860–1940
	Edgecombe County Volume II
B.T. Fowler	*Raleigh: North Carolina's Capital City in Postcards*
Gayle Hicks Fripp	*Greensboro Volume II: Neighborhoods*
John Hairr	*Harnett County*
	Outer Banks
Fred W. Harrison Jr.	*Martin County*
Todd Johnson	*Johnston County*
Stephen E. Massengill	*Around Southern Pines: A Sandhills Album*
John R. Rodgers	*Charlotte: Its Historic Neighborhoods*
Amy T. Rodgers	*Charlotte: Its Historic Neighborhoods*
Lynn Salsi	*Carteret County*
Susan Goodman Sides	*Salisbury and Rowan County Postcards*
James Vickers	*Chapel Hill*

Historical Organizations

Many of the following organizations have multiple accreditations. In order to conserve space, the names of these organizations have been abbreviated.

Amon Carter Museum
Arizona Archives
Barnhill Contracting Company
Beaufort Historical Association
Blount-Bridges House (BBH)
Braswell Memorial Library
Cape Lookout National Seashore
Carteret Community College
Carteret County Historical Society
Charlotte Observer
Columbus County Historical Society
Core Sound Waterfowl Museum
County Doctor Museum
Duke University
East Carolina Manuscript Collection
East Carolina University Special Collections
Edgecombe County Historical Society
Edgecombe-Martin Electric Co-op
First Baptist Church
Forsyth County Genealogical Society
Greensboro Historical Society
Johnston County Room
Lewisville Historical Society
Martin County Historical Society
Nash Community College
Nash-Rocky Mount School School System (NRMS)
NC Division of Archives and History (NCDAH)
North Carolina Maritime Museum
Perkins Library
Rockingham County Community College Library & Archives
Rockingham County Historical Society
Rocky Mount Arts Center
Rocky Mount Telegram
Royal Photographs Center of Williamston
Second Ward High School Alumni Foundation
Sprint/Carolina Telephone and Telegraph
Tobaccoville Historical Society
Town of Macclesfield
Tufts Archives
U.S. Coast Guard
Washington D.C. National Archives (NA)
Wesleyan College Library
West Edgecombe Library
Wilmington Star News
Wilson Library at UNC-Chapel Hill
Edgecombe Community College Library
Edgecombe County Memorial Library (ECML)
Everett Library at Queens College
First Savings Bank of Southern Pines
Forsyth County Library (FCL)
Howard Memorial Presbyterian Church
Joyner Library at East Carolina University
Martin Community College Library
May Museum
Nash General Hospital
New Hanover County Library
North Carolina Fisheries Association
North Carolina State Museum of Natural History
Public Library of Charlotte and Mecklenburg County

One

To Shining Sea:
Along the Coast

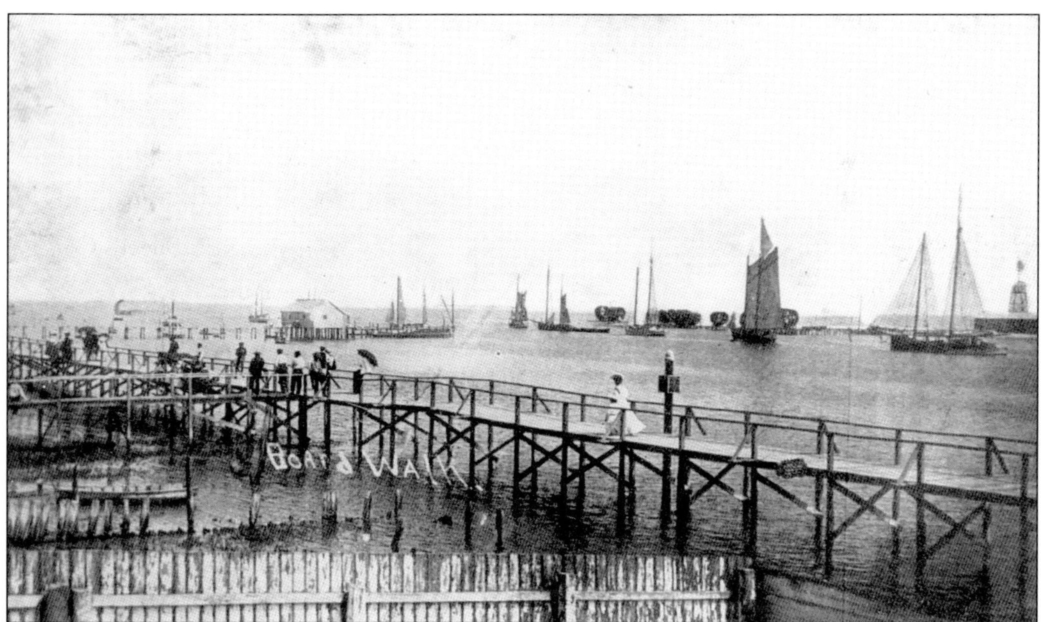

Around 1900, the old Beaufort boardwalk ran parallel to the waterfront with fingers that extended into Taylor's Creek. It was "the place" for a Sunday afternoon stroll along the "beach." Shortly before the turn of the century, Beaufort gained a reputation as a popular resort area for the elite. The boardwalk was enjoyed by visitors and townspeople. (Courtesy North Carolina Maritime Museum.)

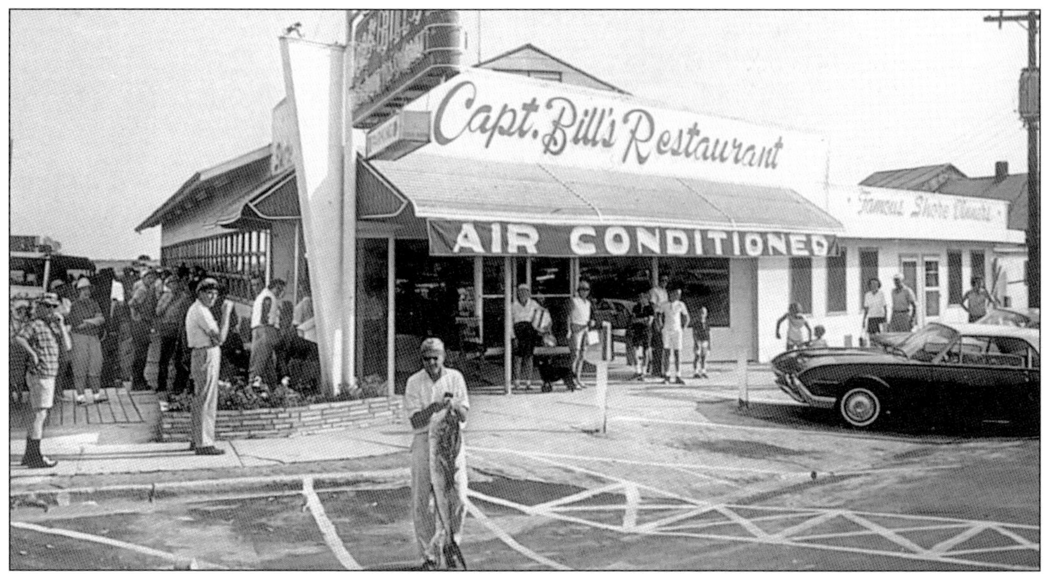

Captain Bill Headen Ballou remodeled a sailing club that had been an old fish house into a restaurant in 1945. Captain Bill's Waterfront Restaurant was one of the first in the area to have air conditioning. (Courtesy Billy Piner, private collection.)

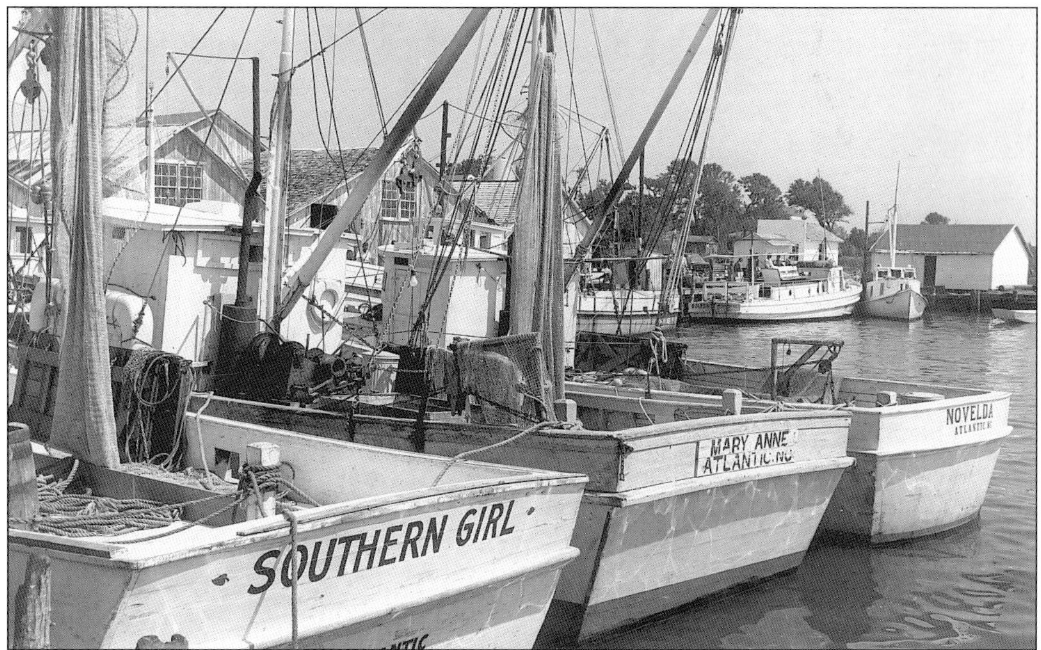

Commercial fishing is an important way of life and has always been vital to the Down East communities. Commercial fishing boats have filled community harbors since the first settlers, and boats and fishing have been a traditional part of daily life in the Atlantic community. Boats are pictured here in the Atlantic harbor in the 1940s. (Courtesy Carteret County Historical Society; photograph by Jerry Schumaker.)

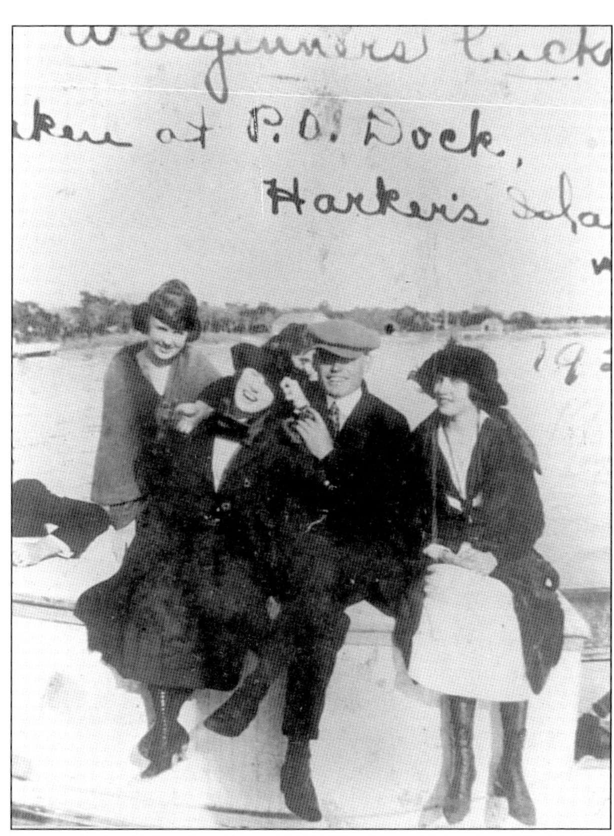

There was no road to Harkers Island when these schoolteachers arrived at the post office dock. The mailboat carried visitors, goods, and the mail from Beaufort to Harkers Island. (Courtesy Core Sound Waterfowl Museum.)

The Blessing of the Fleet was a tradition which encompassed all faiths. Held at the beginning of the fishing season, prayers are said for the boats and crew, the fishing nets, and for daily work. In the photograph below, the parade of boats are blessed and participants pay tribute to those whose lives have been lost at sea by throwing wreaths into the water. The Blessing of the Fleet in Morehead City is held on the first Sunday in October. (Photograph by Frances Eubanks.)

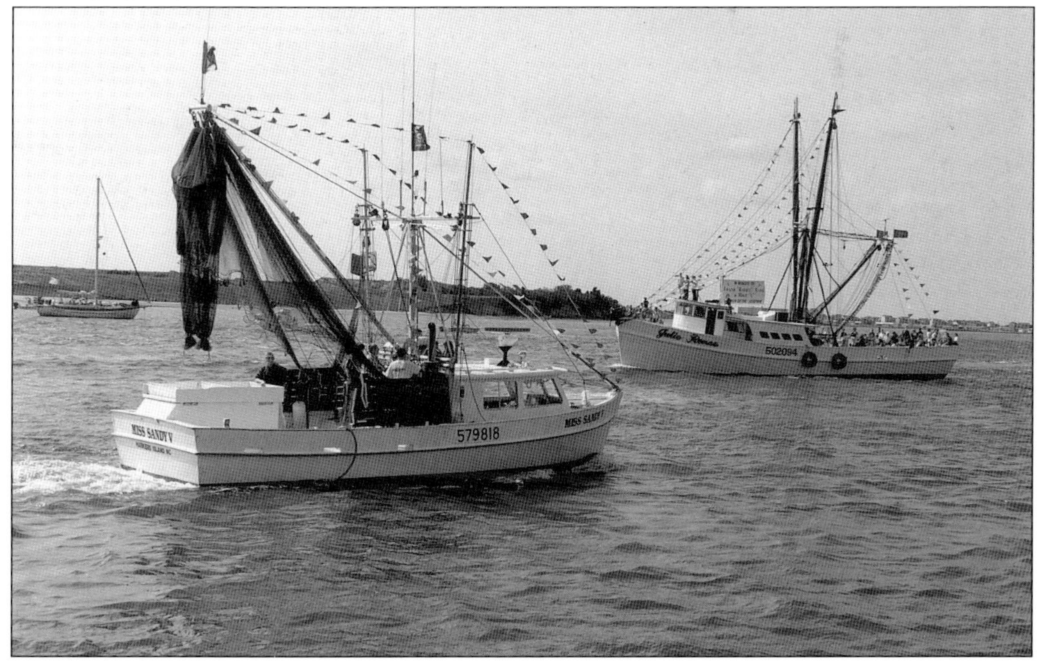

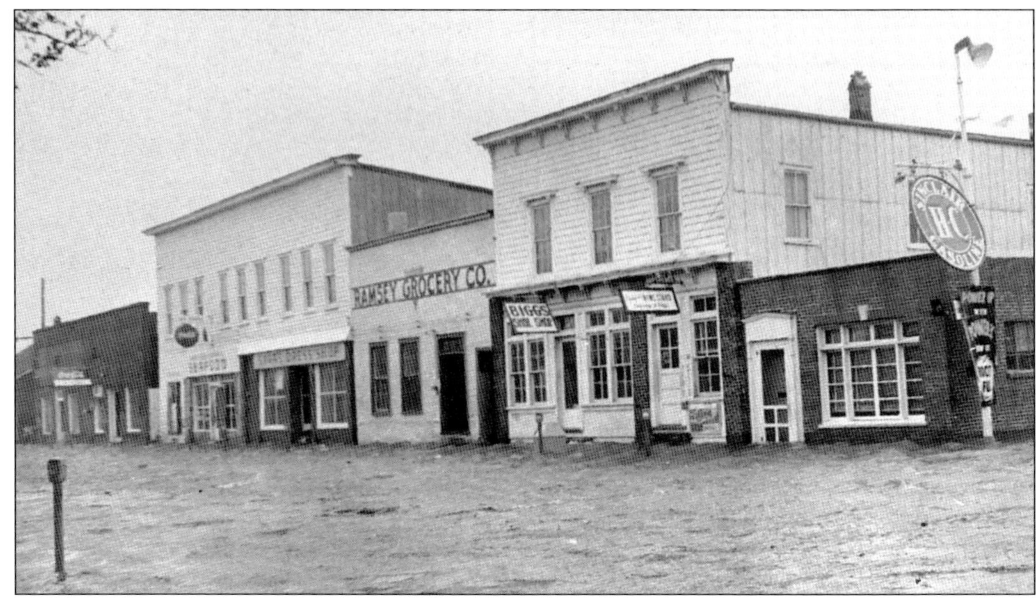

Hurricane Hazel was a category four hurricane and remains as one of the most intense and deadly storms ever to strike the United States. Pictured is Front Street in Beaufort, which went under water. Notice that water is nearly over the parking meters. The surge struck at the exact time of the highest lunar tide of the year—the full moon of October—and was the greatest surge in recorded history. (Courtesy *Carteret County News Times*.)

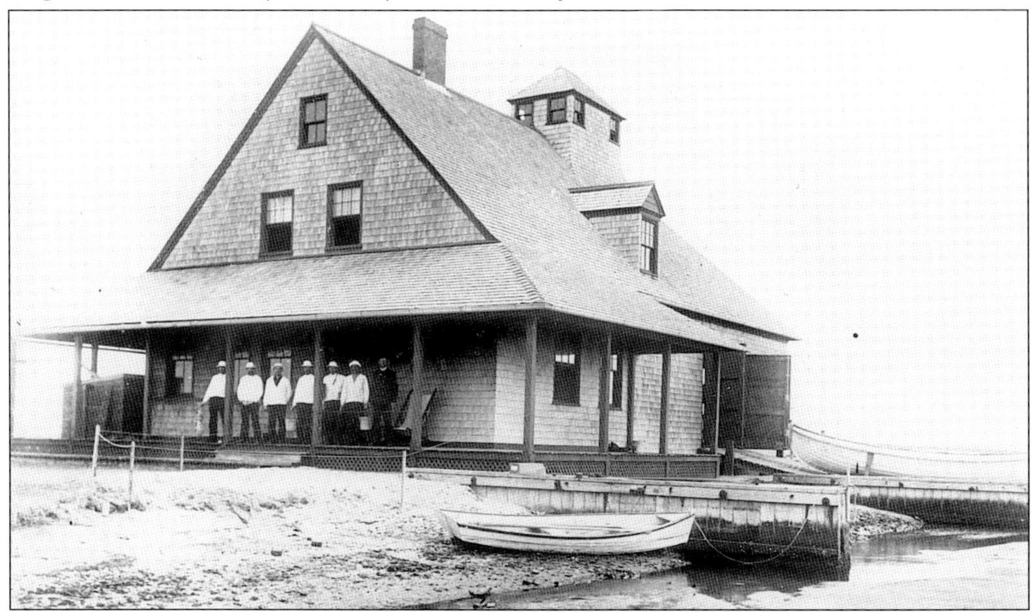

On July 15, 1893, the U.S. Secretary of the Treasury gave permission for part of the Marine Hospital grounds to be used as a site for building the Portsmouth Lifesaving Station. The station saw service into the twentieth century and then became the United States Coast Guard. (Courtesy North Carolina Department of Archives and History.)

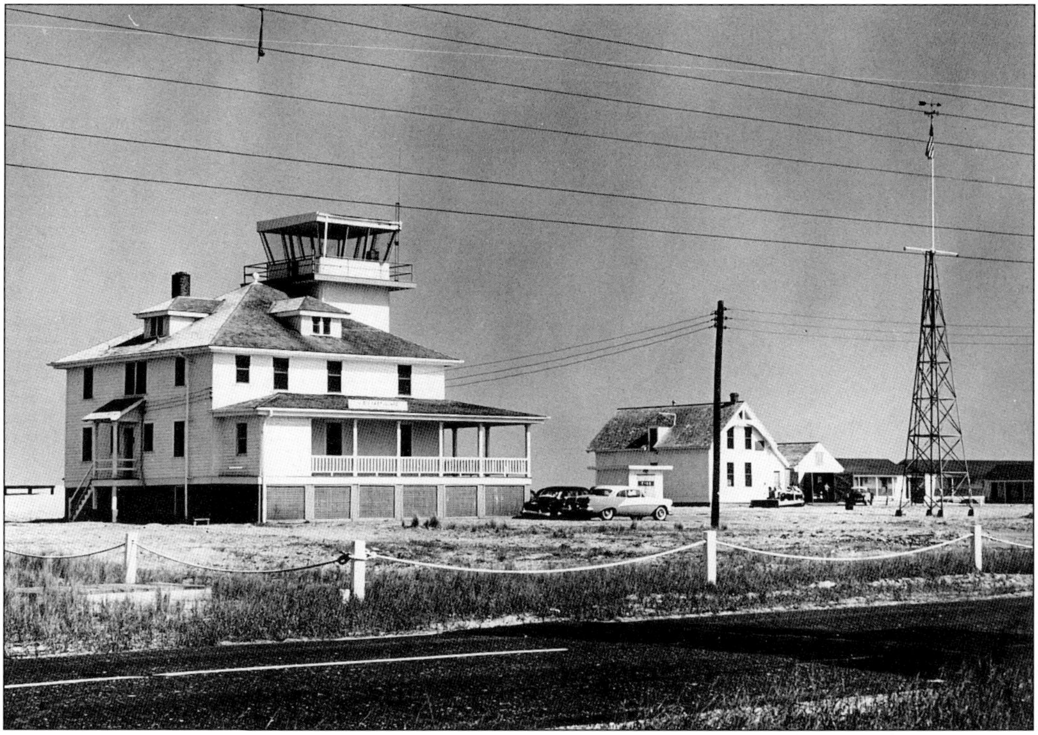

Kill Devil Hills Coast Guard Station was located 4 miles south of Kitty Hawk. (U.S. Coast Guard.)

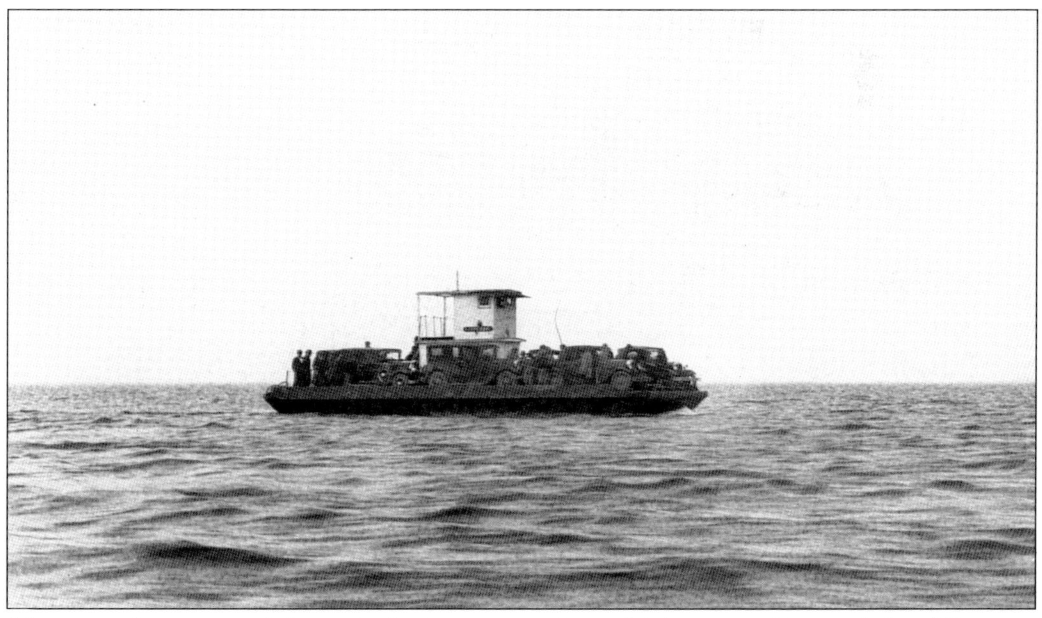

This view shows one of the early ferries transporting vehicles across Oregon Inlet. (Courtesy North Carolina Department of Transportation.)

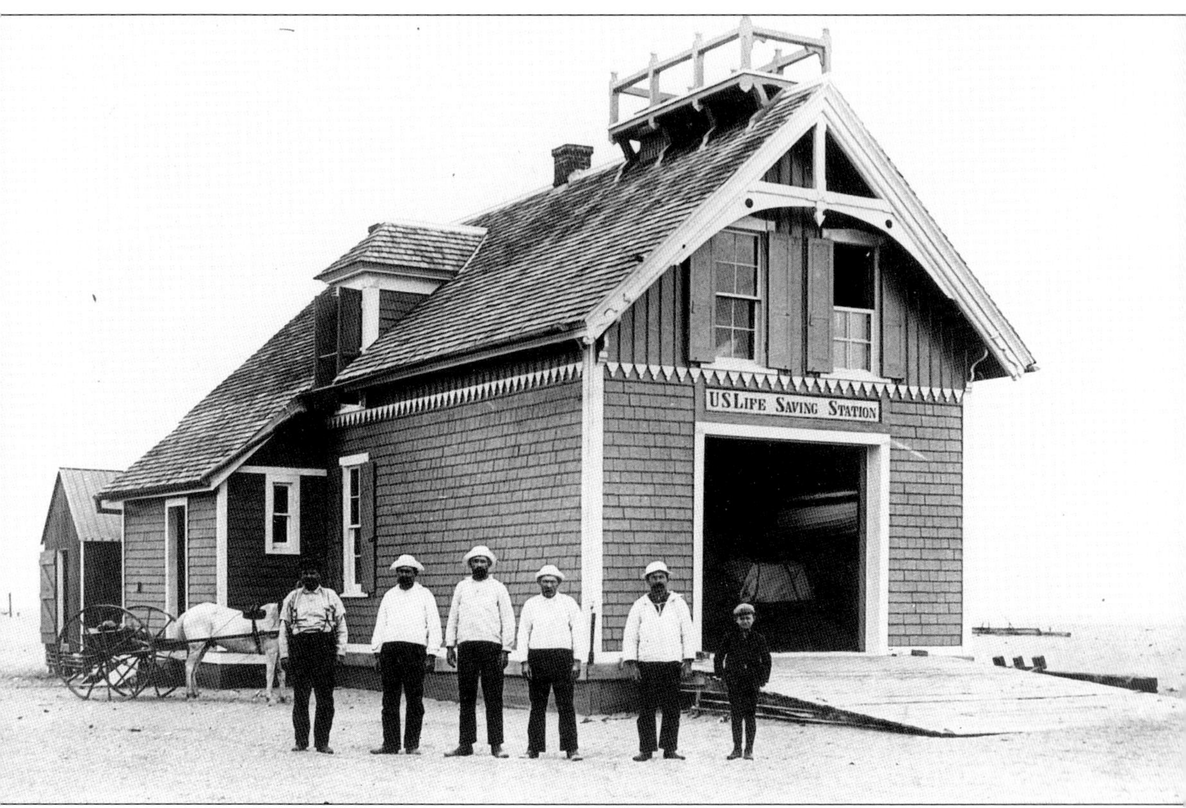

The Little Kinnakeet Lifesaving Station appears in this *c.* 1895 photograph. The original station at this site was erected in 1874. (U.S. Coast Guard.)

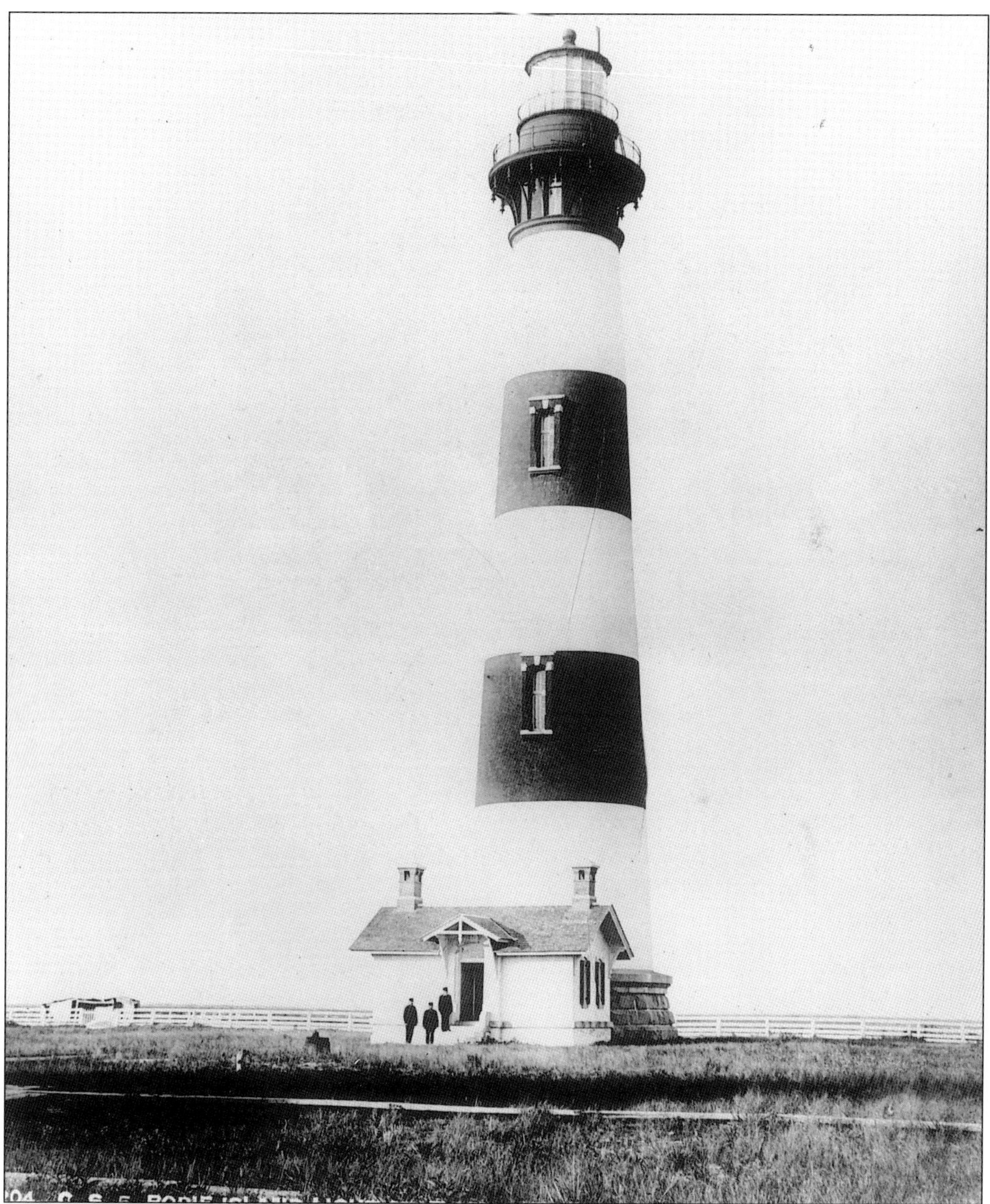

Bodie Island Lighthouse stands 166 feet tall. This is the third lighthouse built on Bodie Island. The first, a 54-foot-tall brick structure, was approved in 1837 and completed in 1848. A year after its construction the tower began listing to one side, thanks to an inadequate foundation. The structure was abandoned in 1859 and eventually fell into the sea.

The second lighthouse at Bodie Island was completed in 1859. The 80-foot-tall brick tower with cast iron lantern and third-order Fresnel lens was destroyed by Confederates in 1861, shortly after the fall of Fort Hatteras. (U.S. Coast Guard.)

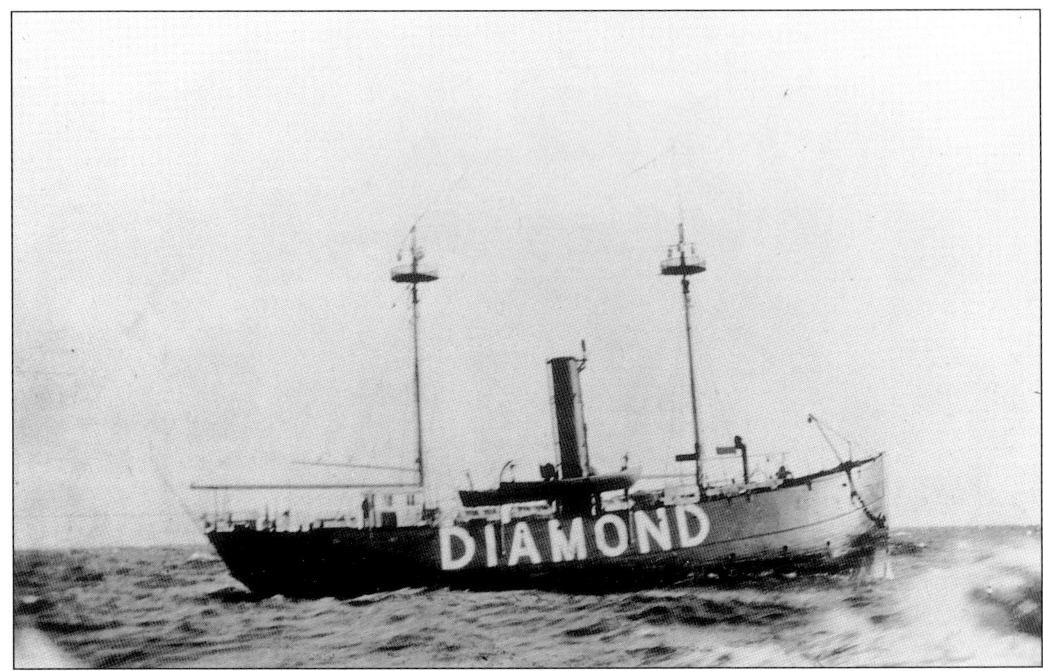

The *Diamond Shoals Lightship* was sunk by the *U-140* on August 6, 1918. The lightship reportedly drew the ire of the German commander by wiring the news of an attack upon a freighter by an enemy submarine. The *U-140* fired six shots at the lightship at approximately 3:25 p.m. from a distance of approximately 2 miles. According to a statement from the U.S. Coast Guard, "Two shots passed between the smokestack and the mainmast, two shots struck on the port side filling the spar deck with water, and under the wireless antenna. At 3:30 all hands were ordered in the starboard boat, which was launched and pulled away from the ship." Figuring that he had silenced the *Diamond Shoal Lightship*, Fregattenkapitan Waldemar Kophamel went off in pursuit of other prizes. Its work complete, the *U-140* returned to the lightship and fired seven shots into her, sinking her to the bottom. "At the time the last shots were fired the lightship's men including the mate (in charge), engineer, cook, three firemen, four seamen and two radio operators, the latter Navy personnel, all escaped without injury. While the lightship was sunk, reports indicated that the wireless message she had sent out resulted in about 25 other vessels taking refuge in Lookout Bight and escaping possible attack." (U.S. Coast Guard.)

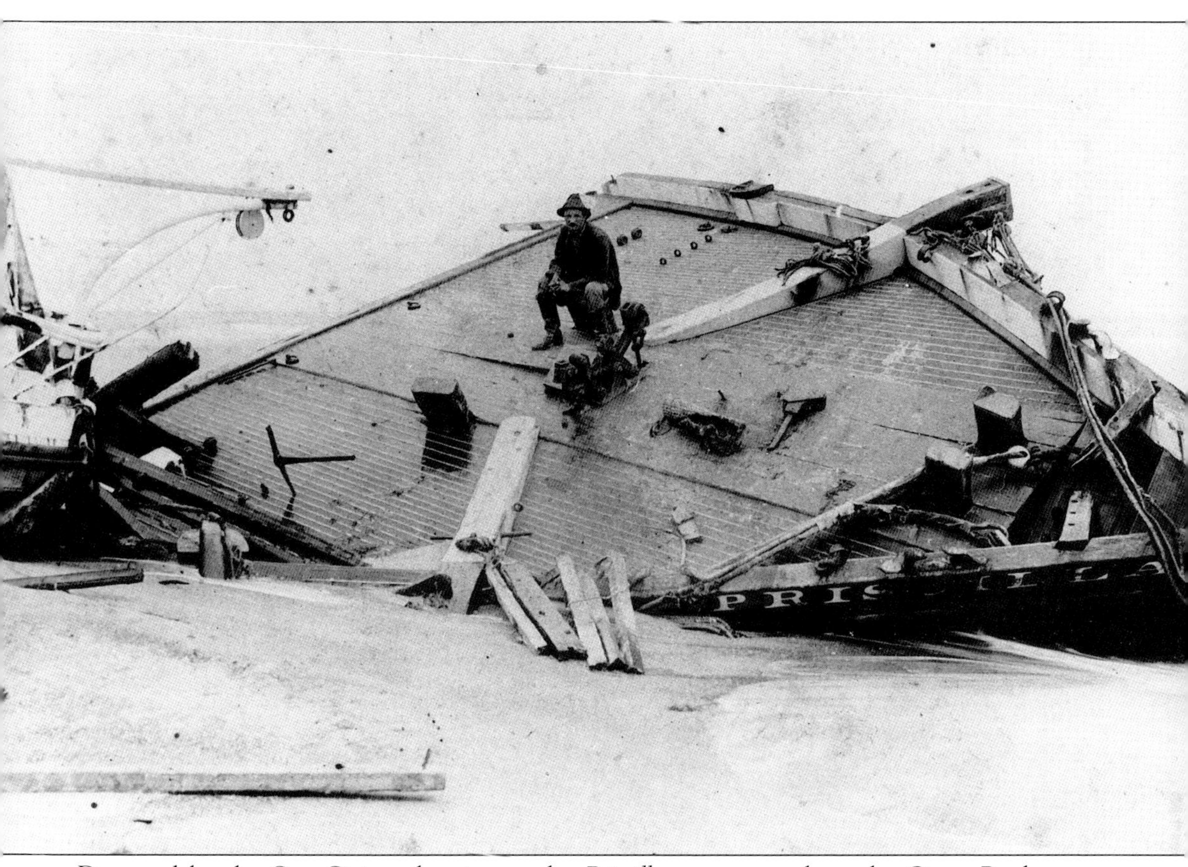

Damaged by the San Ciriaco hurricane, the *Priscilla* ran aground on the Outer Banks near the Gull Shoal Lifesaving Station on the morning of August 18, 1899. Captain Benjamin Springsteen lost his wife, two sons, and his cabin boy in the ferocious surf. Fortunately, the few men who remained were saved from a similar fate when surfman Rasmus Midgett happened upon the site while on routine patrol from the Gull Shoal Station. Midgett single-handedly rescued the crewmen of the *Priscilla*, a feat that earned him the Gold Lifesaving Medal of Honor. (Courtesy North Carolina Division of Archives and History.)

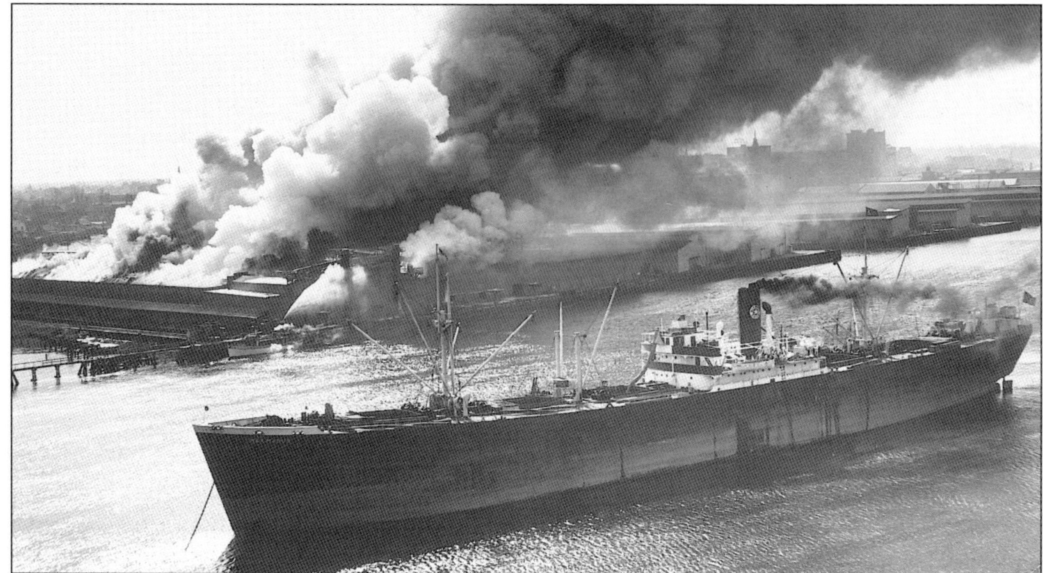

Photographer Hugh Morton bravely snapped this picture of a 1953 fire at the Wilmington Terminal Warehouse as nitrate of soda, sugar, and tobacco burned with a vengeance. An anchor chain holds the ship, *Maxmanus*, which was moved away from the wharf when the fire began. Warehouse owner Peter Browne Ruffin was just thankful the wind was in the city's favor. (Courtesy Hugh Morton.)

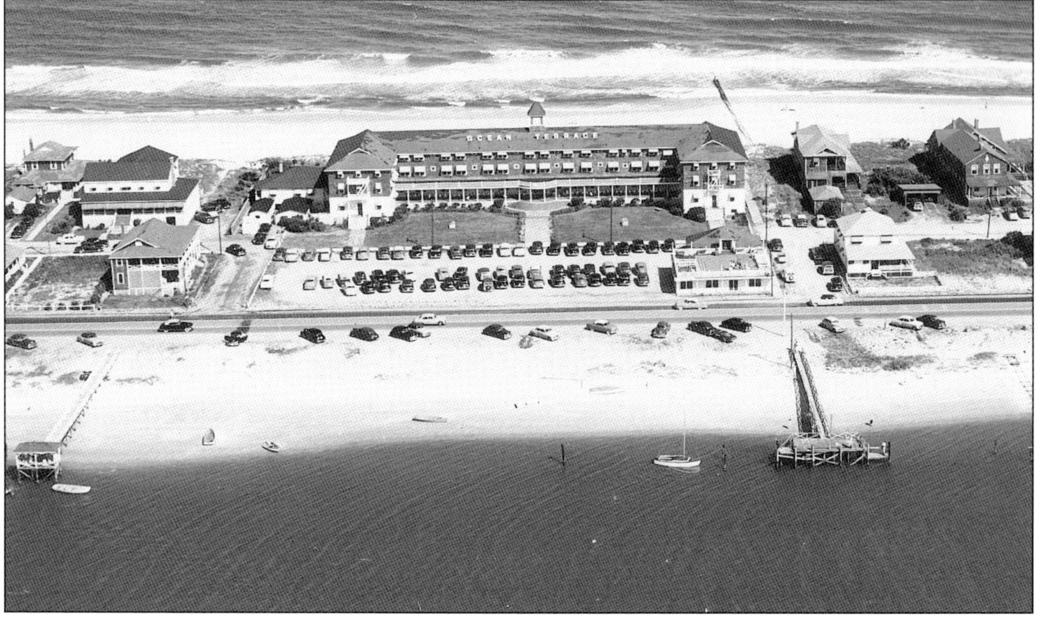

In 1935, the Seashore Hotel was renamed the Ocean Terrace Hotel in a contest won by Virginia Bellamy, who received a $15 prize for her creativity. This photograph was taken by Hugh Morton *c.* 1945. Hurricane Hazel damaged the building in 1954; a year later, it burned to the ground. In 1964, it was replaced by the Blockade Runner. (Hugh Morton.)

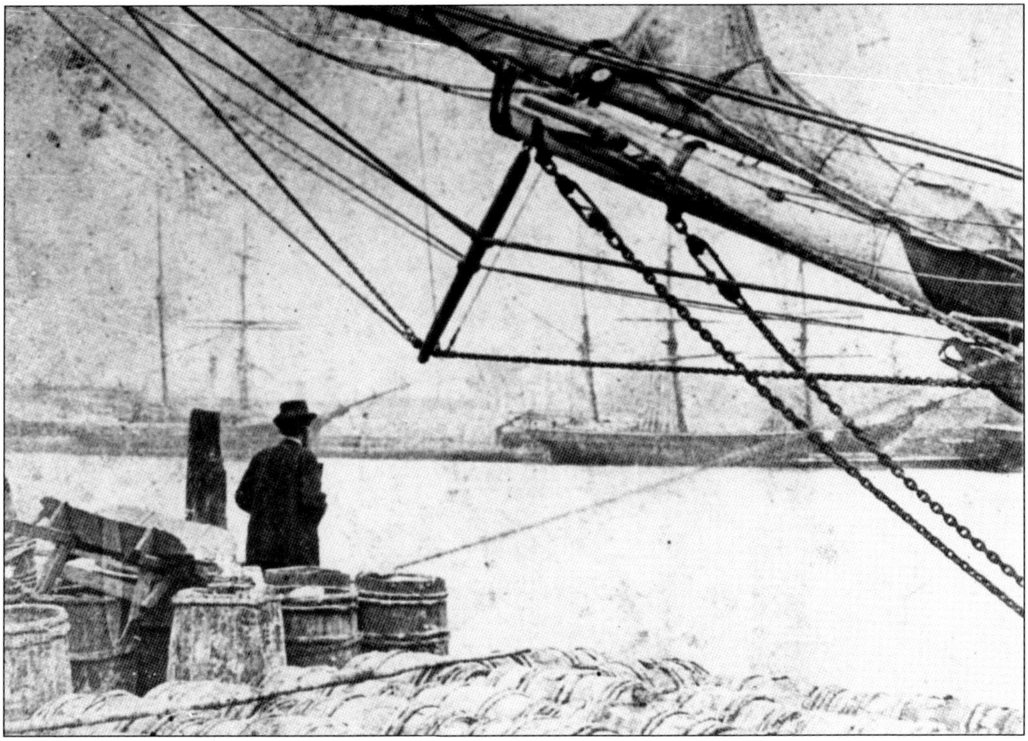

Rufus Morgan photographed this scene on the Cape Fear River in 1873.

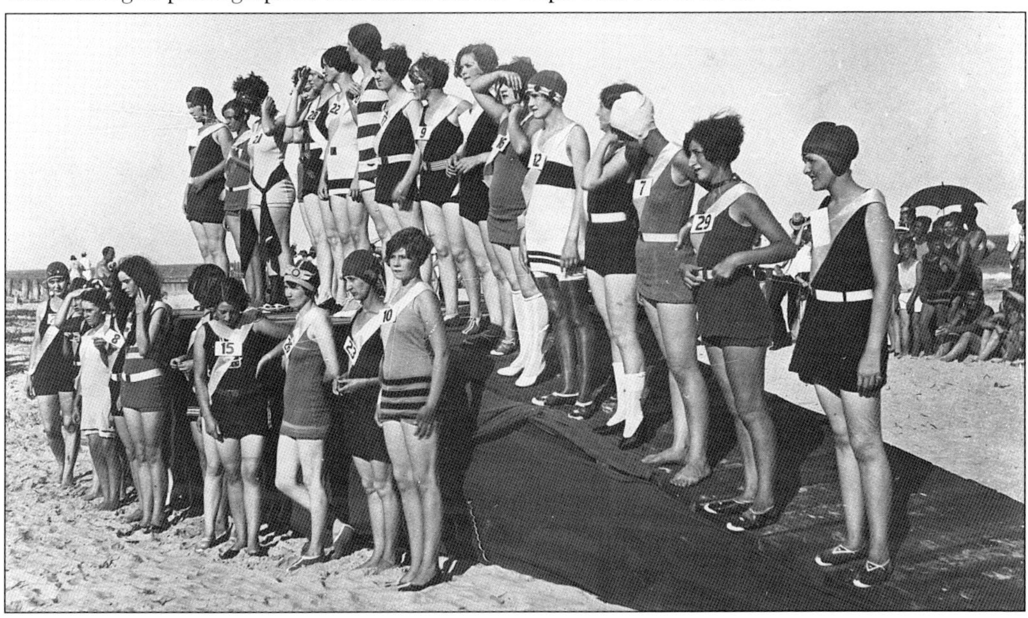

Assuming an array of postures and dress, bathing beauties competed at Wrightsville Beach in the 1920s. Lumina was the venue for varied competitions, including boxing and wrestling matches and greased pole climbs.

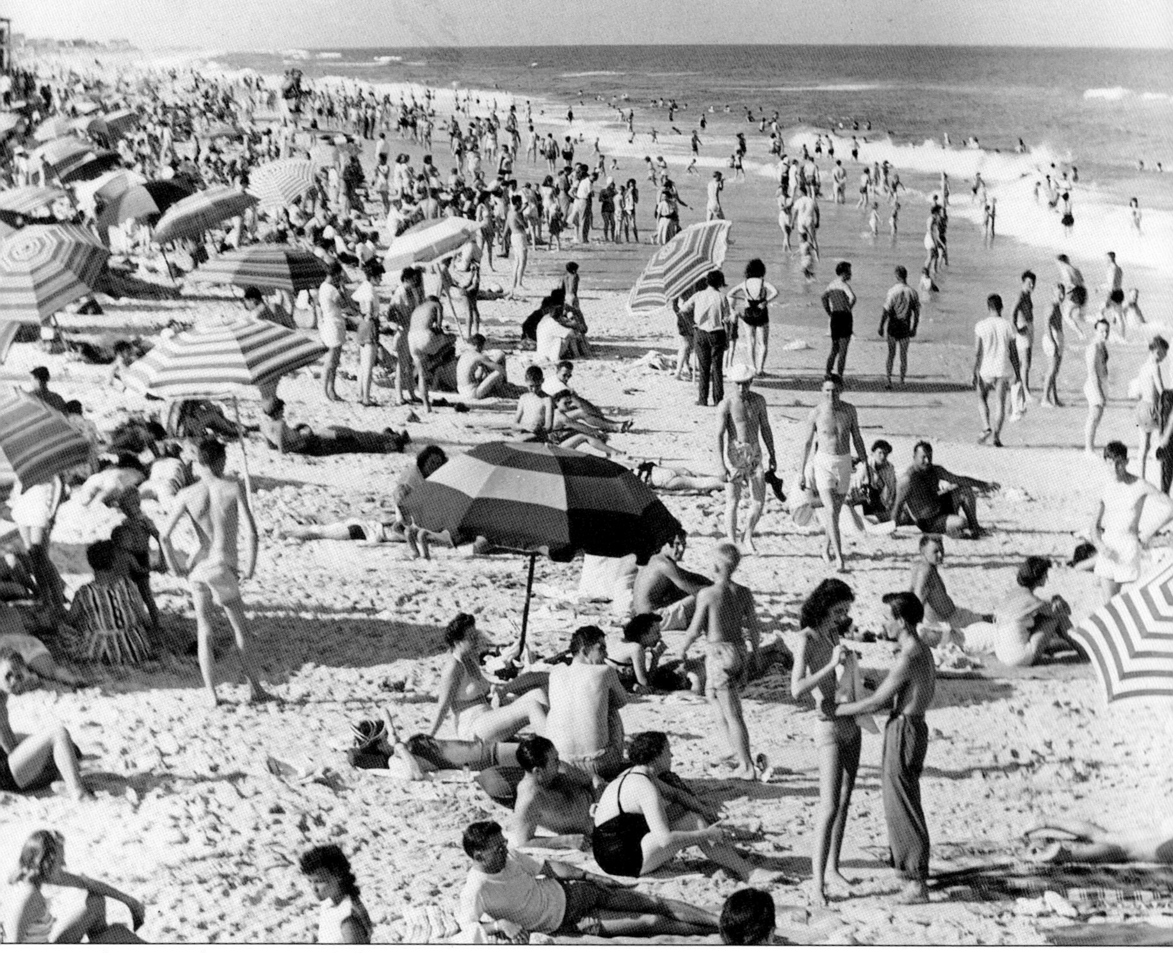

The strand just east of the Boardwalk at Carolina Beach looks crowded in this photograph taken about 1960, but Chamber of Commerce officials were not entirely happy with the picture Hugh Morton took, insisting that the beach was usually more crowded. Though winters were still quiet there in the 1960s, a large rental market made the population of Carolina Beach explode every summer. Bingo parlors ran out of cards and it was difficult to find an empty table at Mrs. High's Dining Room. At the dance hall, local bands played Beach Boy songs and "Under the Boardwalk" a little too often while sunburned young people shagged and bopped, crammed together on the dance floor.

A carnival atmosphere pervaded the center of town. Many Wilmingtonians visited the beach to people-watch on the boardwalk and to "ride the rides." Cotton candy and snow cones kept things sticky and the merry-go-round was a giant music box thumping out a tune that stayed in your head. The amusement park featured many rides designed to amuse and thrill, but the "Bullet," a rickety rocketship that tumbled its strapped passengers like dice in a parchesi cup, truly terrified. Teenagers couldn't get enough of it.

Two

THREADS OF THE COMMUNITY:
THE CITIZENS

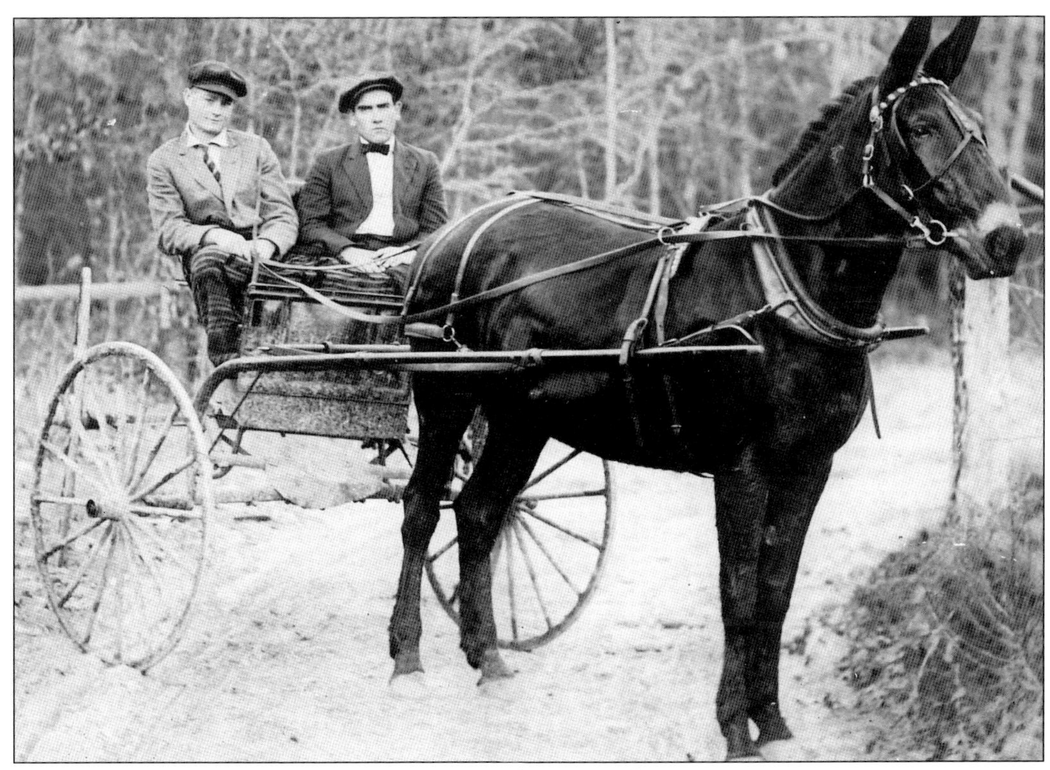

Two unidentified gentlemen enjoy a buggy ride near Duke, *c.* 1910.

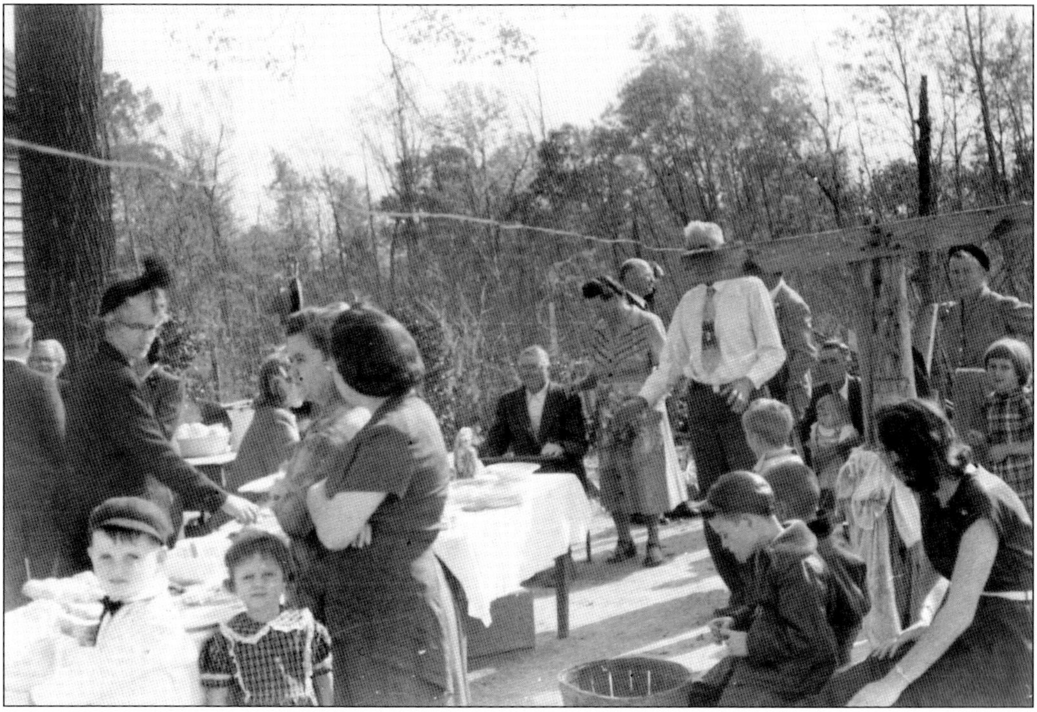

Reunions such as this 1945 family gathering were a common part of the social life for Harnett residents.

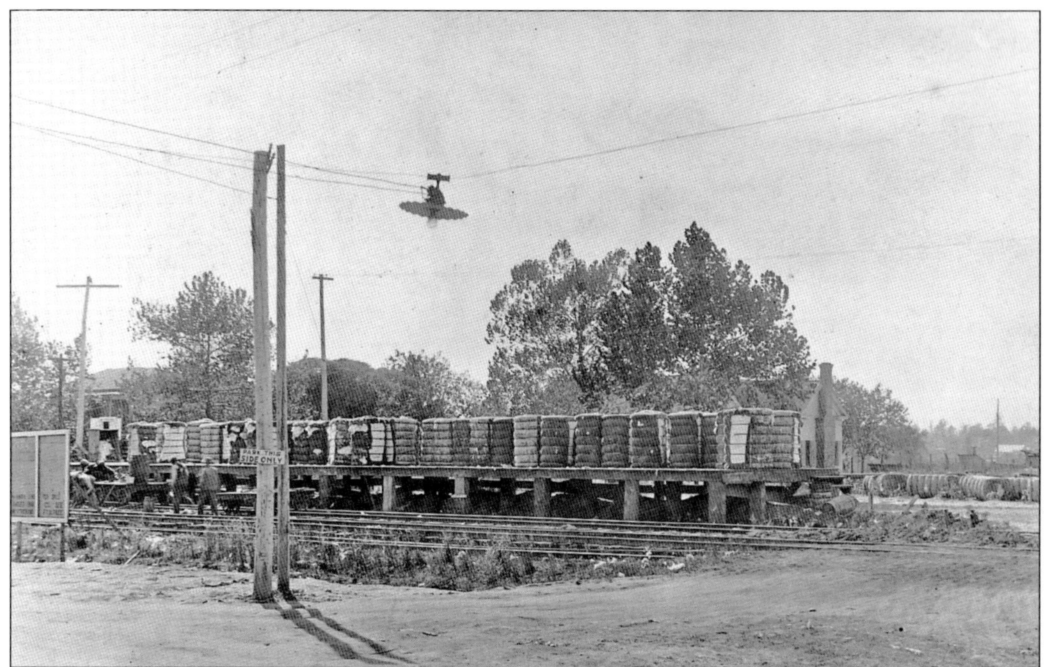

Cotton waits by the tracks for shipment in Angier, 1975.

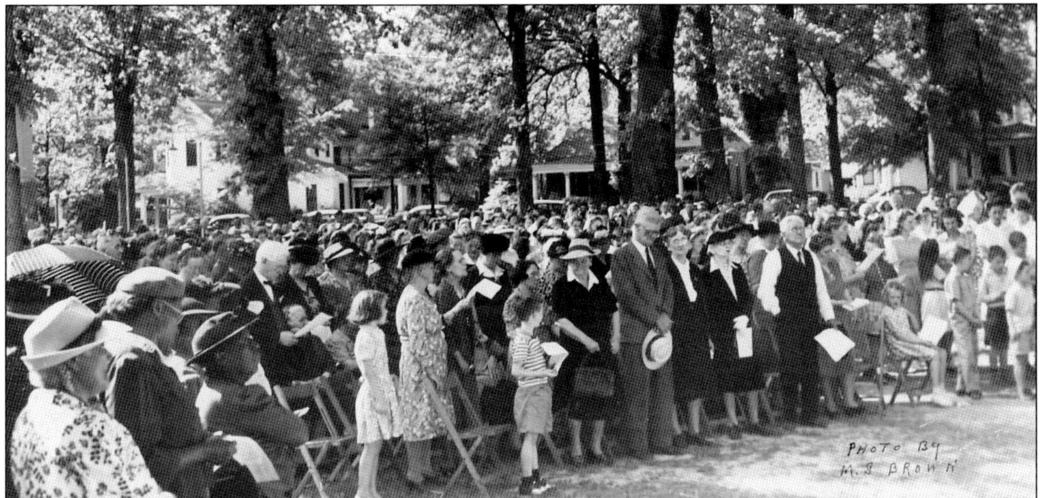

Citizens of Edgecombe County came together on the Town Common in November 1945 to hold a county-wide service of prayer giving thanks that the war was over and that most of the 4,428 men and women serving in the war had returned home. (BBH-photo by M.S. Brown.)

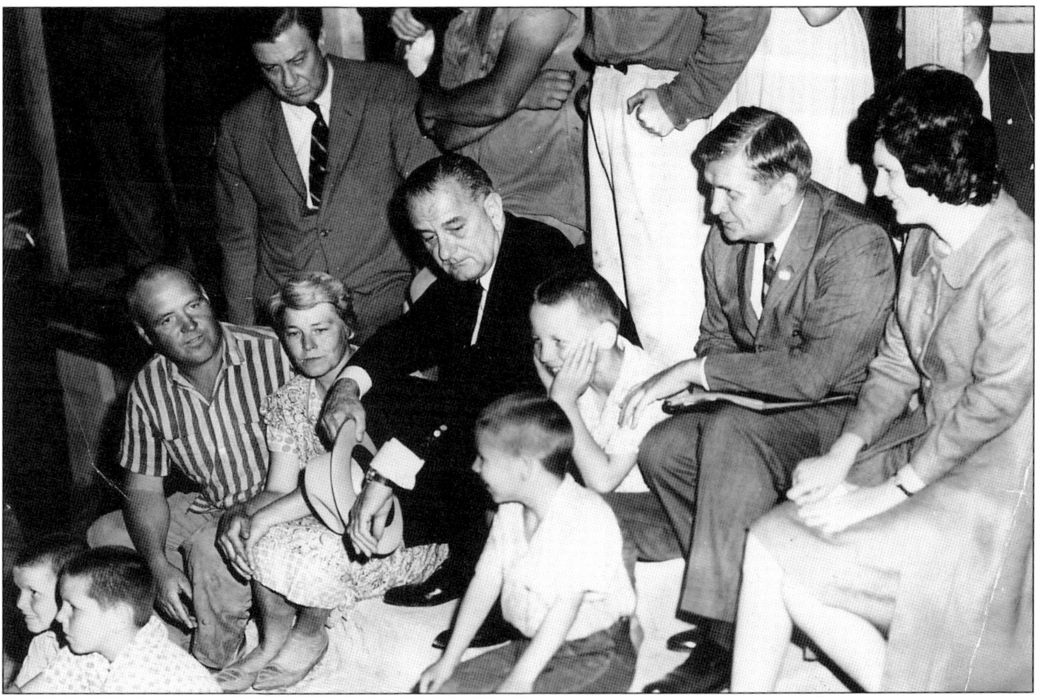

President Lyndon Johnson visited the William D. Marlow farm near Rocky Mount after the 1964 election. To introduce his War on Poverty, he sat down with "poor people" and promised to make life better for millions of Americans living below the poverty level. The rural areas of this and surrounding counties often qualified as impoverished by government standards. To the right of Johnson is Terry Sanford. In a later interview, one of the Marlow children remarked, "We didn't know we were poor until the President told us we were." (ECML.)

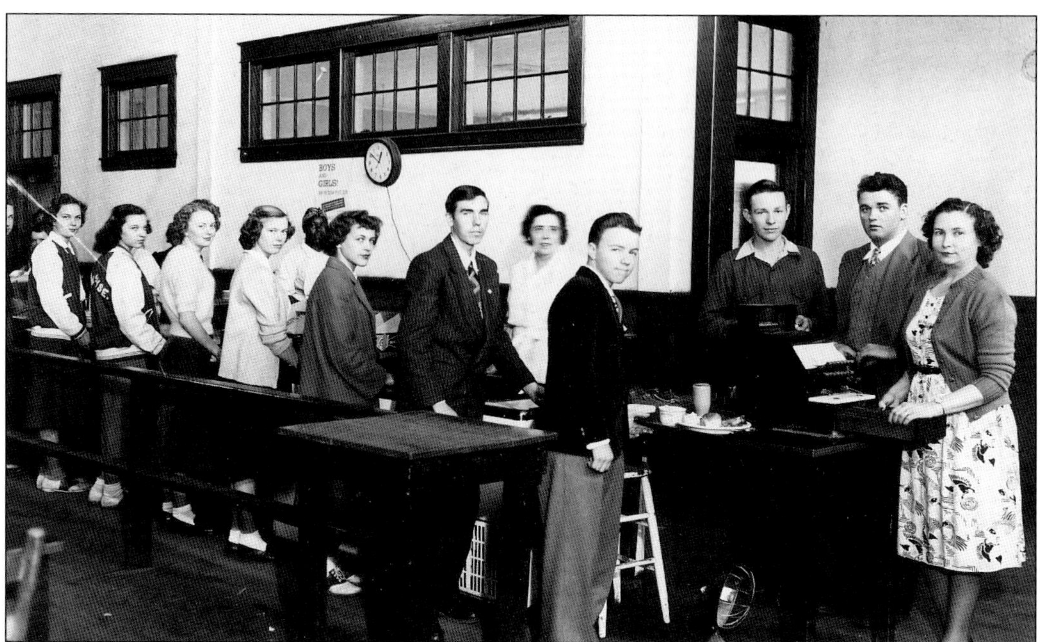

Beginning in the 1930s, WPA programs provided public schools with cafeterias for serving lunch to students. This is the lunchroom at West Edgecombe around 1950. West Edgecombe served grades 1–12 until the 1970s when integration reorganized the county schools. The high school students moved to the new Southwest Edgecombe High School in 1979, and West became a middle school for grades 3–8. (PC-West Edgecombe.)

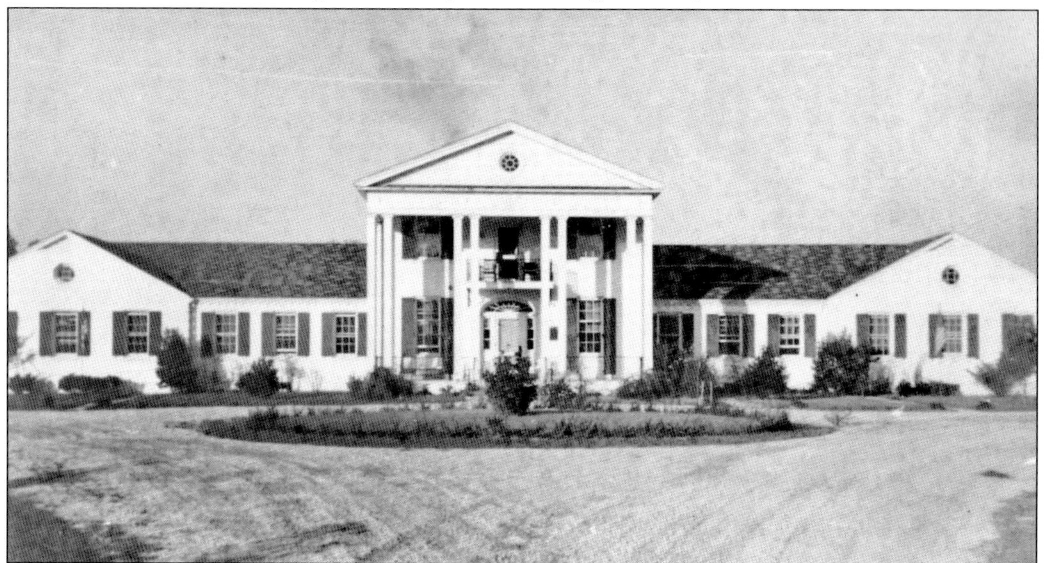

Another project of the federal and local governments was the establishment of a county home for the poor. Located east of Tarboro on County Home Road, the facility served as a home for the poor and veterans without families. Miss Mattie Shacklelford ran the home for a number of years. (ECML.)

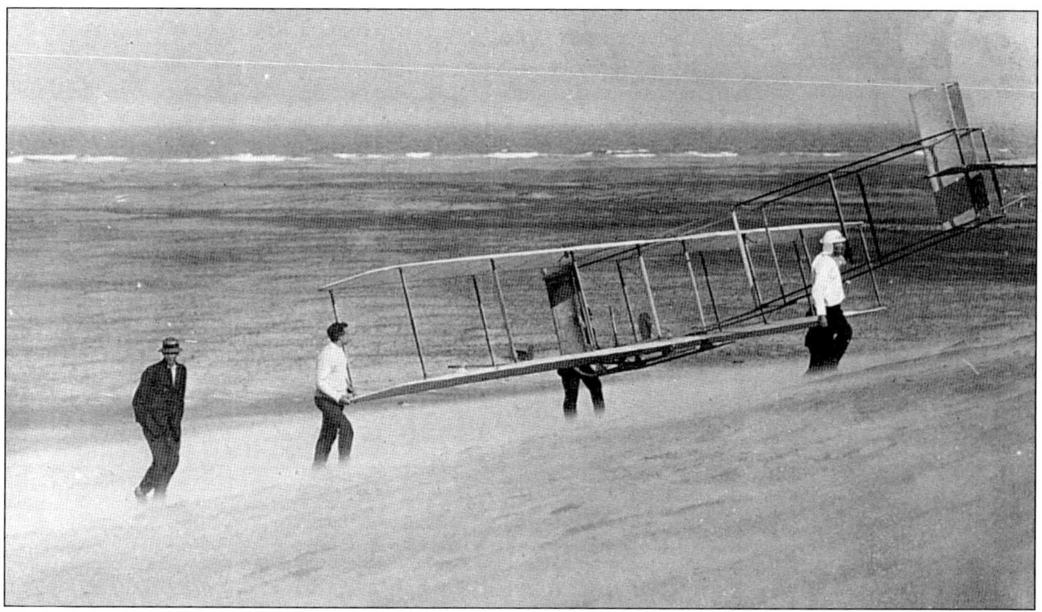

Orville Wright was back on the Outer Banks experimenting with a new glider in 1911. (Courtesy Library of Congress.)

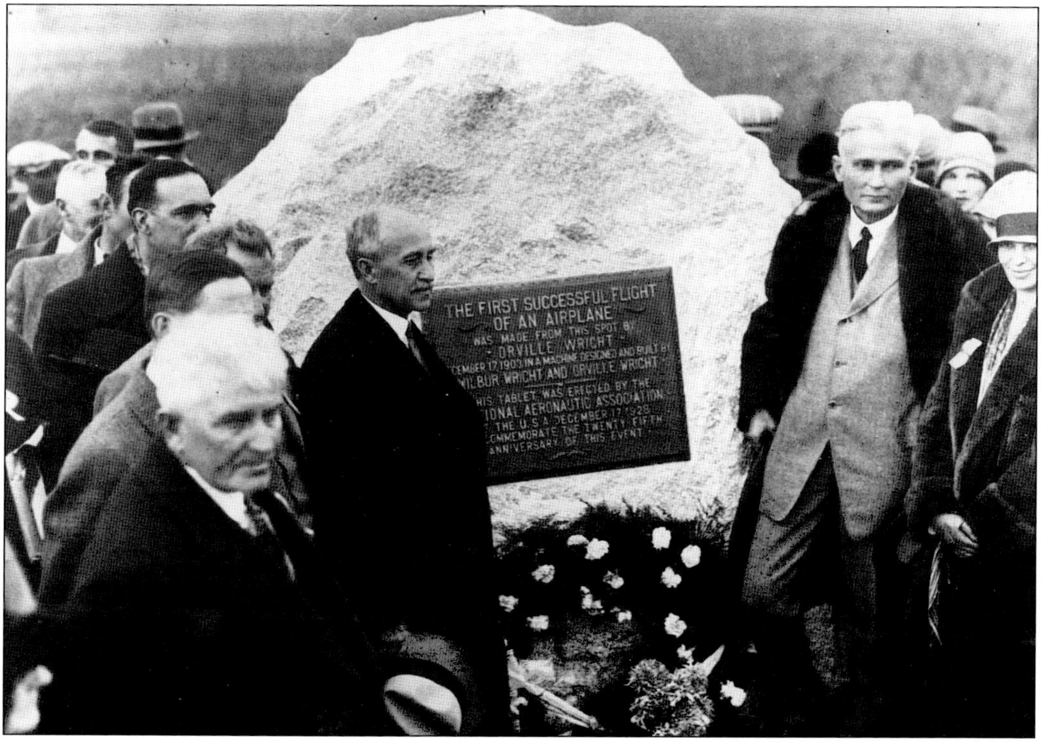

Orville Wright was on hand December 17, 1928, at the dedication of this monument, which marks the site of the first flight. (Courtesy North Carolina Division of Archives and History.)

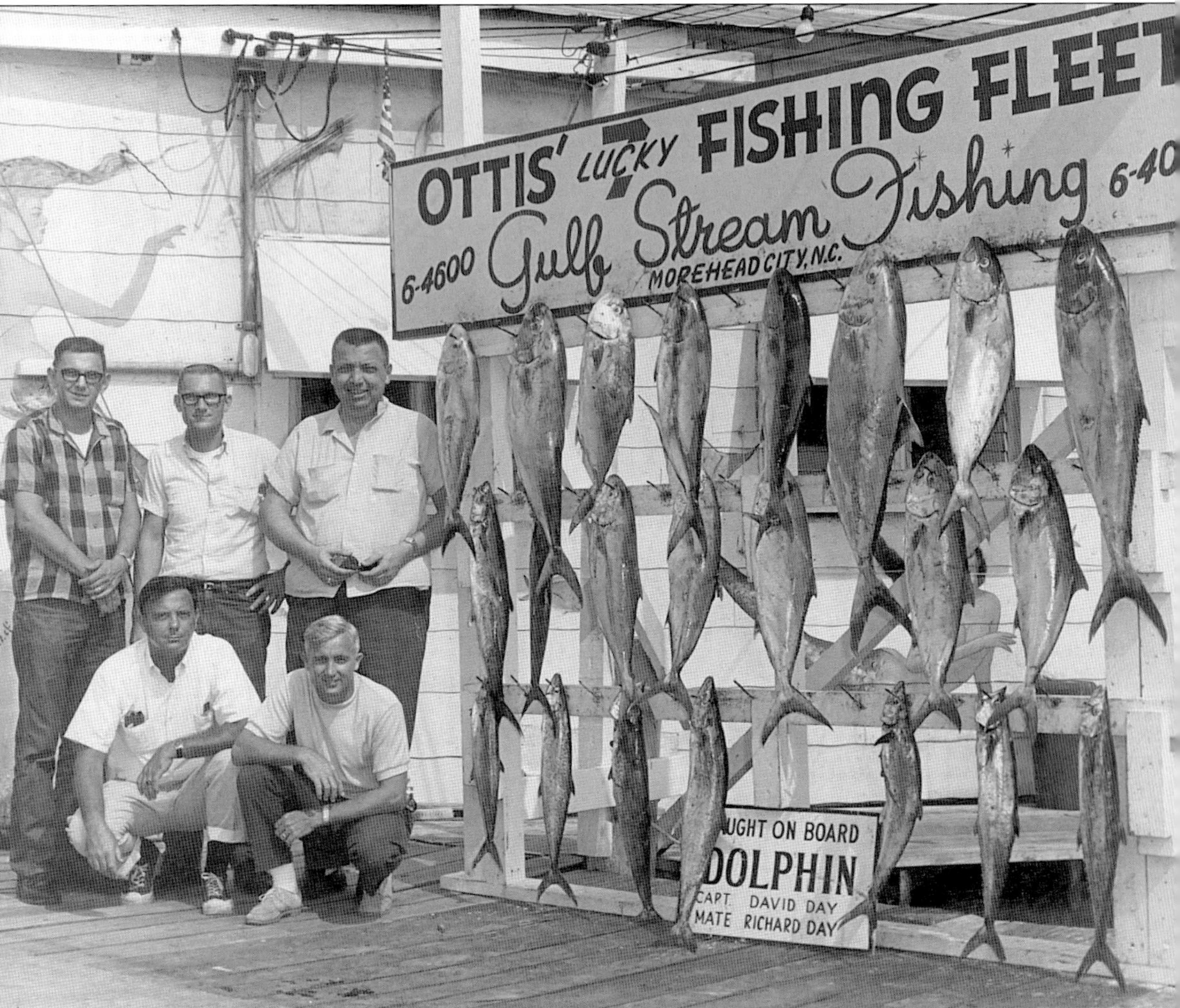

A lucky group of anglers are back from a successful day's fishing in the waters of the Gulf Stream.

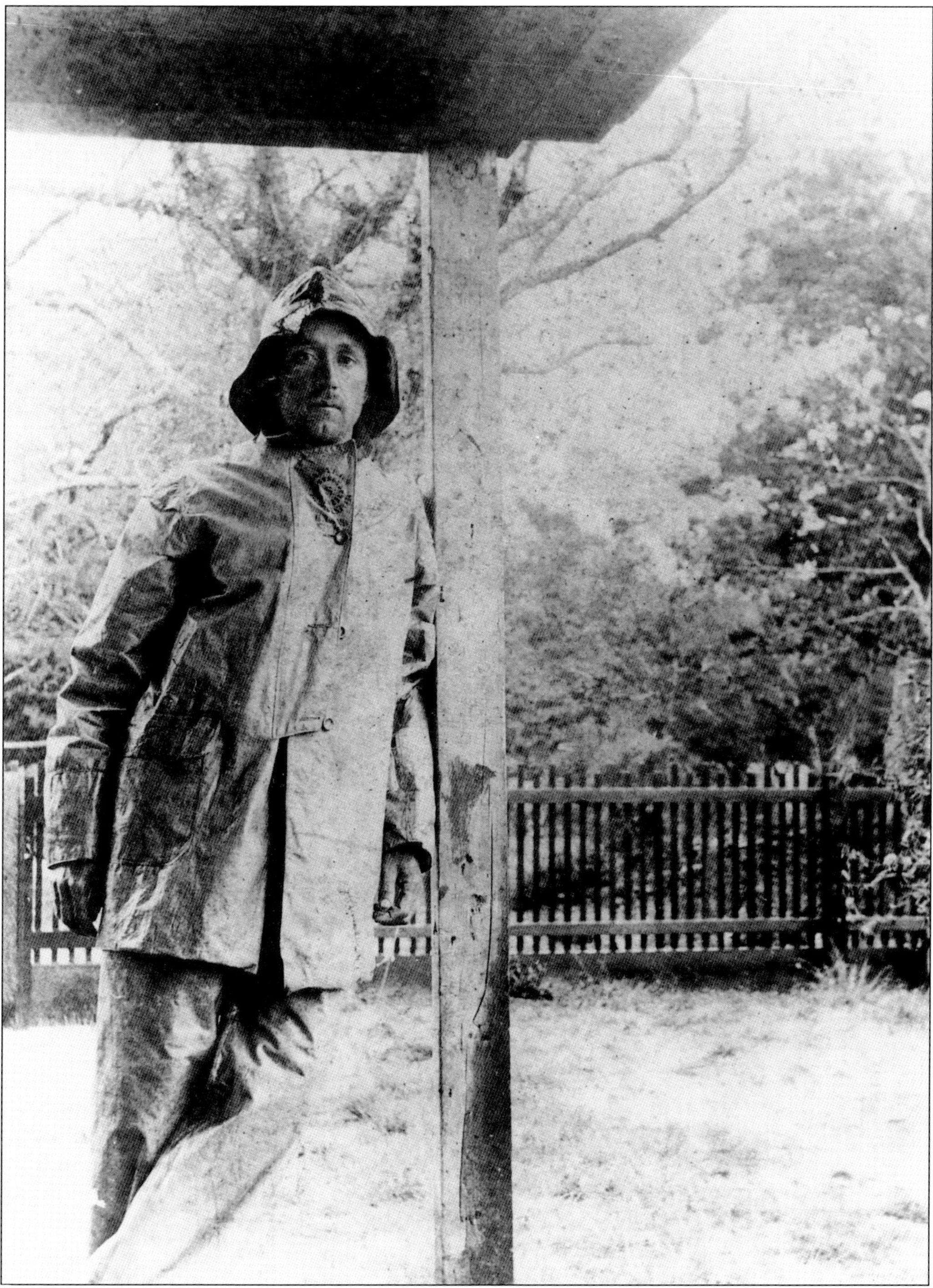

H.H. Brimley labeled this photograph "Nase Jeannette, game warden at Cape H. 1900–1905." (Courtesy North Carolina Division of Archives and History.)

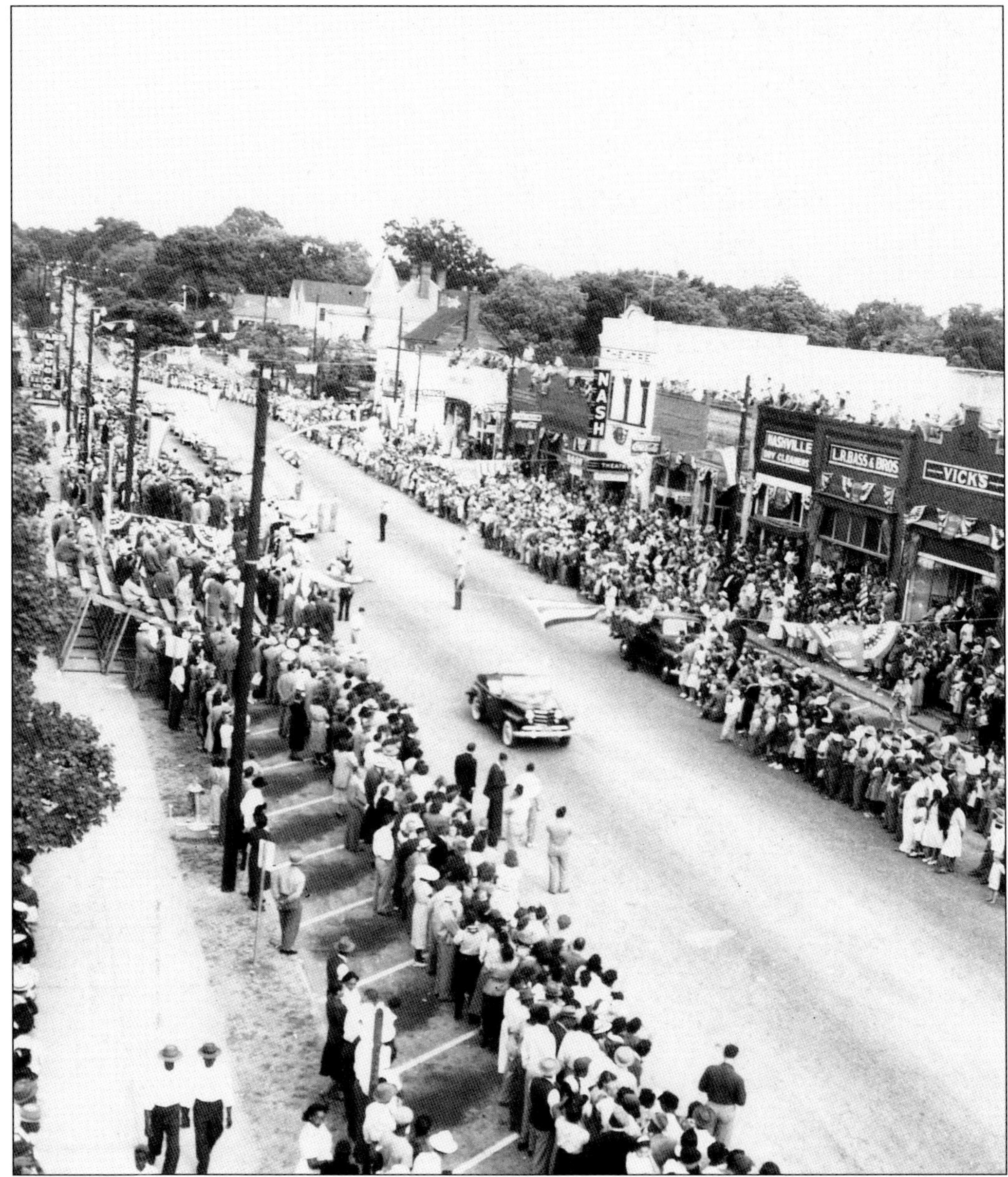

Nashville residents line up along Washington Street for the annual Harvest Festival. Businesses in the 1940s included the Nash Theater, Nashville Dry Cleaners, and L.R. Bass & Brothers. In 1905, P.A. Richardson had a barbershop, and J.D. Barnes was the undertaker. The county seat boasted Nashville Collegiate Institute and Oak Level High School. S.R. Hilliard operated Hilliard Hotel, M.E. Collins ran the Collins Boarding House, and Mrs. M.C. Brake owned the other boardinghouse. J.T. Strickland and James P. Battle provided medical services, and T.T. Ross was the town dentist. General stores included Arrington-Bissett Co., Brooks Son & Co., Griffin & Ward, J.D. Winstead and Co., M.C. Yarboro & Co., and F.B. Cooper Co. Wallace Batchelor managed the livery stable. The town also had three sawmills and a shuttle factory. (NCDAH.)

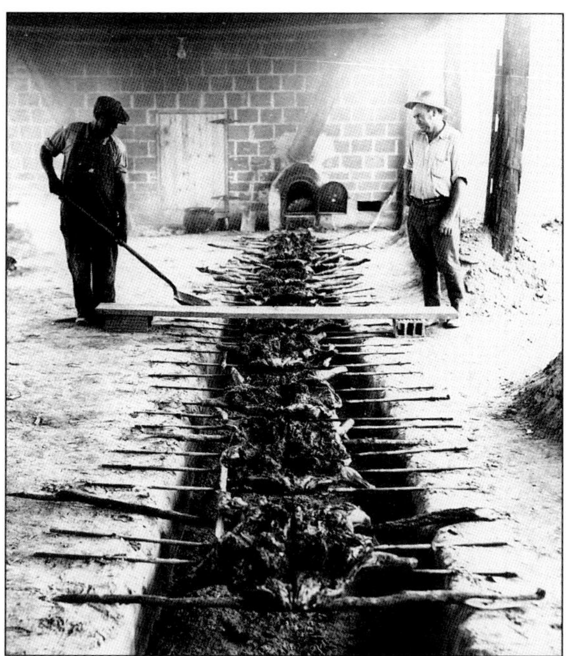

An old Southern tradition, dating back to the 1700s, is a barbecue. Whole hogs are split and cooked over wood coals for most of a day and seasoned with a vinegar-based sauce. Then the diners either picked the meat off the pigs, hence the term pig-picking, or it was chopped into fine meat and served with cole slaw, potatoes, and Brunswick stew. (NCDAH.)

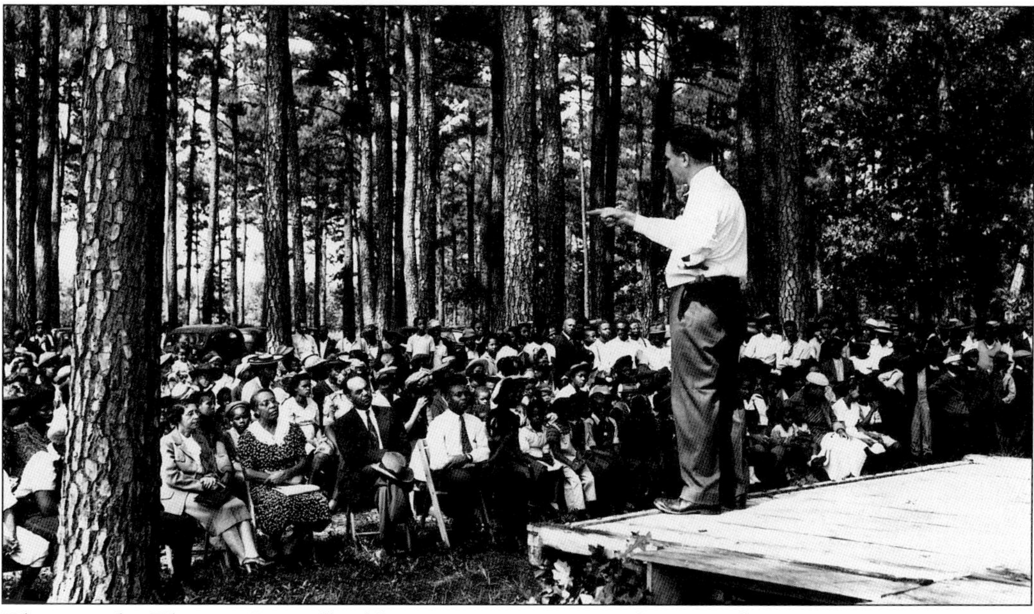

This may be Thomas Pearsall addressing citizens in northern Nash County at a community meeting on the Braswell Farm in the 1940s. Born in Rocky Mount, Pearsall attended Rocky Mount Senior High School and UNC-Chapel Hill, where he earned a law degree. He was appointed to the North Carolina General Assembly and elected for three more terms. Pearsall was Speaker of the House in 1947. Instrumental in the integration plan in North Carolina, Pearsall helped reorganize the UNC system and establish North Carolina Wesleyan College. (NCDAH.)

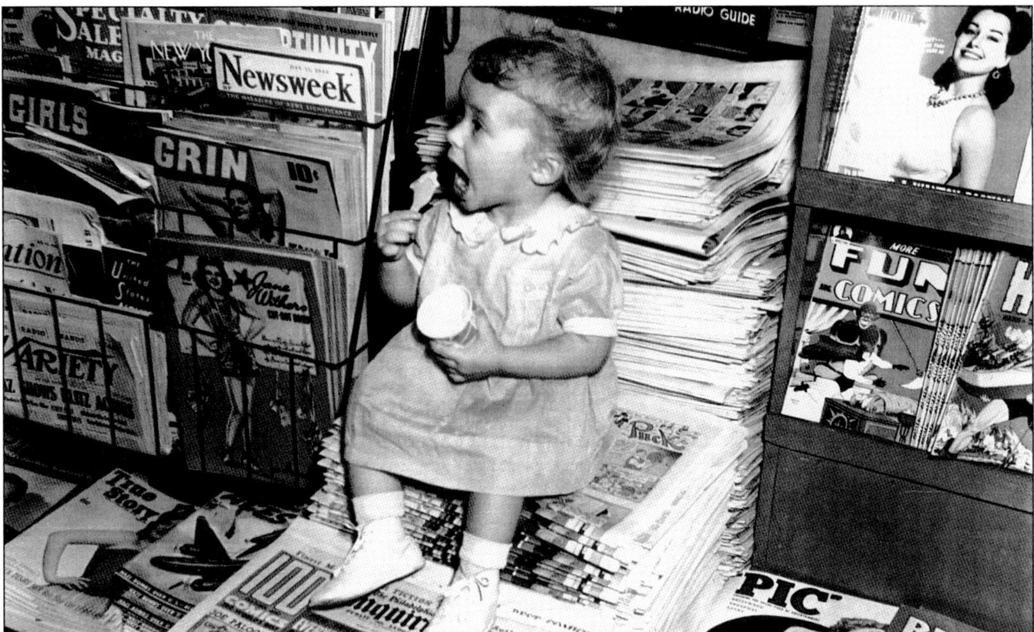

In 1946, Buggs won a photographic press award with this photo of a newsstand and its young customer. (Barringer.)

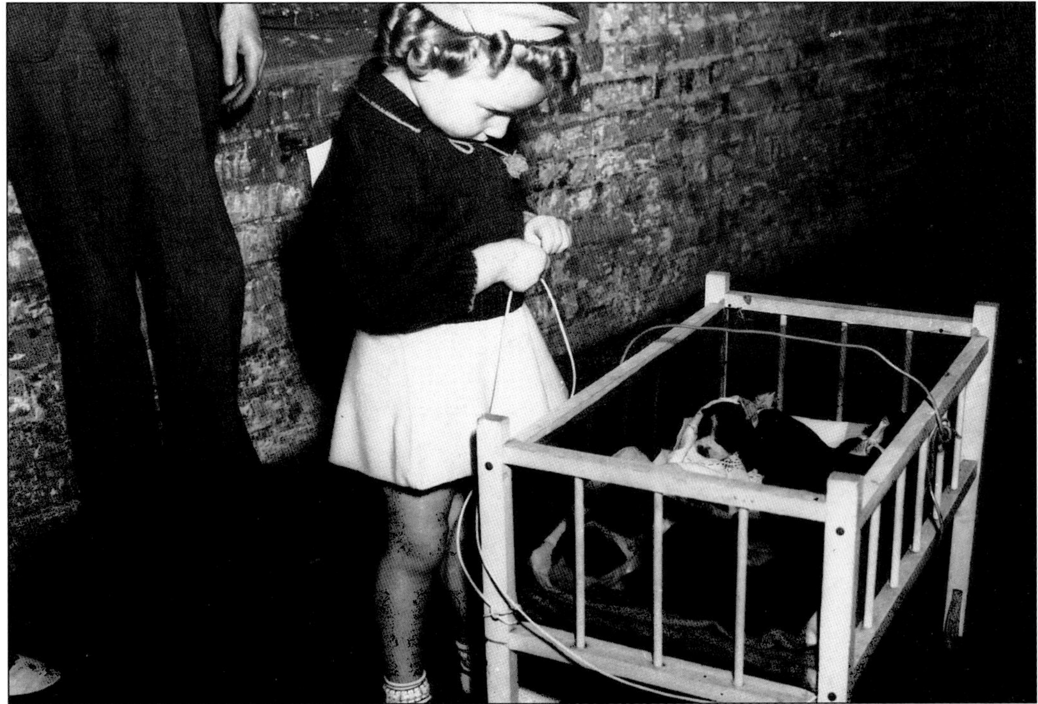

In 1946, Buggs won a photographic press award with this photograph of a newsstand and its young customer. (Barringer.)

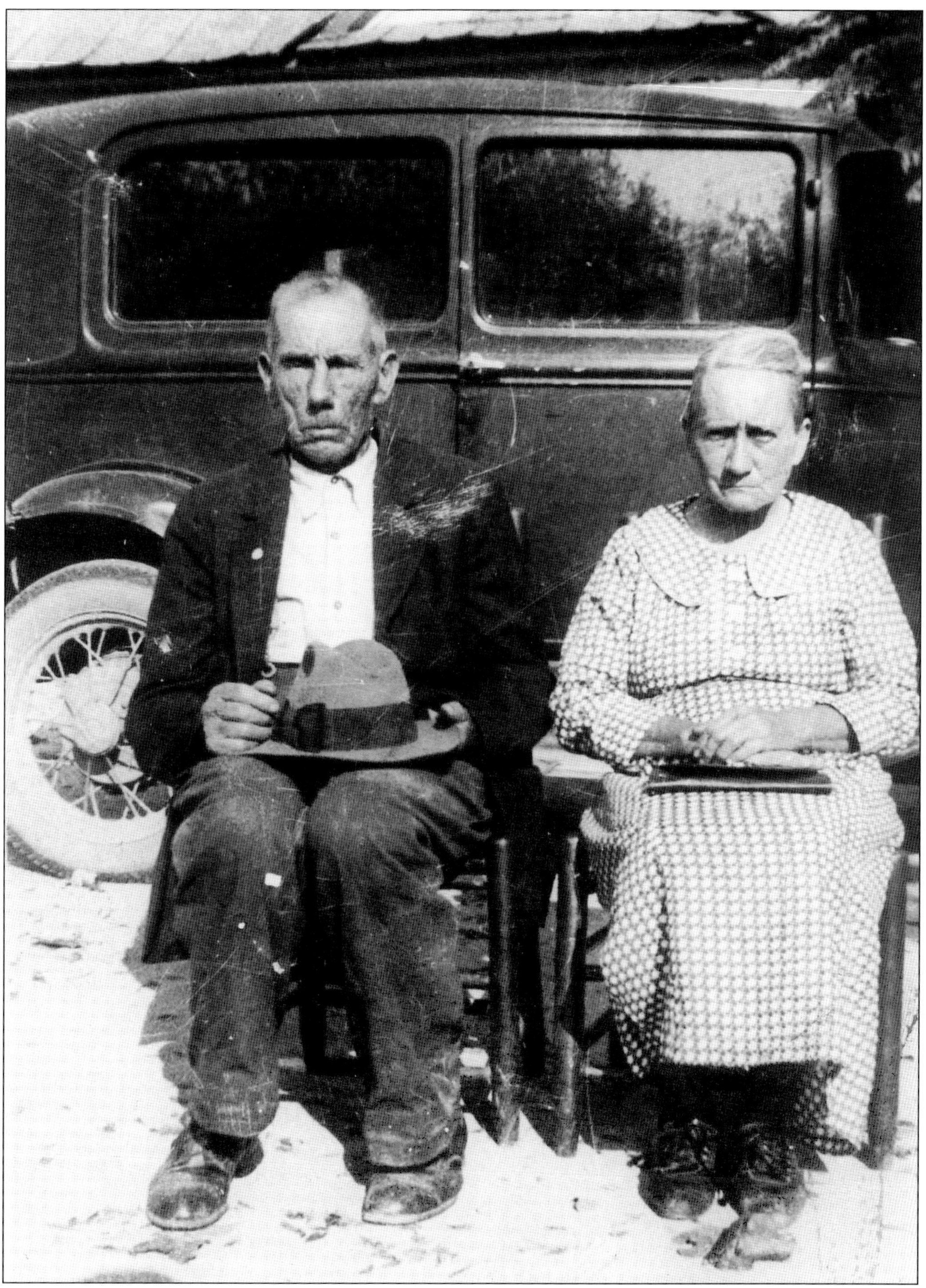

John Washington Lucas and His Wife, Sarah Faircloth Lucas, on their farm near Erwin.

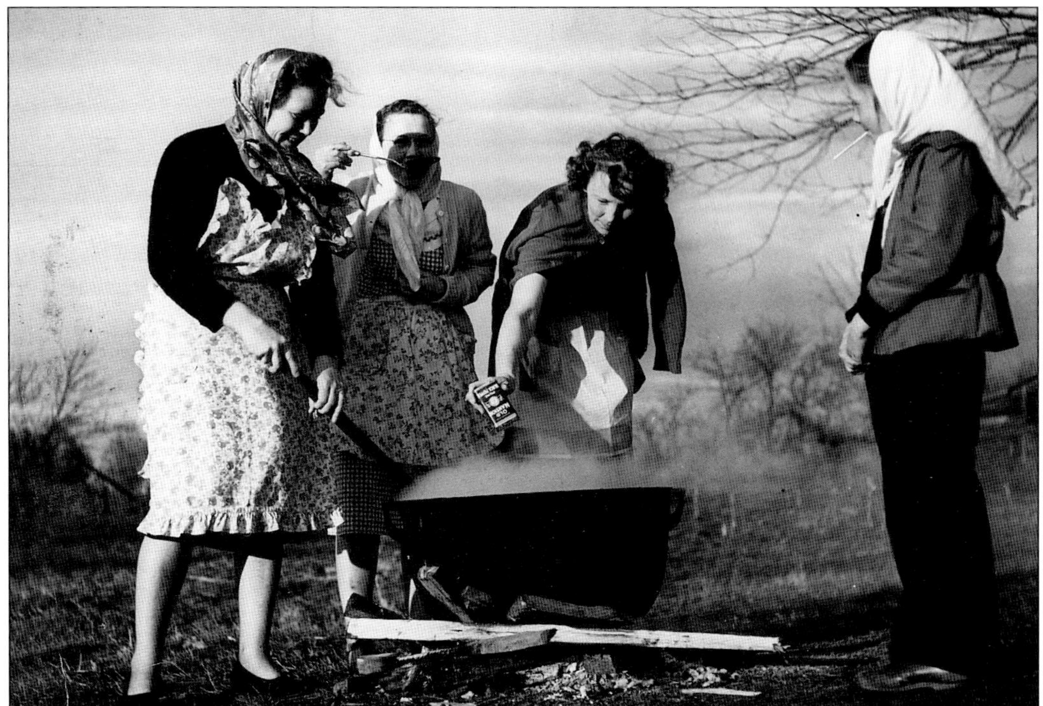

Lela Lewis, Nita Harrell, Sara Burnett, and a neighbor prepare a pot of Brunswick Stew for a stew sale, a traditional area fund-raiser. The Town of Macclesfield used the funds from the stew sale to improve the community. (MAC.)

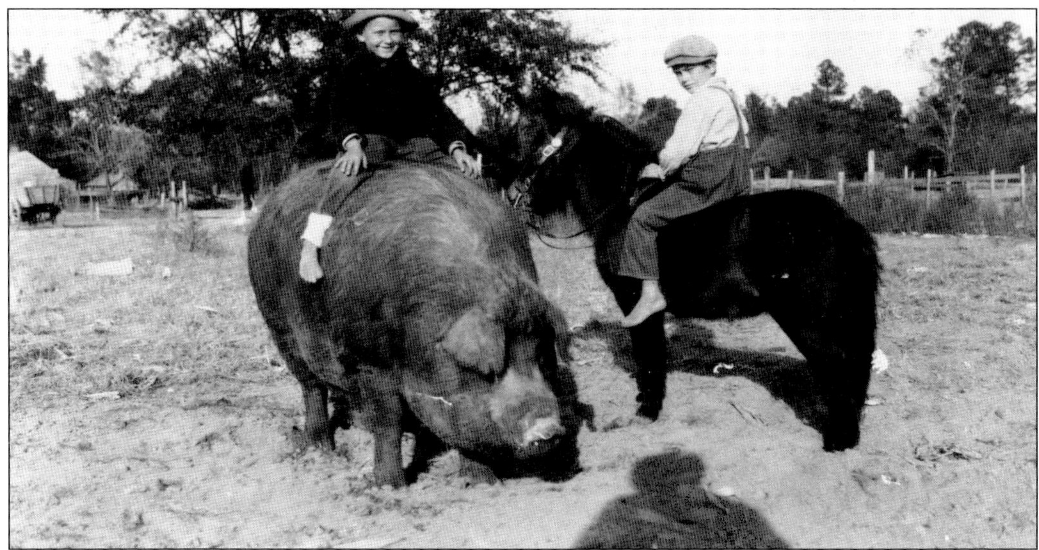

Most Edgecombe County farmers raised animals and grew vegetables for their families as well as raising crops for sale. Hogs and chickens could be found on most farms. Here young Sam Easton sits atop his 1,134-pound pet Duroc hog in 1928 while his brother Austin rides a pony. The hogs were usually slaughtered or sold before reaching this size. (PC Mayo family.)

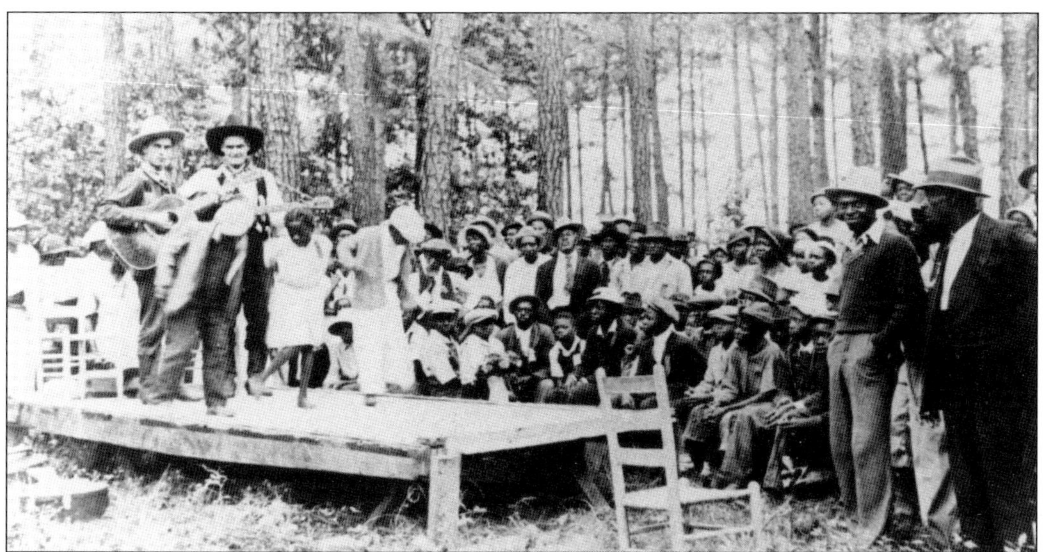

Live entertainment was not limited to the stage at The Opera House; traveling shows of all types made the circuit in the first quarter of this century. Here, three children dance on stage as a crowd enjoys the music of traveling singers. (ECML)

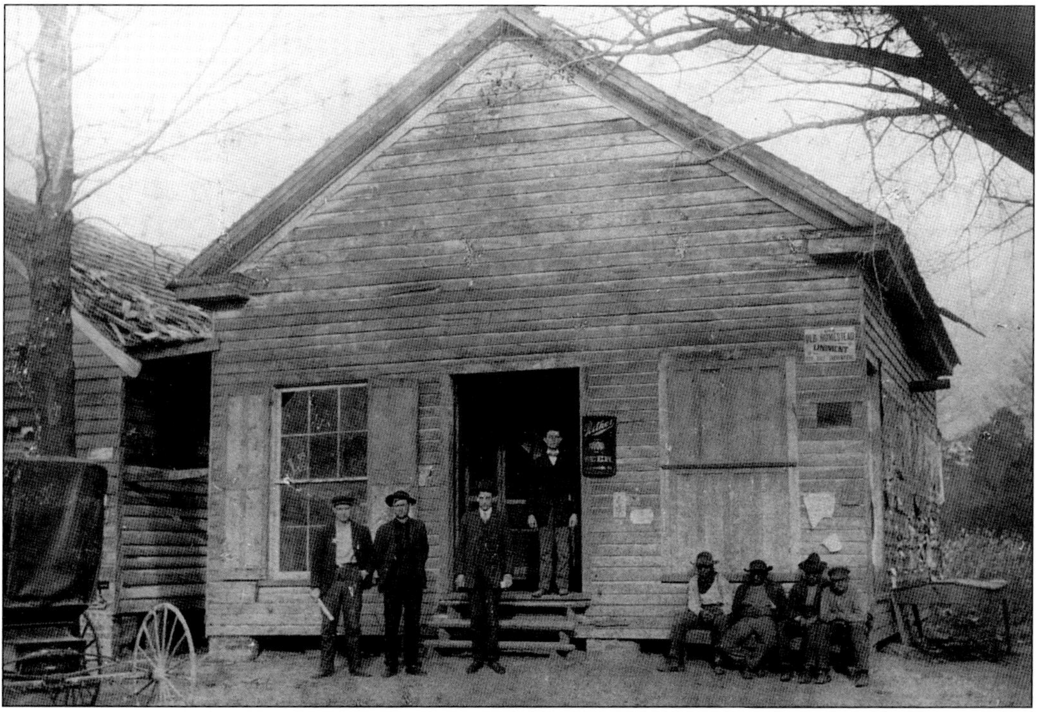

Standing outside the J. Edwards General Store in Old Sparta in 1908 are G.C. Webb, Tom Exum, T.G. Shelton Sr., and Charles Edwards. The men seated are Nathan Thorn, Write Stincle, Drew Mercer, and Brice Cobb. G.C. Webb was Grover Cleveland Webb, better known as "Cheb." He was the last police chief of Old Sparta. (PC Webb.)

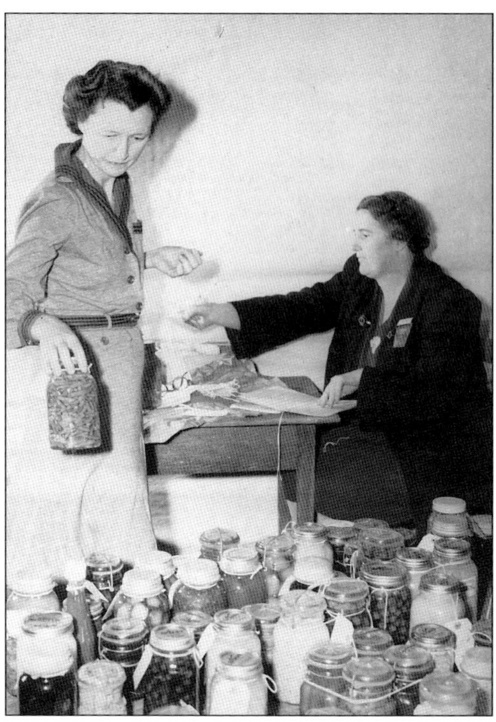

The Rocky Mount Fair has been hosting contests and rides at the fairgrounds every fall since the 1930s. Here, two women prepare the exhibit of award-winning canned goods. Women in the 1930s and 1940s took pride in producing pickles, okra, cucumbers, beets, beans, and many other vegetables for their families. (NCDAH.)

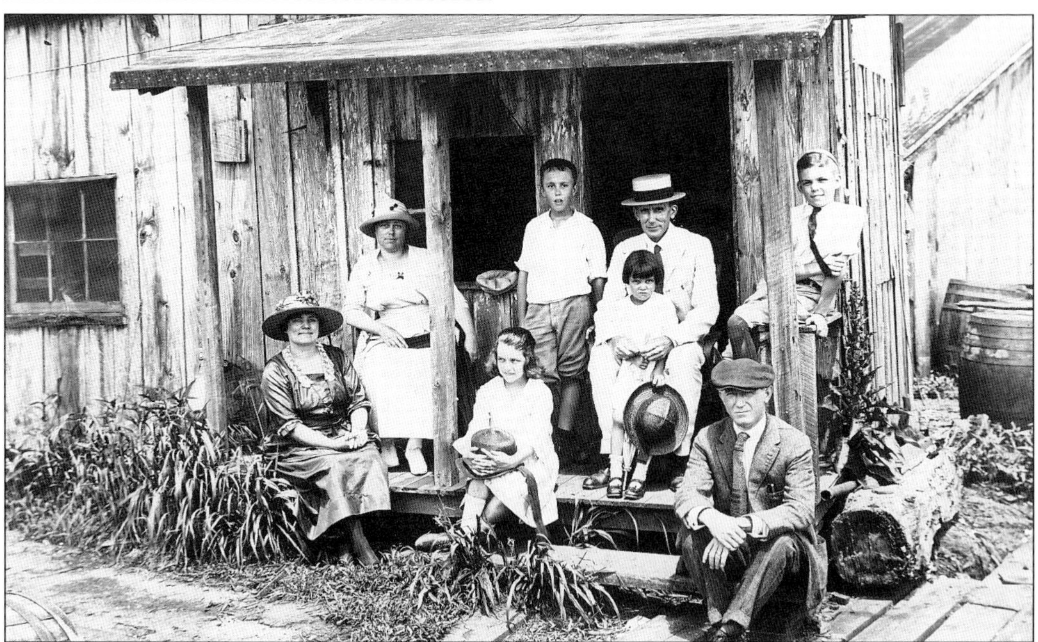

In 1920, the Frank Thompson family posed in front of what truly looks like a "cottage industry." Naval stores like the ones Mr. Thompson processed on Eagles Island were once numerous and strategic to the economy of Wilmington. The rich resin of the longleaf pine was processed and sold to be used in paint, medicine, caulking, and many maritime products.

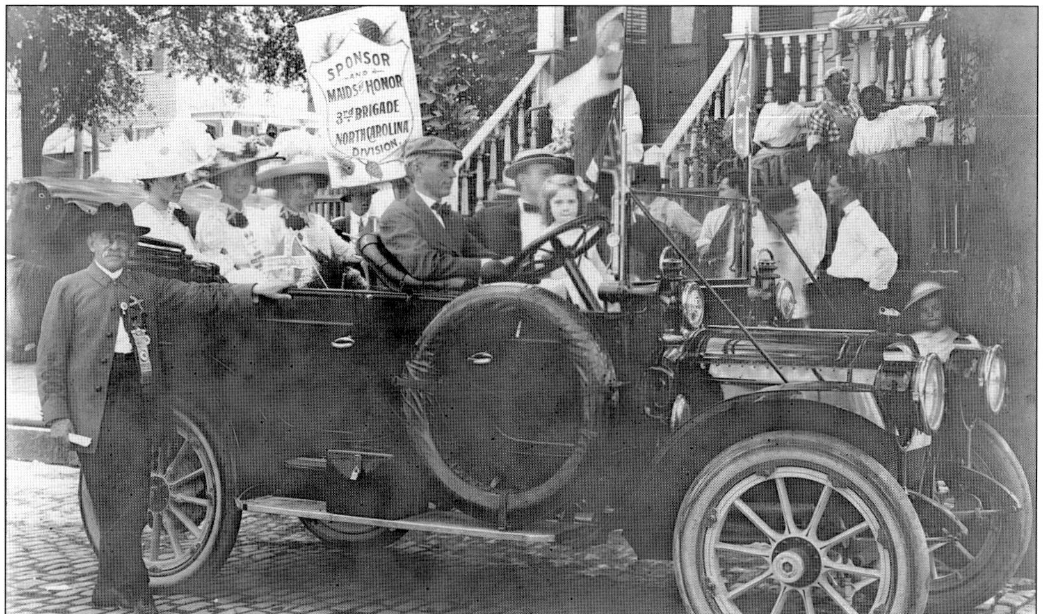

When pretty much any old car was a rarity, this Packard "18" driven by automobile dealer W.D. MacMillan Jr. in 1911 must really have turned heads. Only 2,493 versions of the full-size "18" were produced by Packard, the luxury car benchmark of the day. Each sold for a whopping $4,200. Mary Wiggins Davis and Alice Davis Peck were two of the maids of honor, all three of whom were granddaughters of George Davis, attorney-general for the Confederacy.

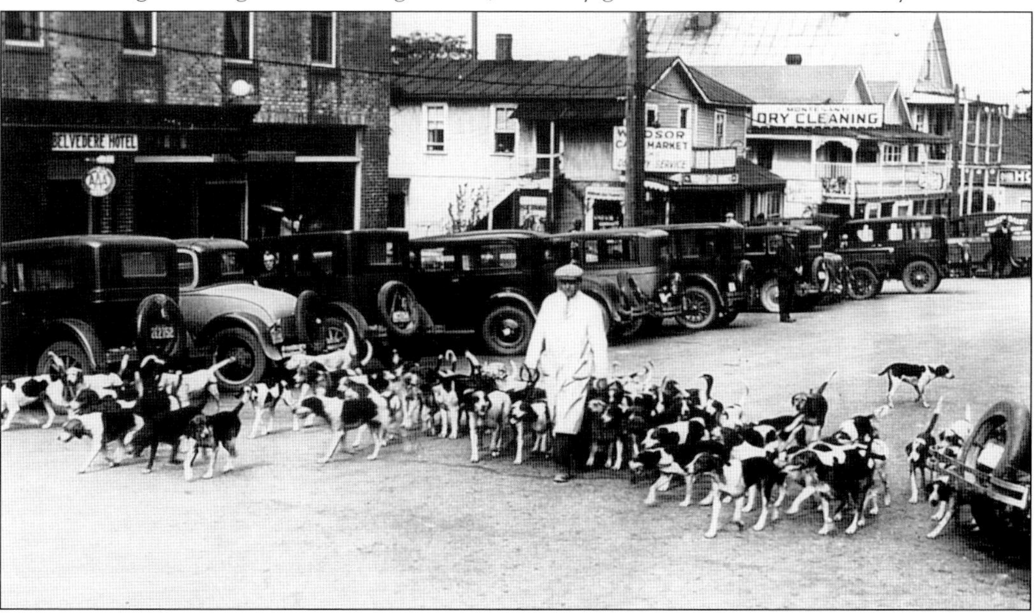

This real-photo postcard features huntsman Harry Knott "roading" the hounds near the entrance of the Belvedere Hotel on Pennsylvania Avenue in the late 1920s. The landmark two-story brick hostelry opened in Southern Pines in 1917. (Courtesy of Willard E. Jones.)

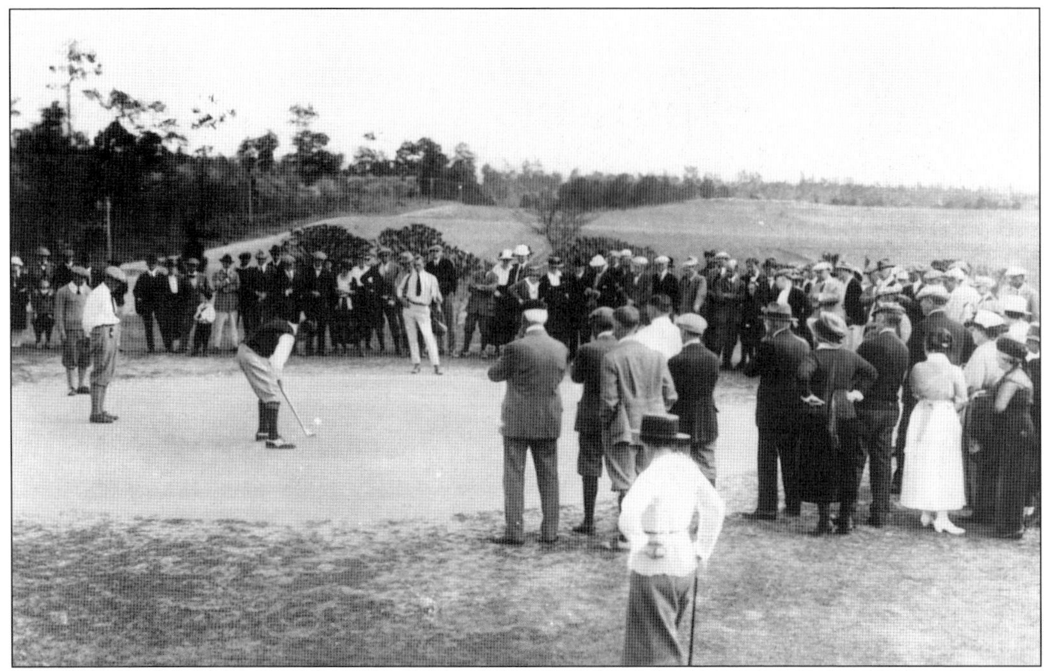

Spectators encircle a sand green to watch golfers putt during a tournament at Southern Pines Country Club before 1920. At that time, greens were covered with sand instead of grass. Eddy photographed numerous amateur and professional golfers in the Sandhills and even took up the game of golf himself in the fall of 1909. (Courtesy of North Carolina Collection.)

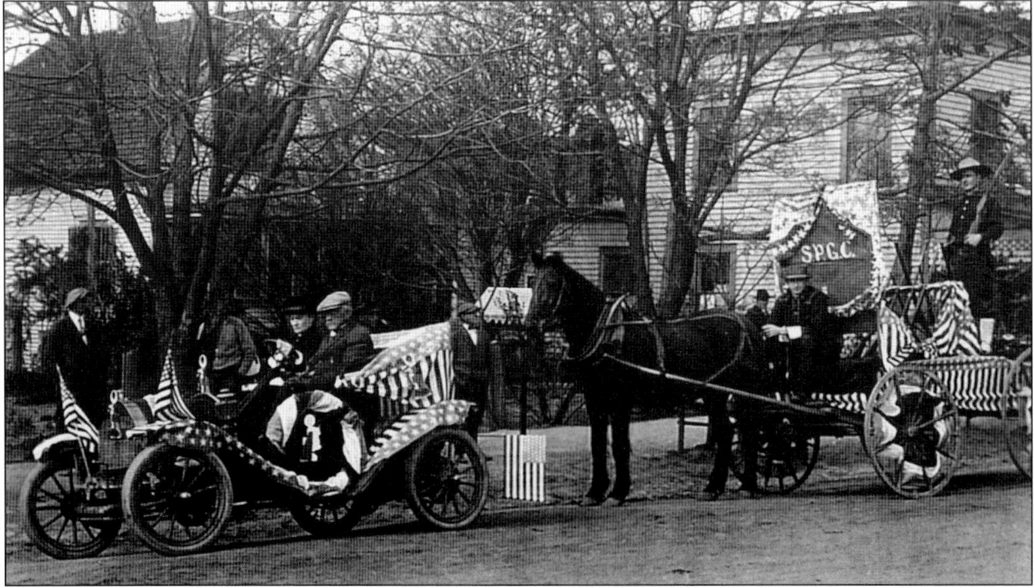

These patriotically decorated floats were on display in the parade of the Firemen's Carnival in Southern Pines in March 1915. The horse-drawn vehicle represented the Southern Pines Gun Club. (Courtesy of Gene Hamlin.)

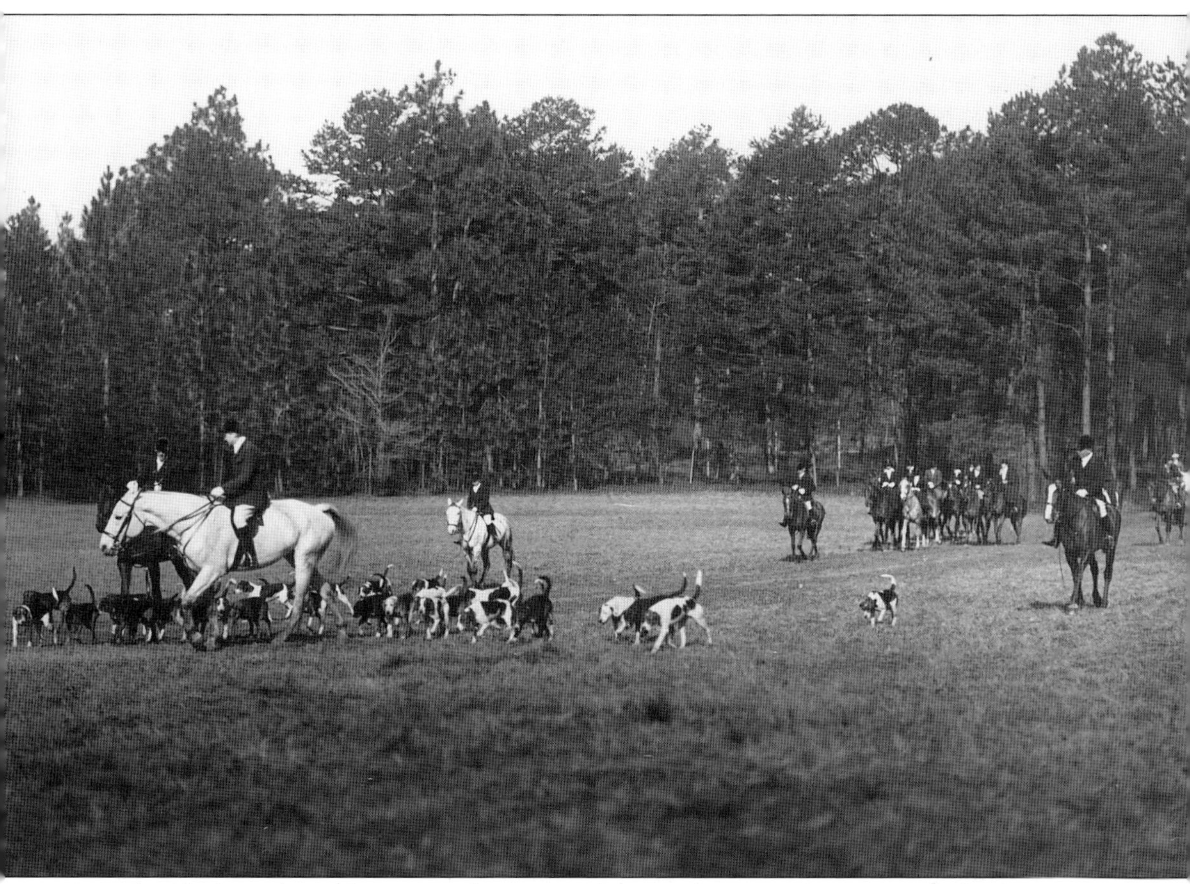

A pack of foxhounds and hunters strike out on a hunt in the 1930s from Weymouth, the estate of the Boyd family at Southern Pines. Eddy admitted that one of his most difficult photograph assignments was mounting a horse with a camera to take pictures of a fox hunt. He failed to get any pictures, and the only result "was the necessity of carrying a pillow to put in every chair [he] sat in for a week." (Courtesy of the North Carolina Division of Archives and History.)

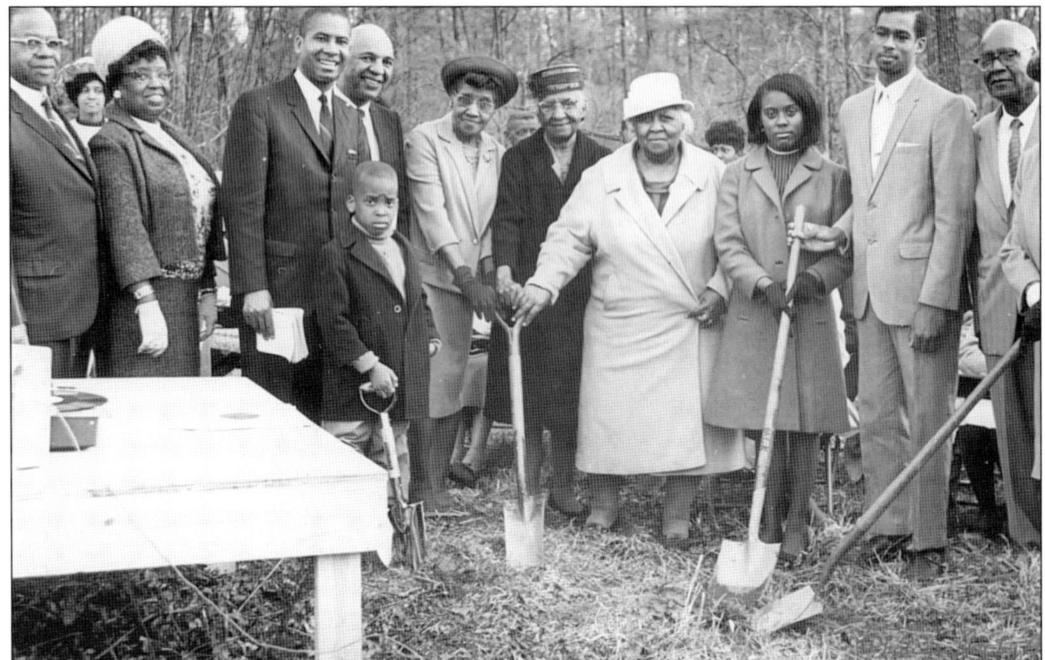

Ground-breaking ceremonies were held on March 30, 1969, for the new White Rock Baptist Church at 3400 Fayetteville Street. In 1971 the congregation moved to its new location after 75 years at the corner of Mobile and Fayetteville Street. (Courtesy of Andre D. Vann.)

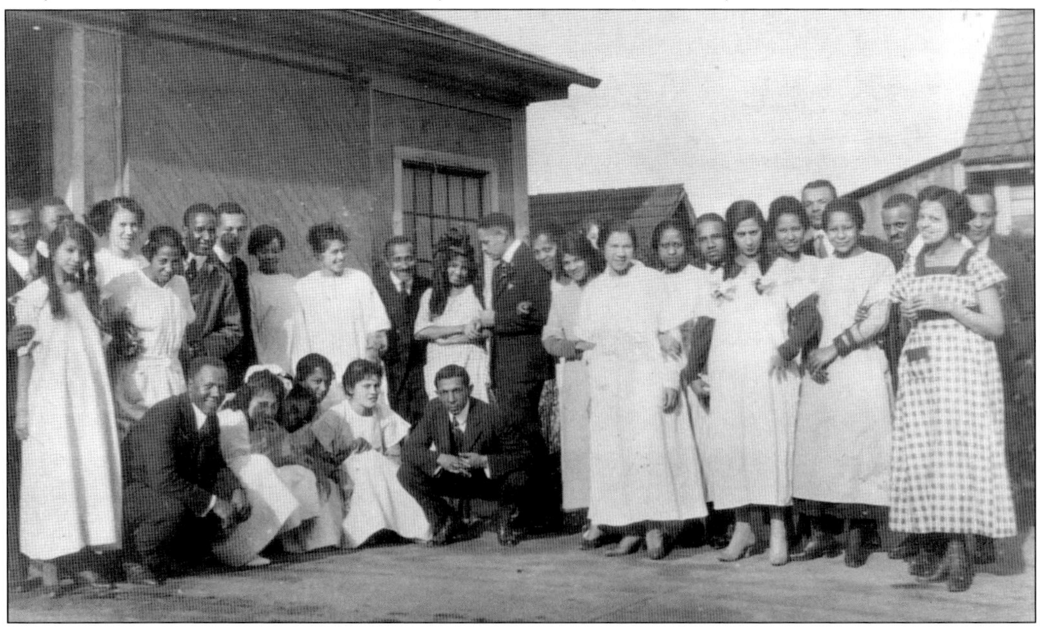

Clyde Donnell and Martha Merrick, daughter of John and Martha Merrick, were married on December 10, 1899. Here friends and family members surrounded the couple. (Courtesy of Andre D. Vann.)

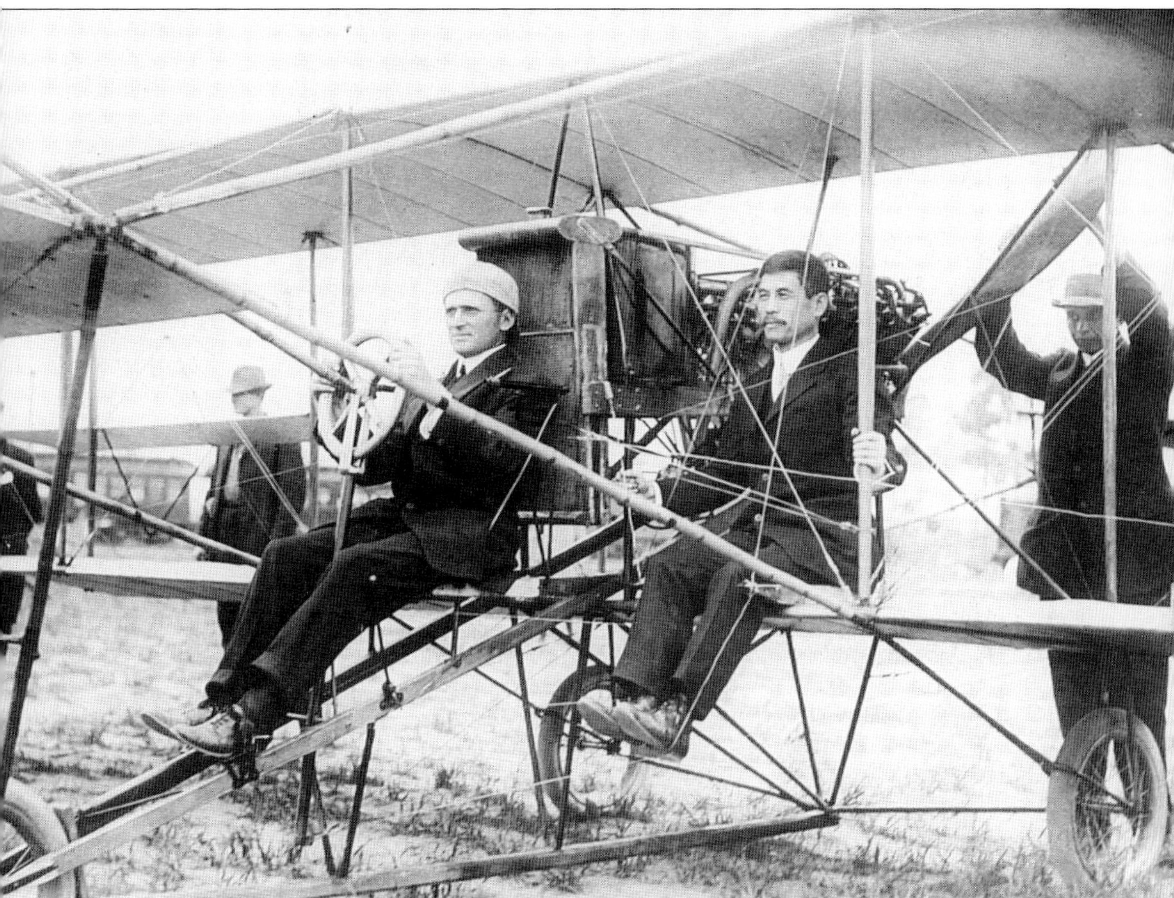

Pictured here with Beachey is Commander S. Saito of the Royal Japanese Navy. The unidentified man at right is about to start the airplane's motor by spinning the propeller by hand. The foreign passenger enjoyed two flights in Beachey's *Buzz Buzzard* in early April 1911. Saito was excited about the aircraft and realized its potential for use by the Japanese military. (Courtesy of Tufts Archives, Pinehurst.)

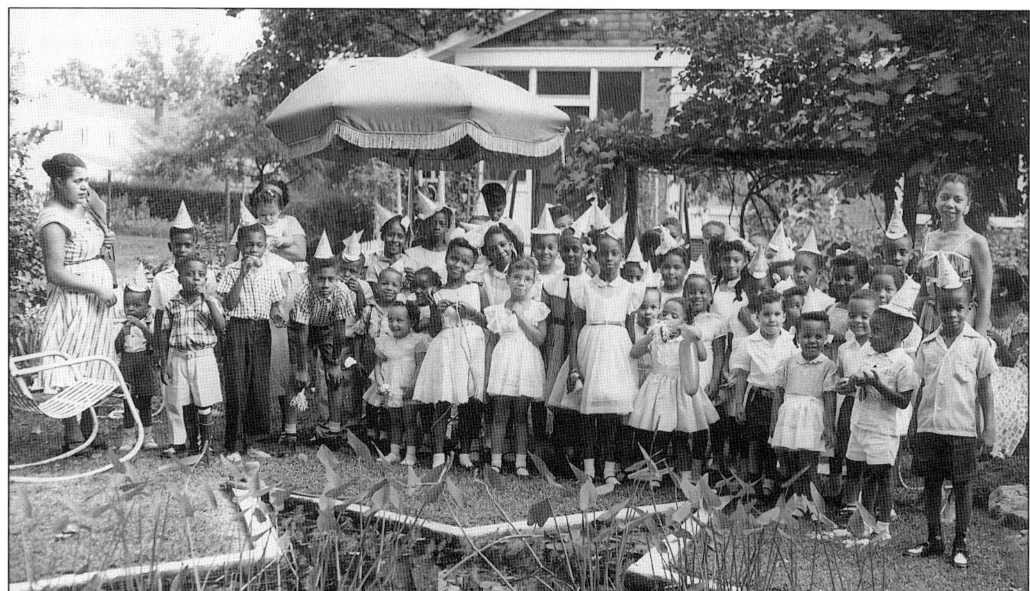

Hayti children enjoy a birthday party at the home of the Rencher N. Harris family on Formosa Avenue. (Courtesy of Ellis Allen / Andre Vann.)

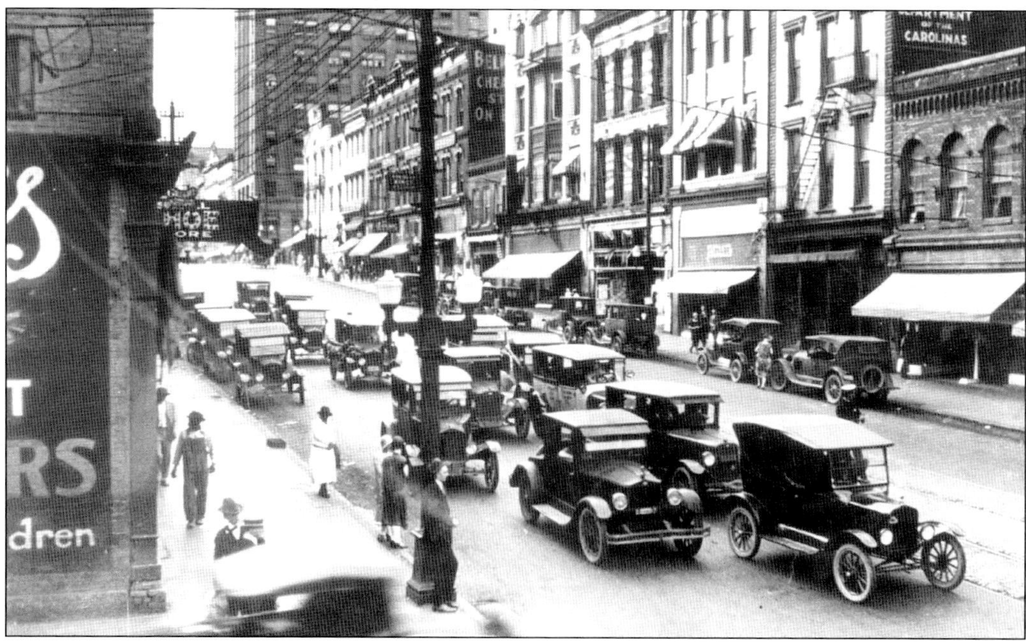

Every imaginable sort of street traffic—pedestrian, streetcar, automobile, bicycle—shared the road in Charlotte's early days. This photograph was taken looking down the first block of East Trade Street toward Tryon Street. Just to the left of the power pole in the center of the image is Kings Business College, shown here in its original location before its move to the Elizabeth neighborhood. (Robinson-Spangler Carolina Room, Public Library of Charlotte and Mecklenburg County.)

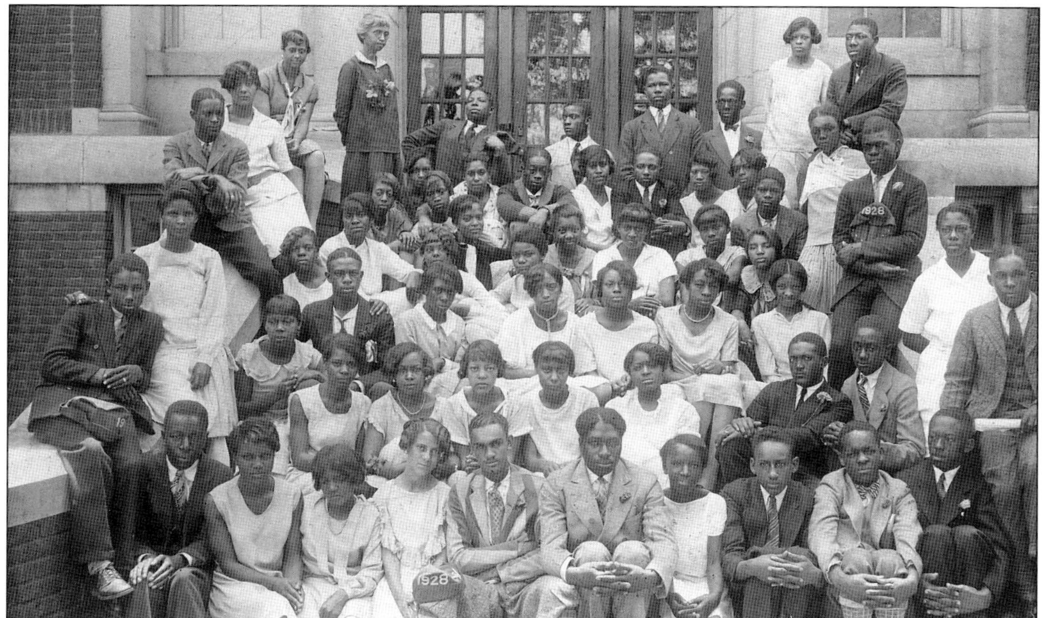

It's May 17, 1928, at Second Ward School, the first public high school for blacks in Charlotte-Mecklenburg. The students, many of whom lived across town in black neighborhoods such as Biddleville and Washington Heights, walked several miles to school each day. Back then, the school offered instruction only through the eighth grade. Students seeking further education had to look elsewhere, and many went on to Johnson C. Smith University, which had a high school division as well as college programs. By the 1940s, Second Ward provided instruction for students through the twelfth grade. The school graduated its last class in 1969. (Second Ward High School National Alumni Foundation.)

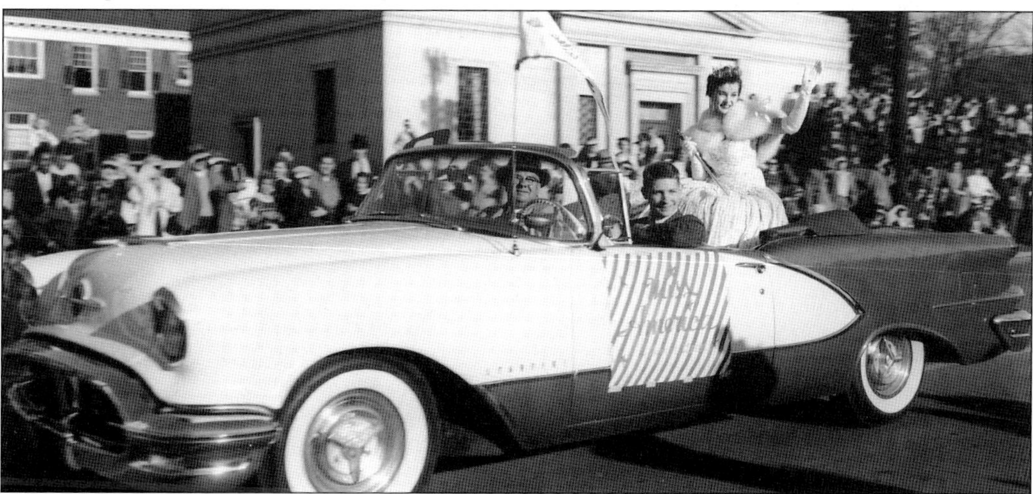

Here's Miss America, Ann Drew, waving to the crowd gathered along the parade route. Whether from the brightness of the afternoon sunshine or the brilliance of the beauty queen and her jewels, many of the onlookers are shielding their eyes as Miss America passes by in this 1950s photograph. (Kugler's Studio.)

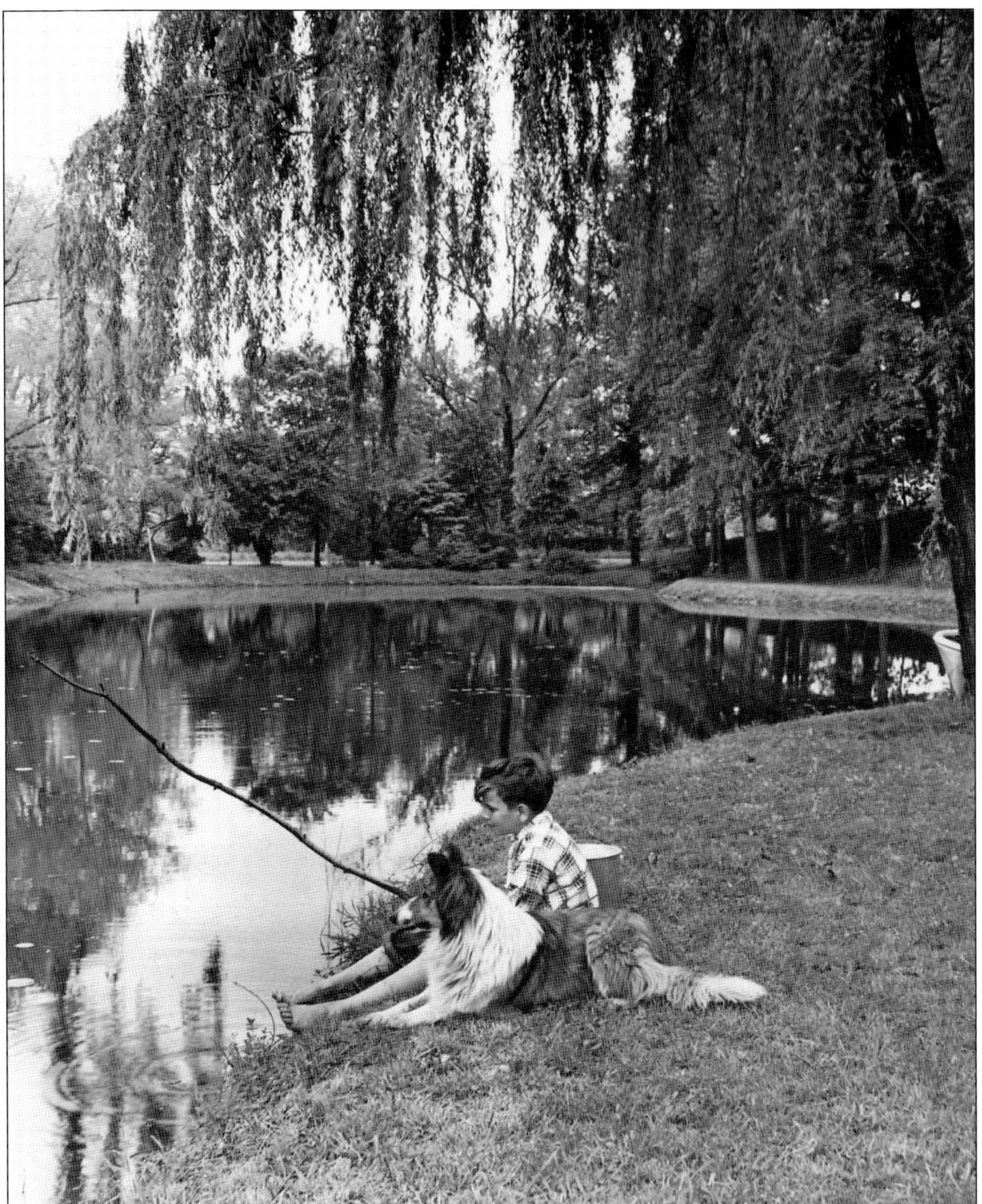

By the 1950s, many of Charlotte's trees had grown up and matured along with the city's young neighborhoods. At the intersection of present-day Park Road and Kenilworth Road, this small pond was visited by hopeful angler Skip Kugler and a canine friend. The pond has since been filled in and developed as part of an apartment complex. (Carey Kugler.)

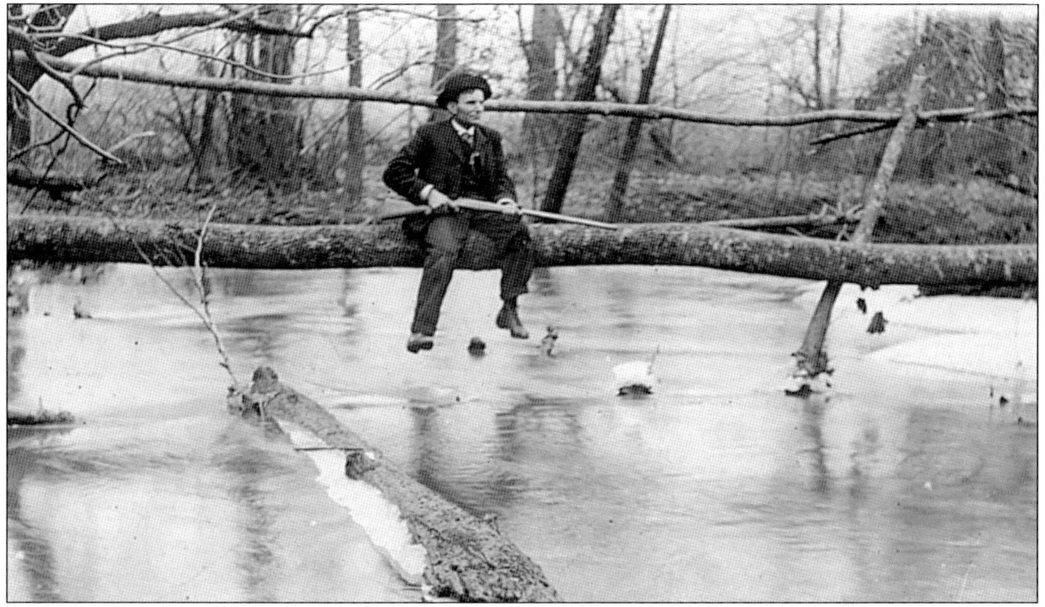

Rowan County's abundant game provided food and sport for many families. This young man appears to be enjoying his solitude in a restful pose over the icy waters.

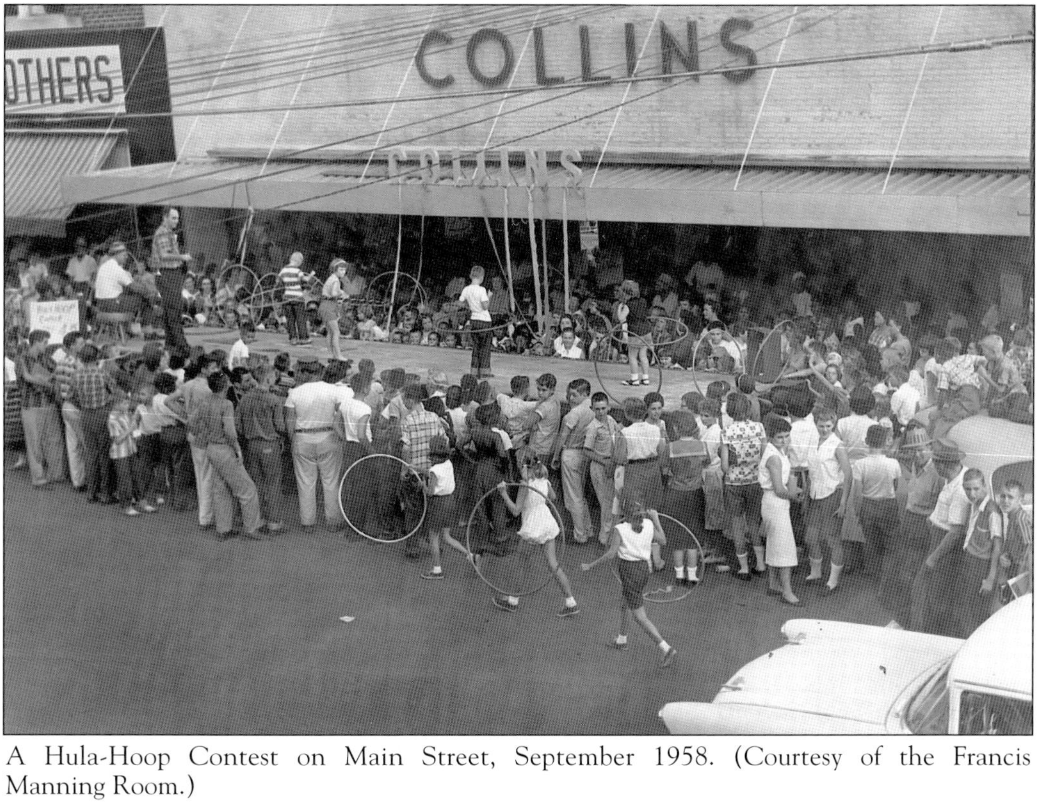

A Hula-Hoop Contest on Main Street, September 1958. (Courtesy of the Francis Manning Room.)

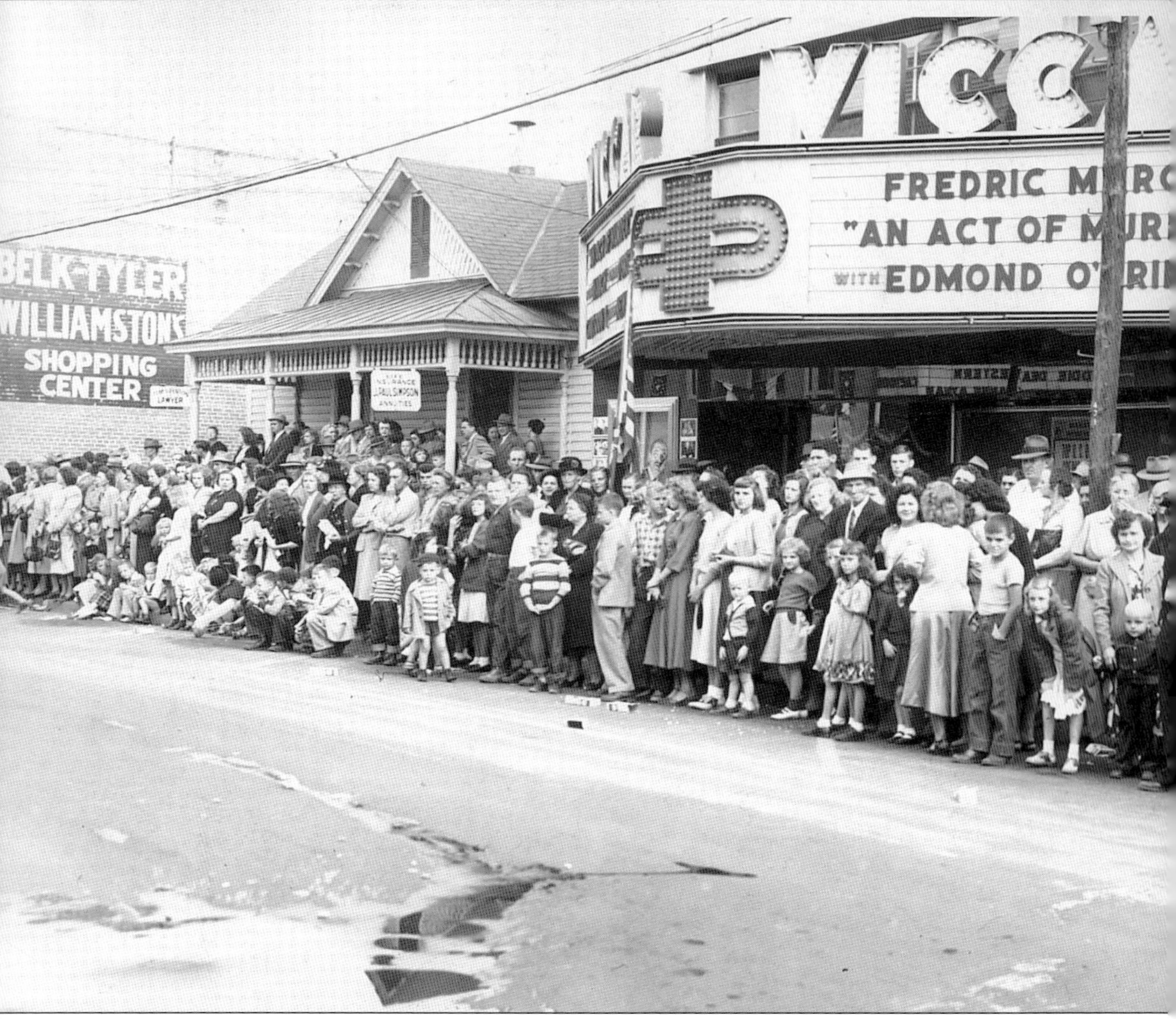

Harvest and Christmas parades began to make a more regular appearance on the Main Street scene after World War II. They initially began as promotional events for commercial activity downtown but have since become annual rituals for community pride. This photograph was taken in 1949. (Courtesy of Francis Manning Room.)

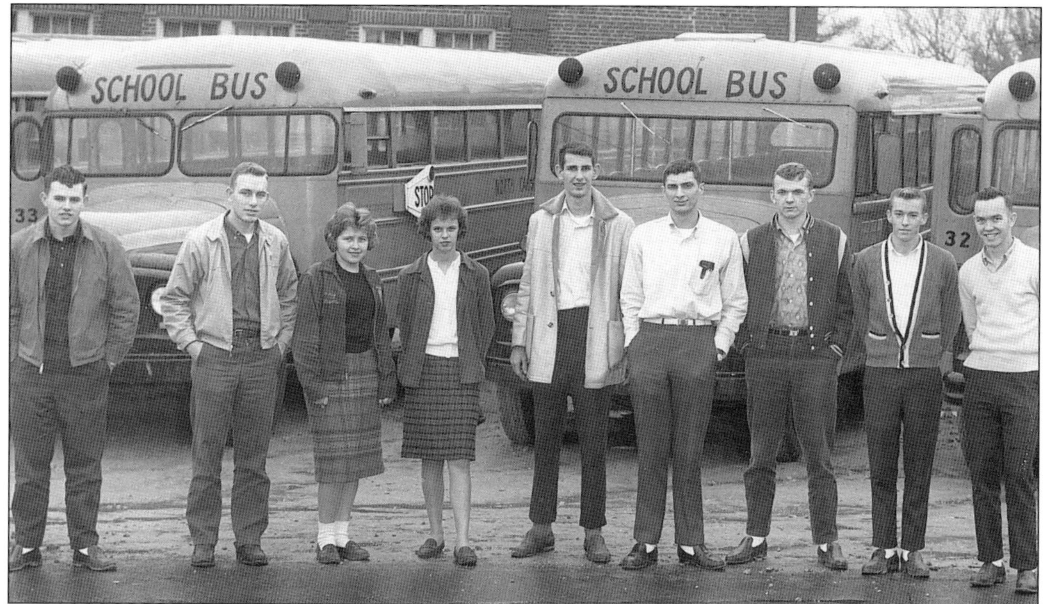

Robersonville High School Bus Drivers, March 1963. (Courtesy of the Francis Manning Room.)

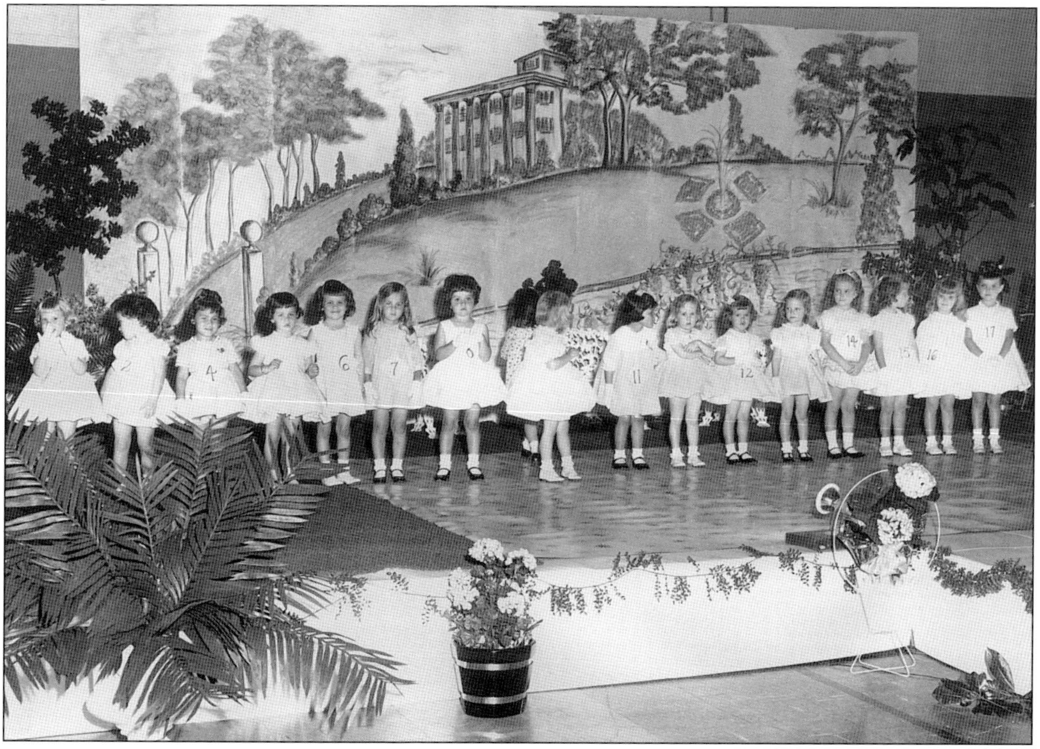

A Youth Beauty Pageant in Williamston, *c.* Mid-1960s. (Courtesy of the Francis Manning Room.)

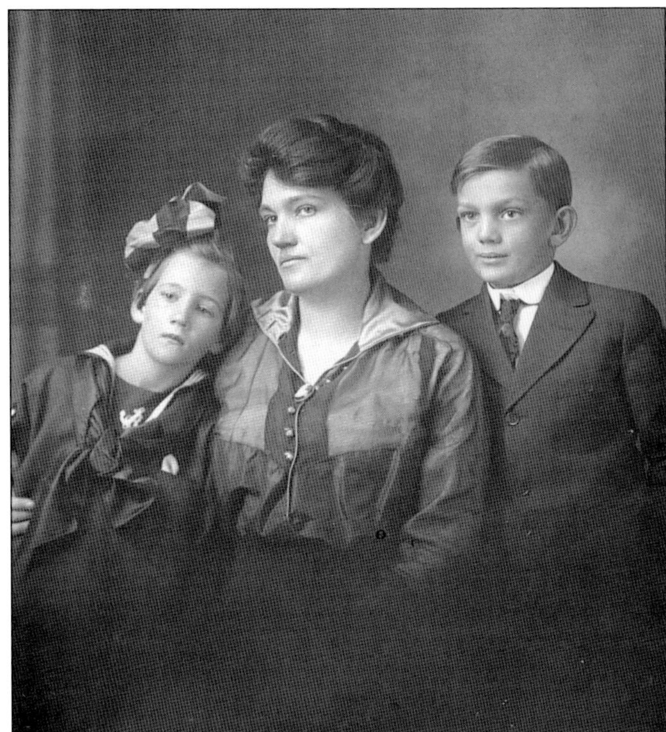

The Lovette Biggs Harrison Family of Williamston, c. 1915. Pictured here are Hattie Harrell Harrison and her children, Evelyn and Bill. (Courtesy of Ann H. McKeel.)

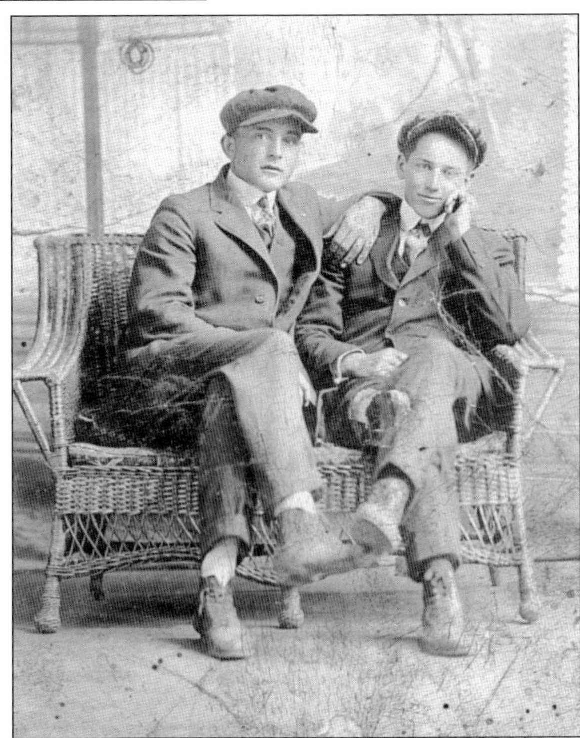

Tommy Lawrence Roberson and Gilbert Rogerson, Bear Grass, *c.* 1917. Roberson was the son of Reddick Roberson, a founder of the town of Bear Grass. (Courtesy of Joyce T. Roberson.)

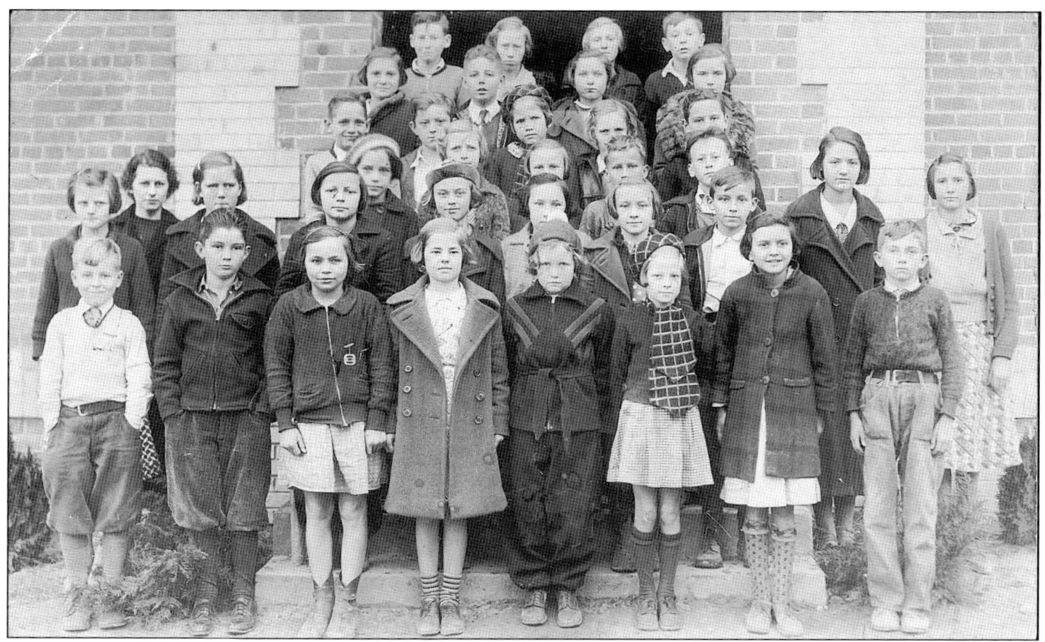

Fourth graders at the old Jamesville Elementary School posed for this class portrait taken around 1934. (Courtesy of Mary G. Dixon.)

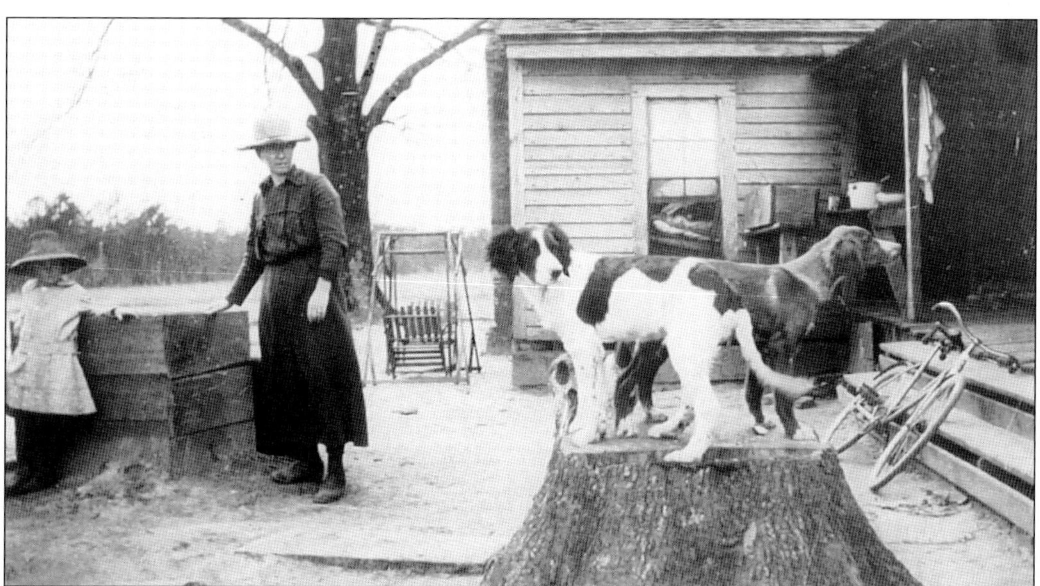

Aunt Duck and child near the back porch of her home, farmville area, 1910s. Notice the dogs on the stump, the bicycle on the steps, and the swing visible farther down the yard. (Courtesy of East Carolina Manuscript Collection, East Carolina University.)

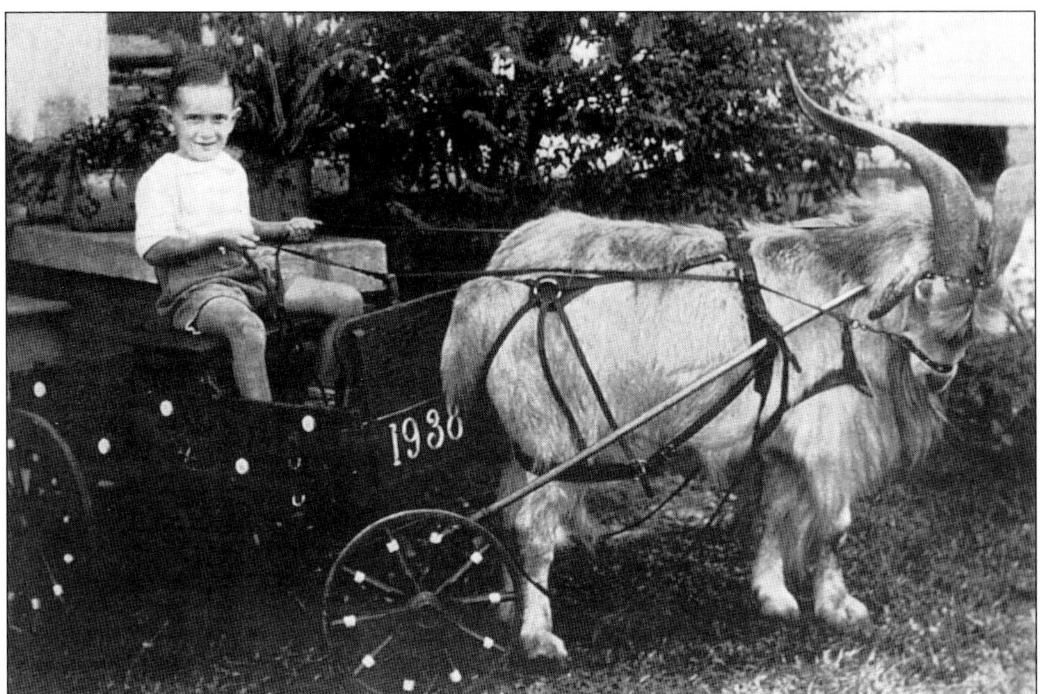

John M. Godwin is seen here in 1938, enjoying his goat cart in front of his house at 1012 Ward Street in Greenville. Pictures of children in goat carts were in vogue at the time. (Courtesy of Jeanne Jenkins.)

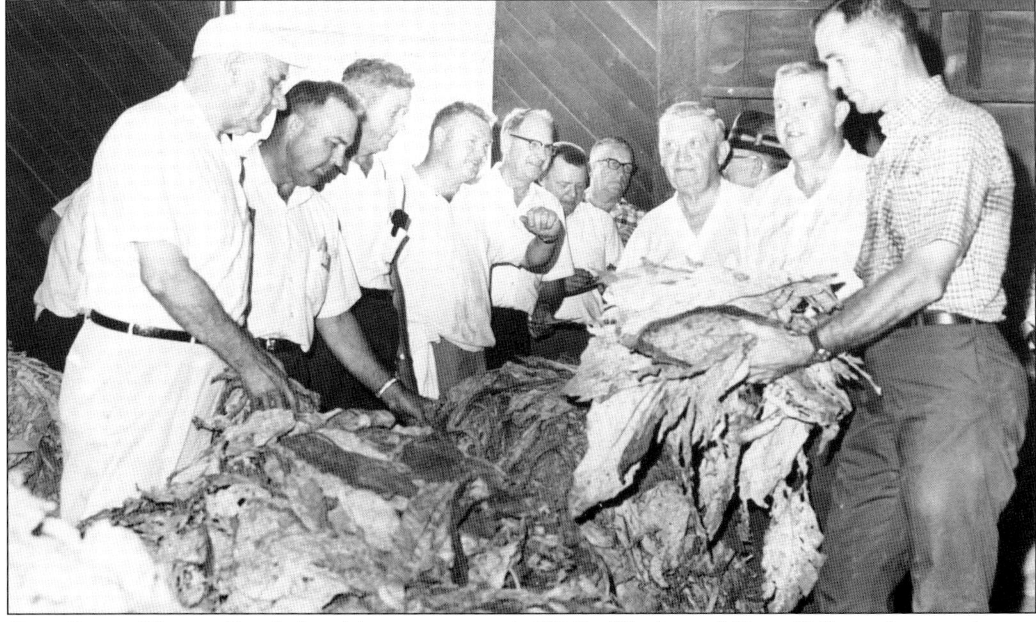

Don Price, Champ Batchelor (the auctioneer), W.G. Clark, and Don Gilliam Jr. are shown here at the opening of the tobacco market. (BBH.)

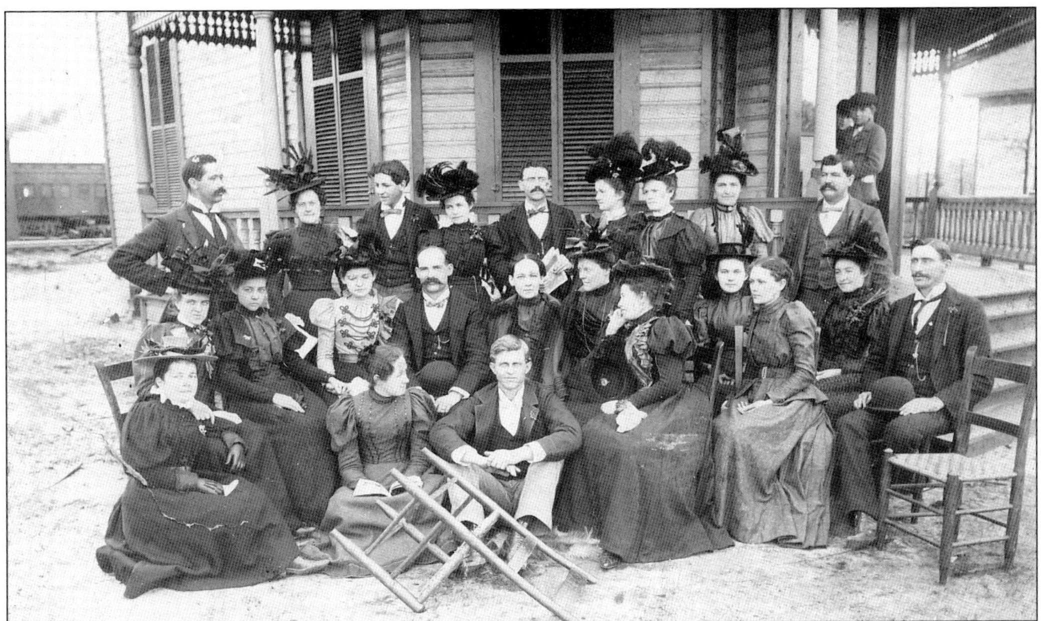

Pictured in front of the town's first library building is the S.A.L. Magrundi Club. The structure was used for a variety of social activities.

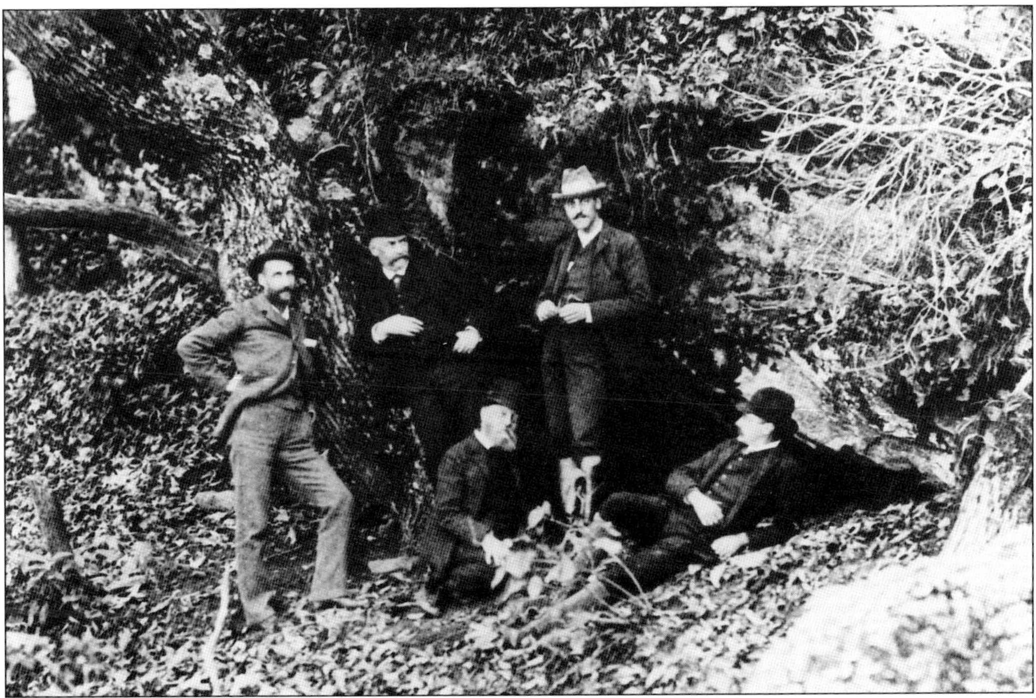

The famed architectural landscape firm of Olmsted, Olmsted, and Eliot was hired by Pinehurst founder James Walker Tufts to design the layout of the village. Pictured in the center of the photograph is Frederick Law Olmsted (seated), with George W. Vanderbilt to his right.

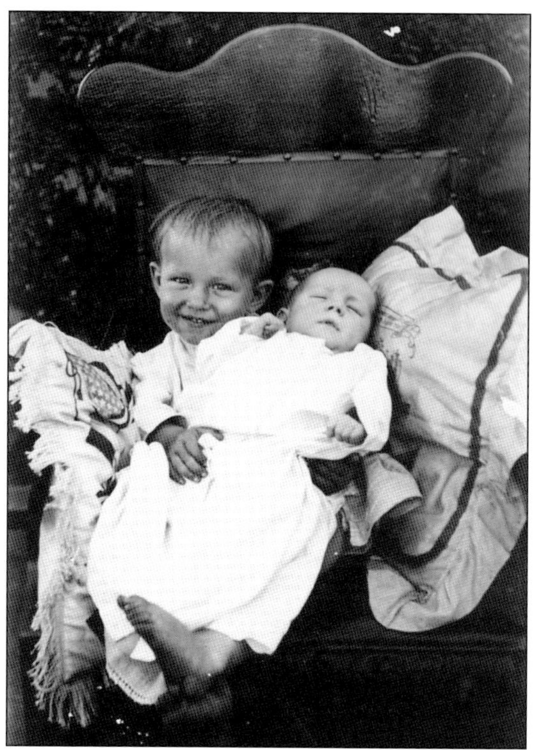

William Aheron holds his sister Sunshine so his Dad can make another 1920s postcard/birth announcement. Dan and Bertha had five girls and three boys during their many years together. (Courtesy of Bertha Vestal Aheron and the Aheron family, Eden, NC.)

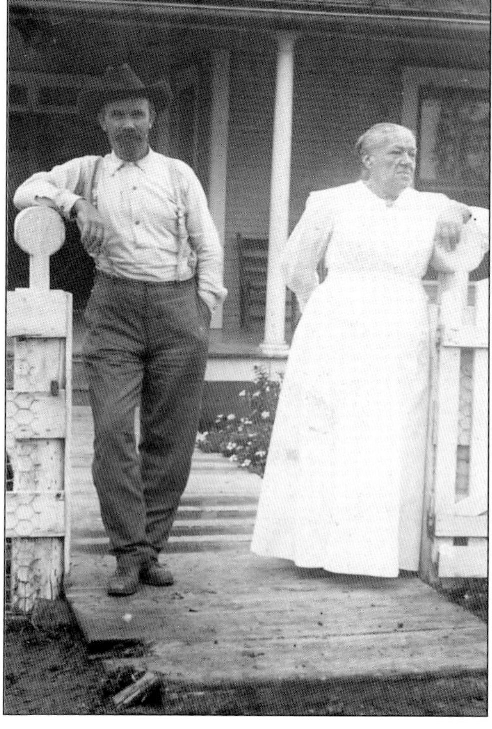

Rubin Hensley Joyce and his wife are the subjects of this postcard dating around the 1870s. The exact location in Stoneville is not known. (Courtesy of the Zelma Joyce Scott Collection, Stoneville, NC.)

Three

More Than Our Bread and Butter:
The Livelihoods

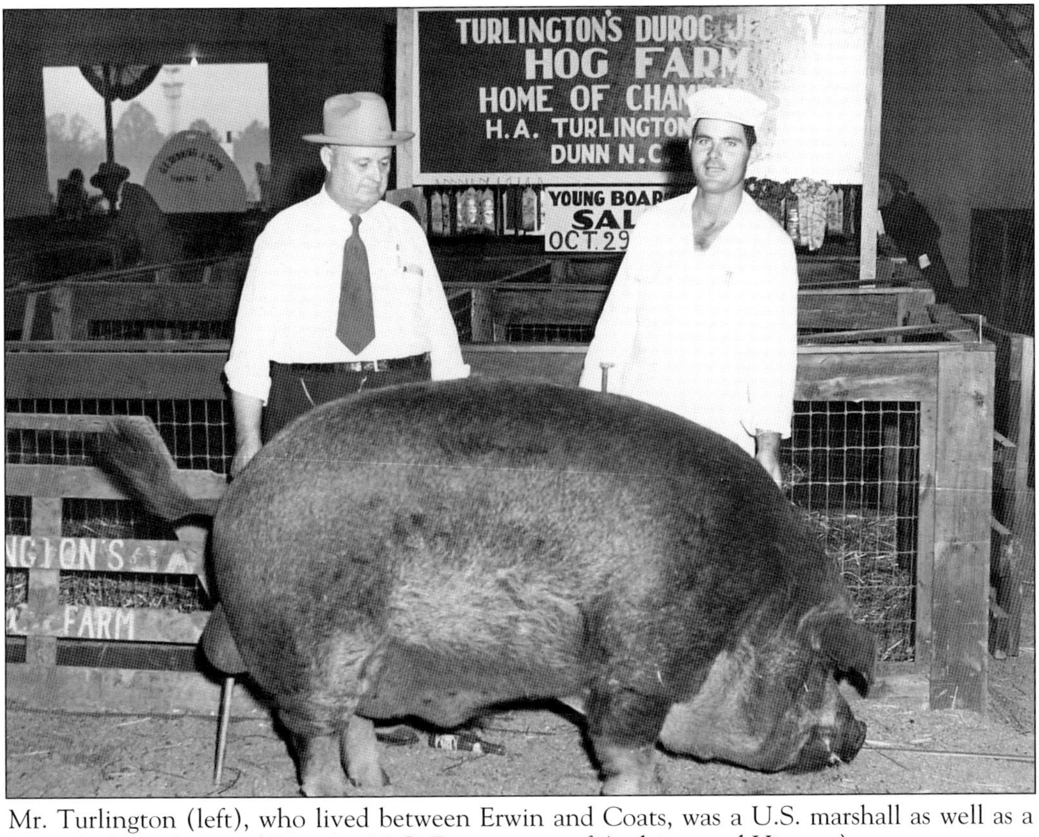

Mr. Turlington (left), who lived between Erwin and Coats, was a U.S. marshall as well as a renowned hog farmer. (Courtesy N.C. Department of Archives and History.)

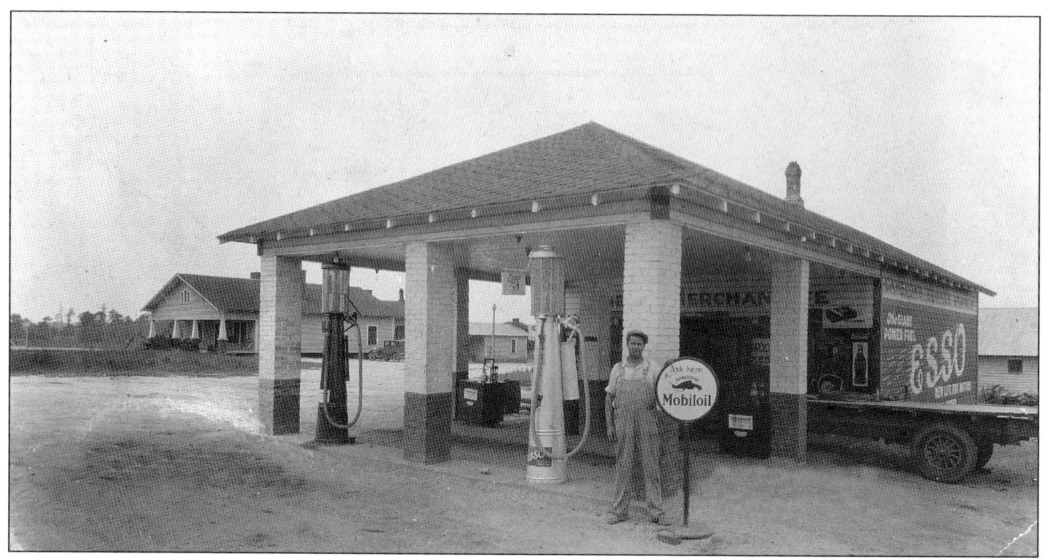

Duncan Cameron's Store in the Boone Trail Community, *c.* 1940.

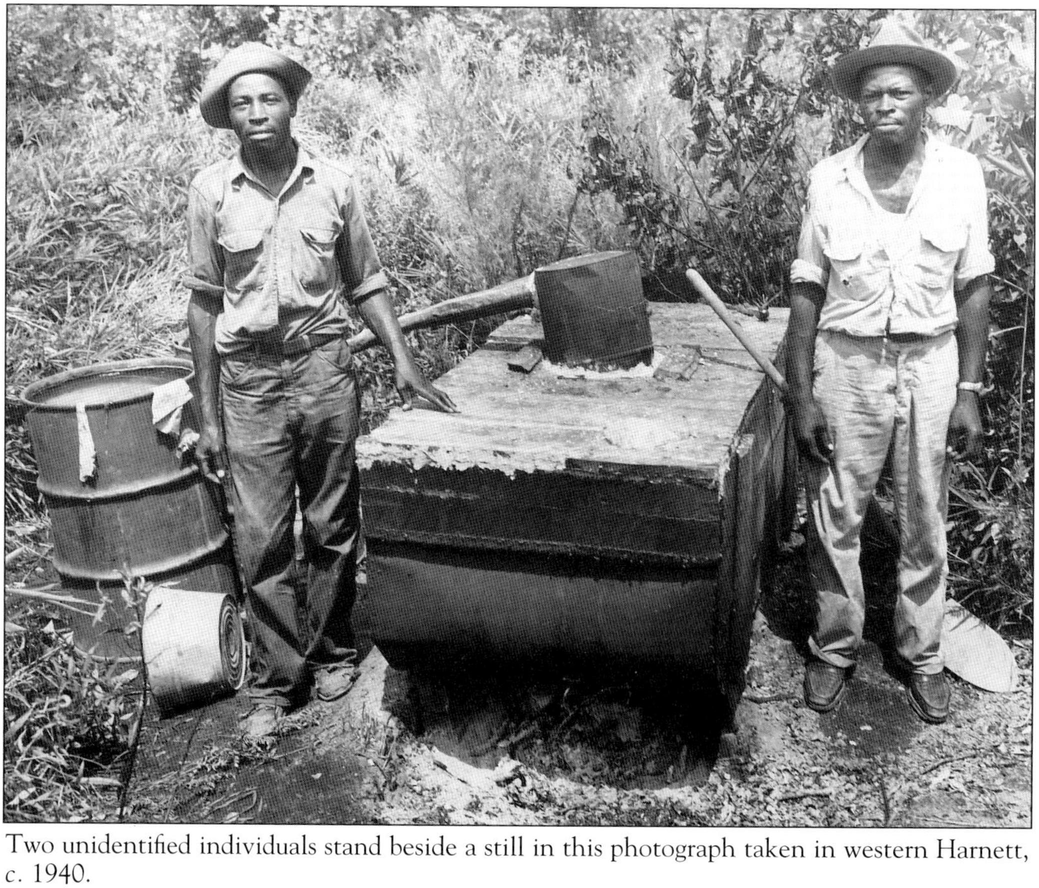

Two unidentified individuals stand beside a still in this photograph taken in western Harnett, *c.* 1940.

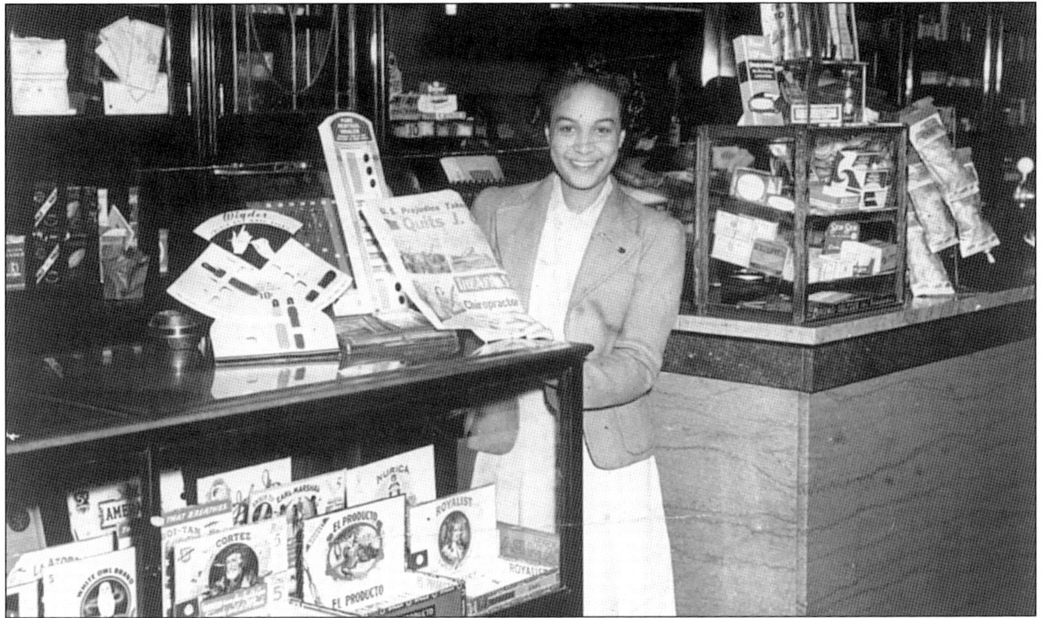

In this 1940 photograph, Gloria Garrett Pratt, daughter of Dr. York David and Julia Williams Garrett, is pictured with newspapers beside a tobacco counter inside the Biltmore Drug Store in the Biltmore Hotel on Pettigrew Street. (Courtesy of the Durham County Public Library.)

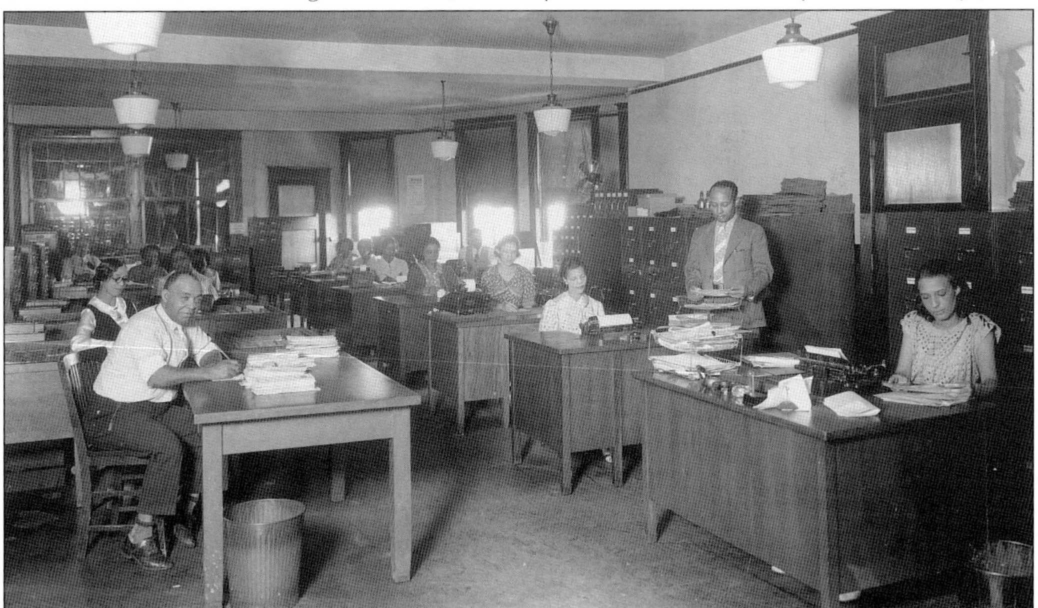

Durham's North Carolina Mutual Life Insurance Company, formed in 1898, became the largest black-owned business in the United States and was a major employer of black professionals. This photograph of clerical workers in the company's "industrial department" was made about 1930. Joseph W. Goodloe, to the extreme right, would go on to become the president in 1967. (Courtesy of Andre D. Vann.)

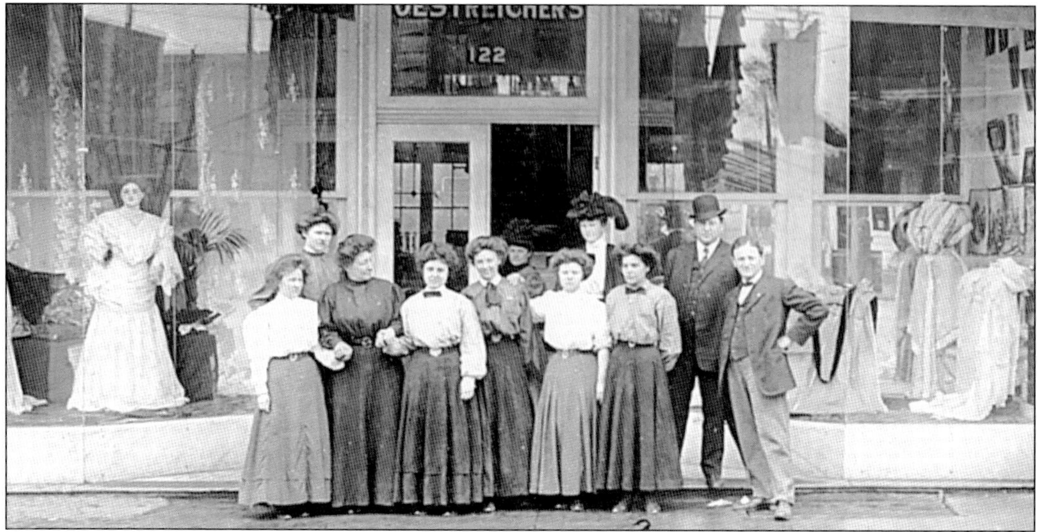

David Oestreicher, on the far right, had a tremendous impact on Rowan County. In fact, Theo Buerbaum moved to Salisbury because of their friendship! Located at 122 South Main Street, Oestreicher's store sold a variety of goods ranging from the beautiful bustle dresses on the left to matting from China, which was used as floor coverings. The tall lady in the second row on the left is believed to be America Aaron Weinbrum, who married Carl Weinbrum. The couple met at Oestreicher's and both worked there approximately 50 years. Oestreicher's, under David and his son Irvin, was for many years one of Salisbury's "fancy stores." (Courtesy of Rachel Oestreicher Bernheim.)

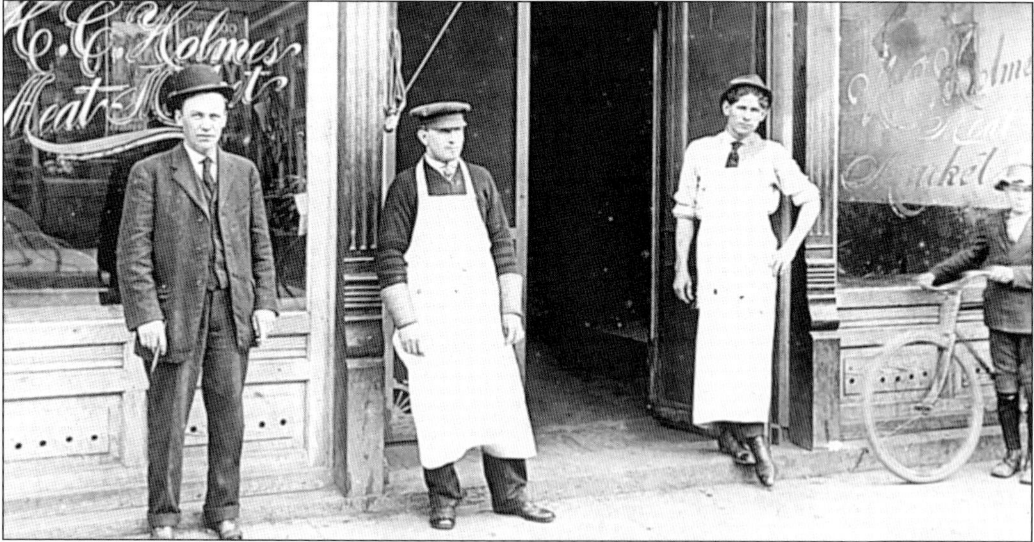

The H.C. Holmes Meat Market was owned by Haden Charles Holmes (pictured on the left), who bought the market from his father in 1904. Holmes served as city manager in Salisbury and died while in office. He was the driving force behind the creation of the City Lake and Park. Holmes was the grandfather of Jim and Gordon Hurley and the late Haden Hurley, Salisbury's prominent newspaper family.

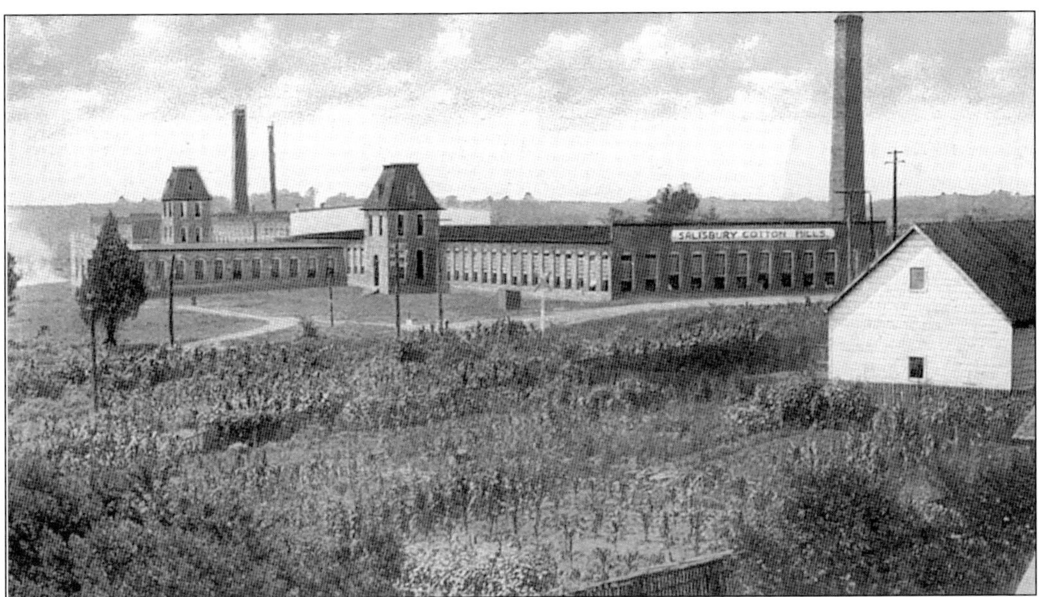

The Salisbury Cotton Mill was built in 1888 as the result of a successful revival. When a traveling evangelist challenged local businessmen to put idle hands to work, they met his challenge. Salisbury's Episcopal priest, Francis Murdoch, was one of the driving forces behind the mill. Eventually, Cone Mills took over the plant. After 110 years of continuous operation in the same location, the mill closed in 1999.

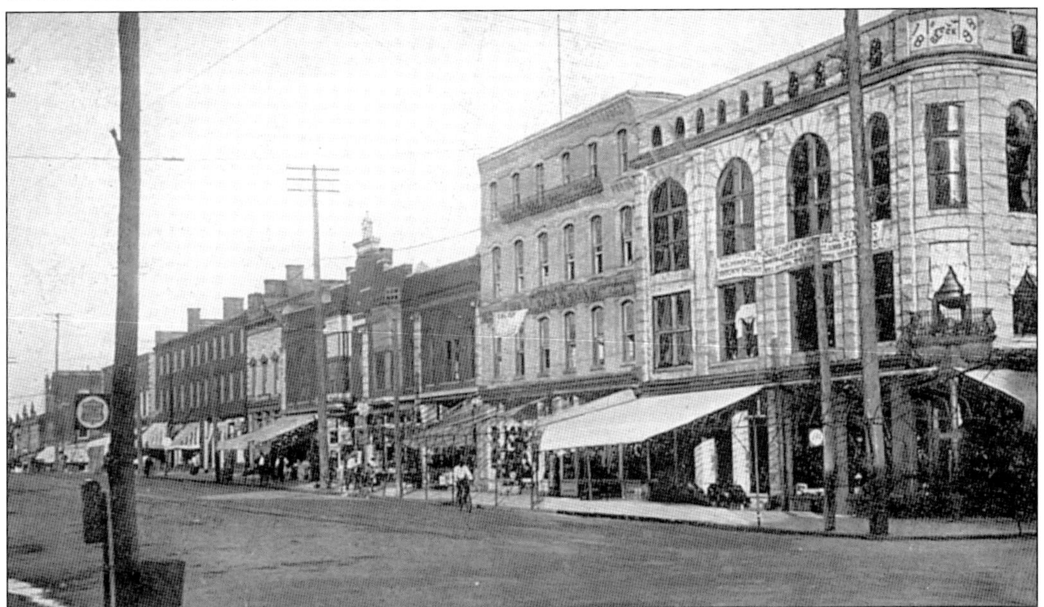

The Bell Block Building on the corner of South Main and East Fisher Streets was built in 1898 for David Gaskill and his aunt, Mrs. Bell. The architect was C.C. Hood of Charlotte. For years, the Belk Budget Shop housed the building. The banner across the front of the building advertises the Southern Commercial School.

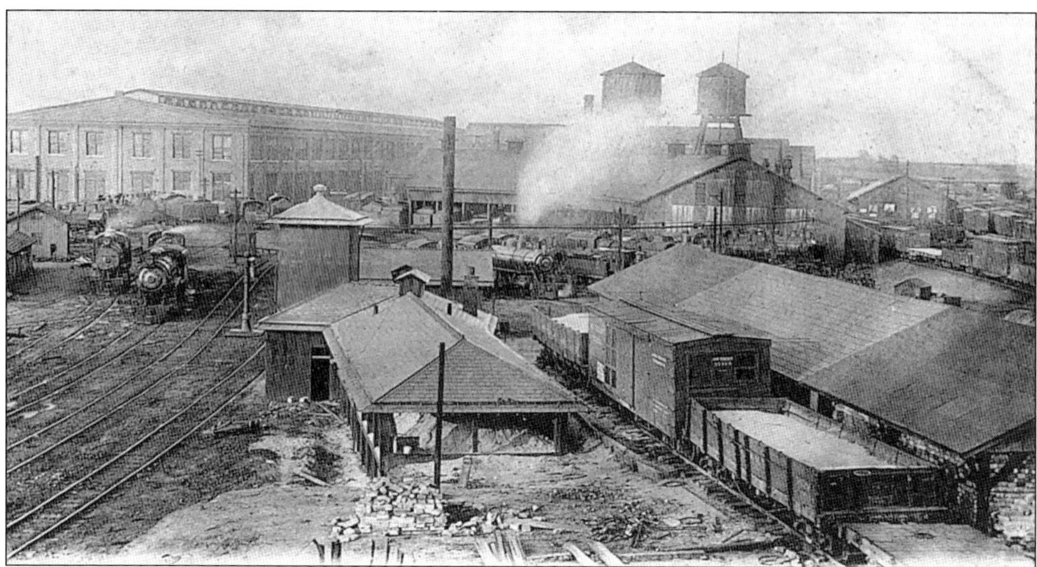

In 1896, 3 miles north of Salisbury, Southern Railroad Company started what became the largest steam locomotive servicing facility between Washington, D.C., and Atlanta, Georgia. Streets were laid out, residences built, and the Town of Spencer—named for Samuel Spencer, president of Southern Railroad—was begun. Today, the facility is known as the N.C. Transportation Museum.

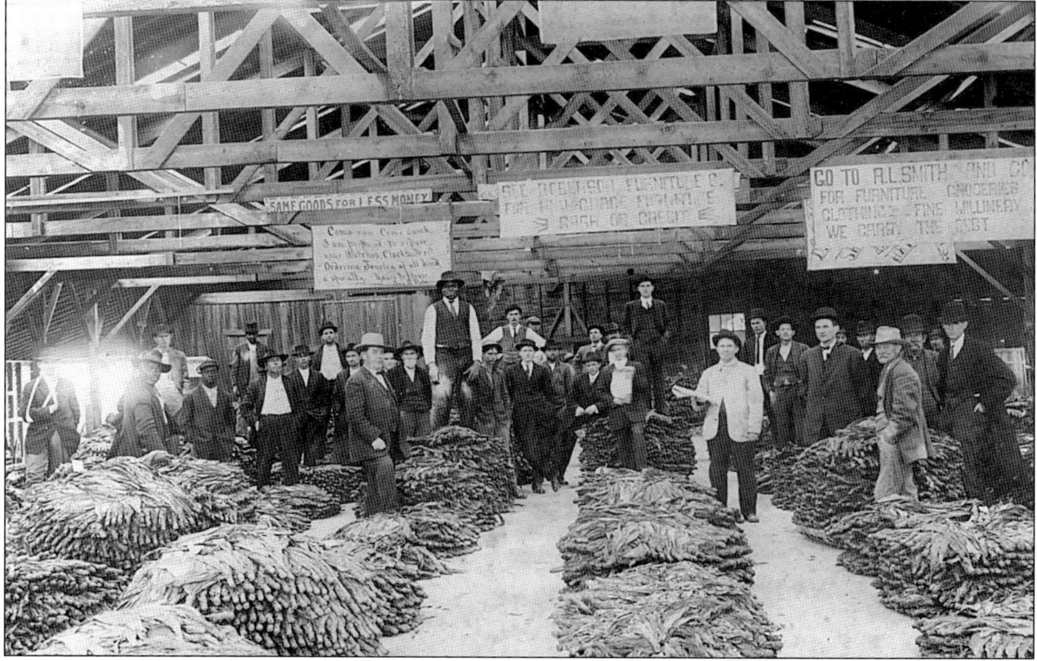

Another Inside View of the Adkins and Bailey Warehouse, c. 1910. The first auction sale of tobacco in Martin County occurred in Robersonville on August 7, 1900. (Courtesy of Doris L. Wilson.)

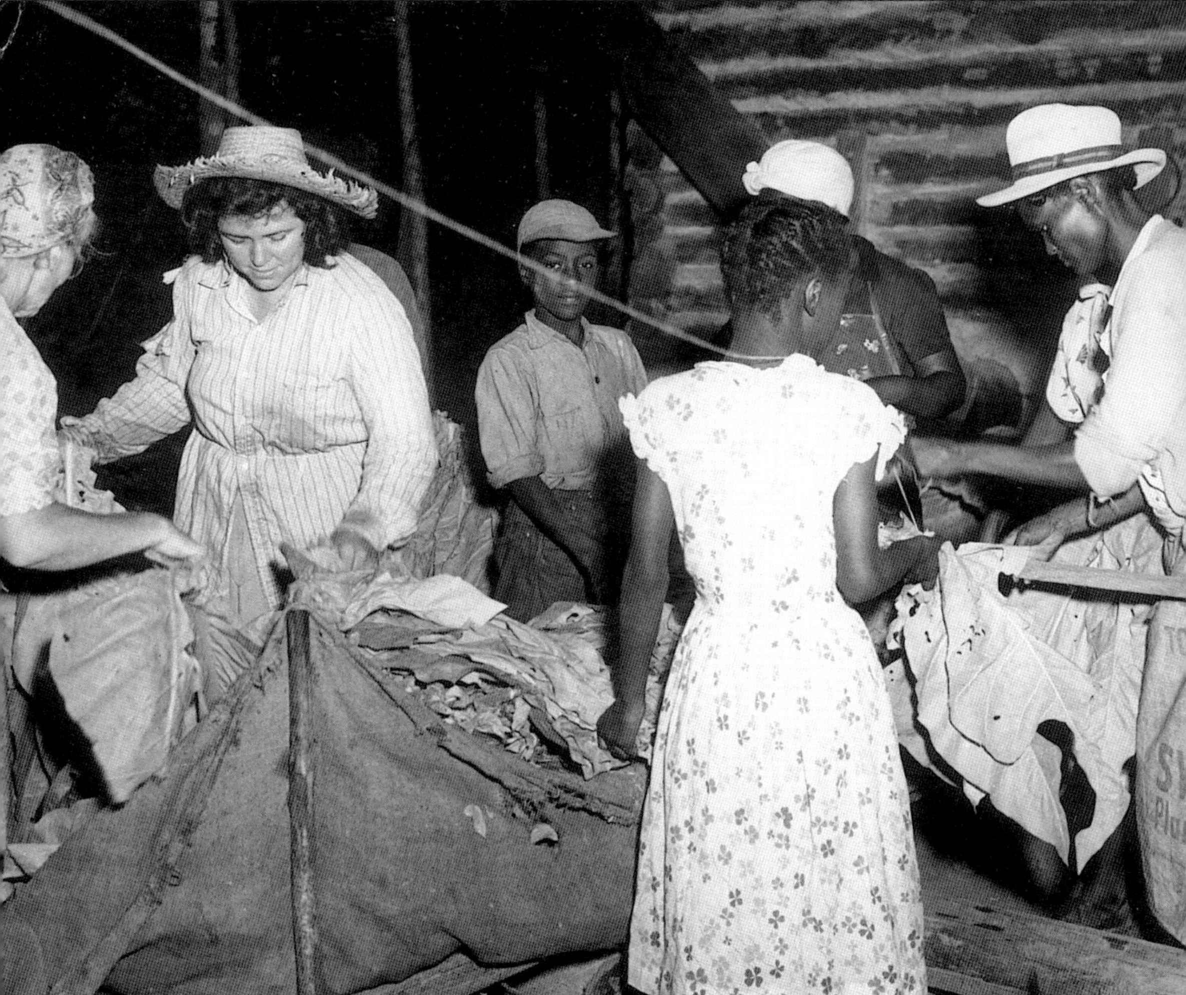

Harvesting tobacco the old way in Martin County, c. 1940s. (Courtesy of the Francis Manning Room.)

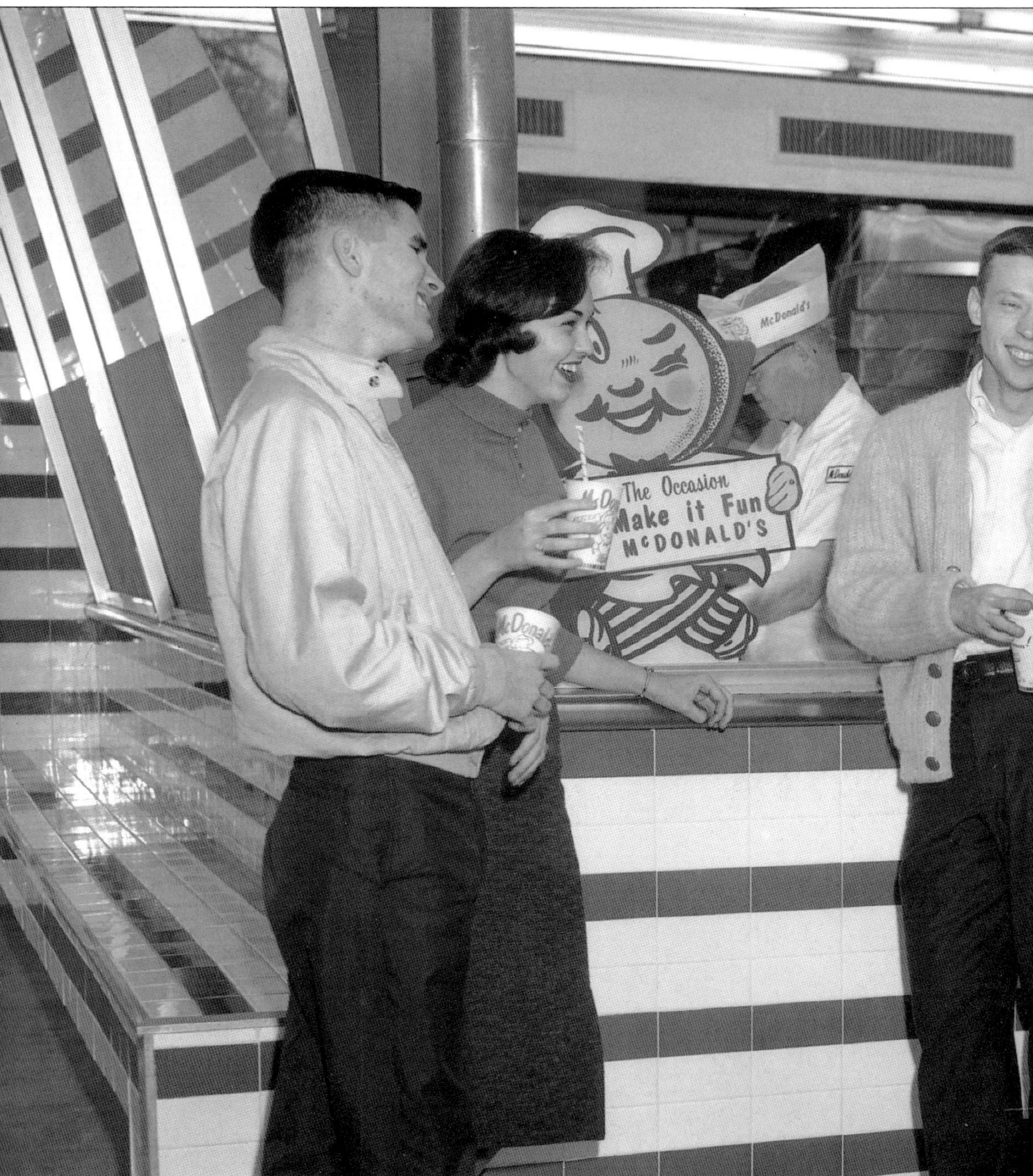

Greensboro has the distinction of being the site of the first McDonald's in North Carolina, which opened at this Summit Avenue location on September 30, 1959. Six weeks later, these Grimsley High School students decided to sample its 15¢ hamburgers, 10¢ fries, and 20¢ milk shakes. McDonald's became a popular hangout, at least for white students; like all the city's

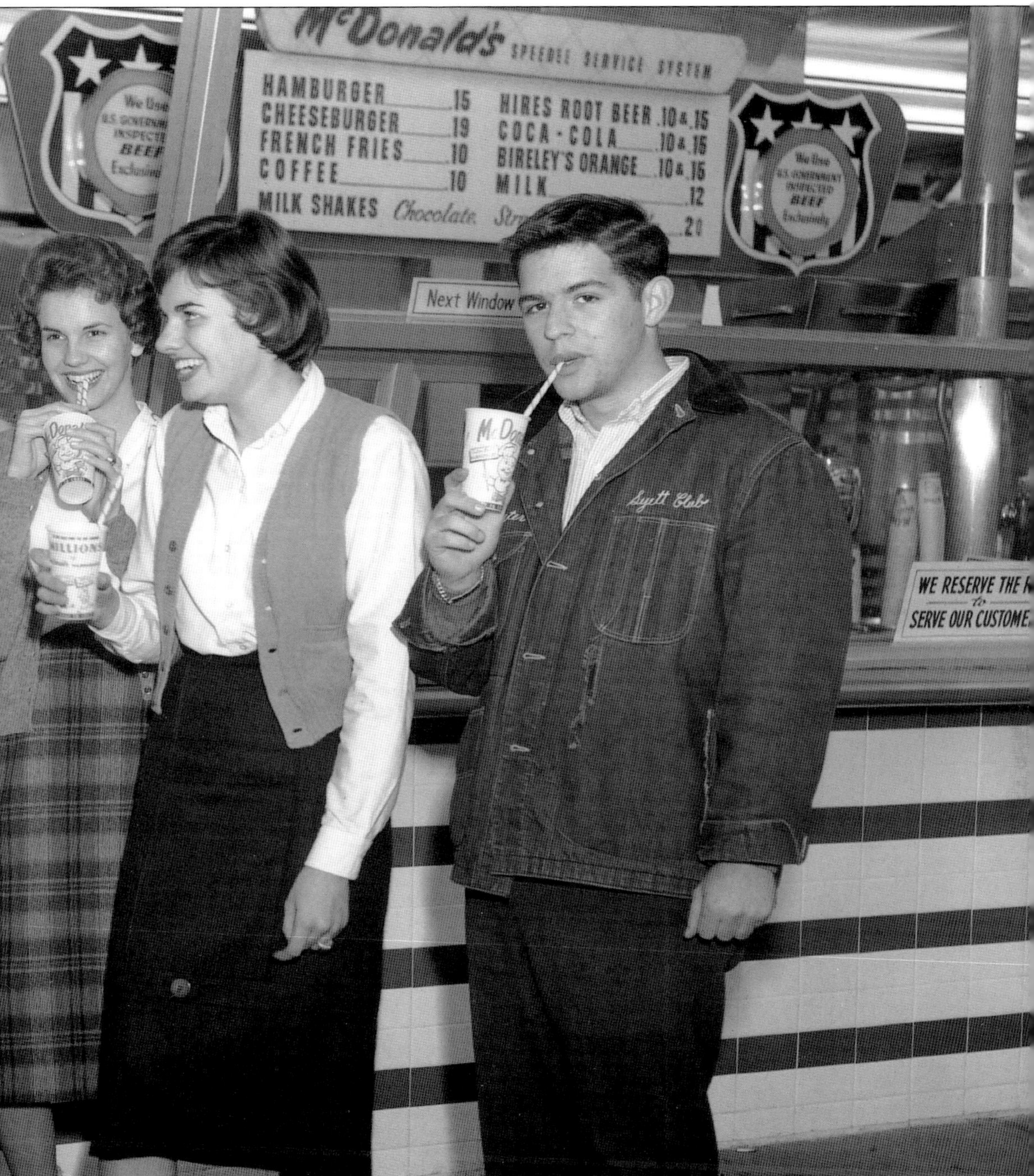

restaurants, it remained segregated until after May 1963, when local civil rights protests finally opened up all eating establishments to anyone who could pay. (© Carol W. Martin/Greensboro Historical Museum Collection.)

Smaller grocery stores, like the Cheek Mercantile Store in Pleasant Garden, were still the norm in April 1947. The range of products was great, but, as seen here, a whole "department" might consist of only a couple of shelves. (© Carol W. Martin/Greensboro Historical Museum Collection.)

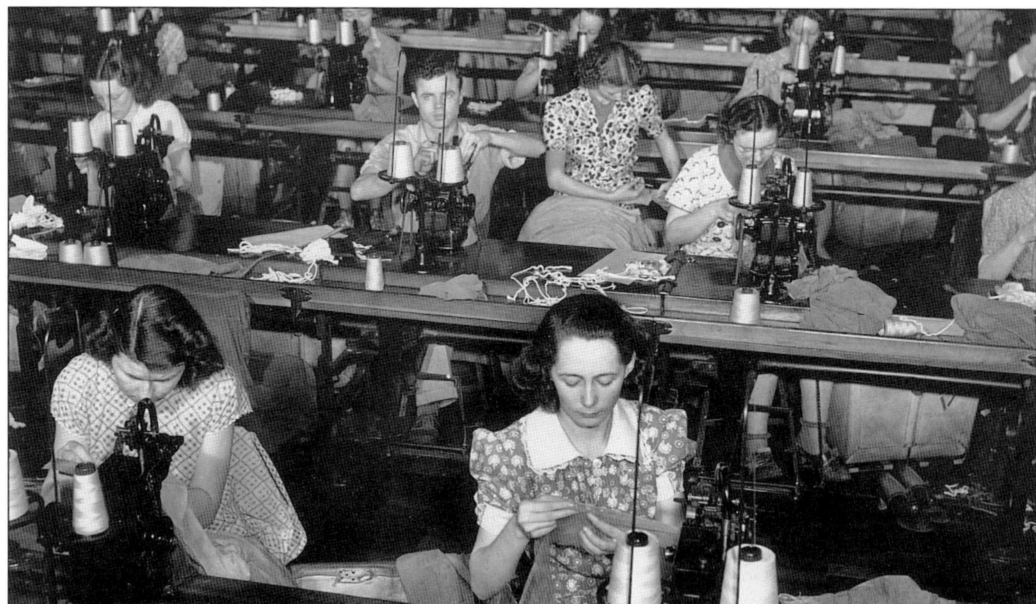

The Mock-Judson plant on Howard Street was a hub of activity on March 11, 1939. The plant began producing silk hosiery in 1926 but, after 1940, "Mojud" began fashioning nylon hosiery and soon became one of the top worldwide makers of women's full-fashioned hosiery. By the 1950s, the company's 2,000 workers, working three shifts, were producing 19.2 million pairs of nylons per year. Kayser-Roth bought Mock-Judson in the 1950s and ceased hosiery production in 1972. (© Carol W. Martin/Greensboro Historical Museum Collection.)

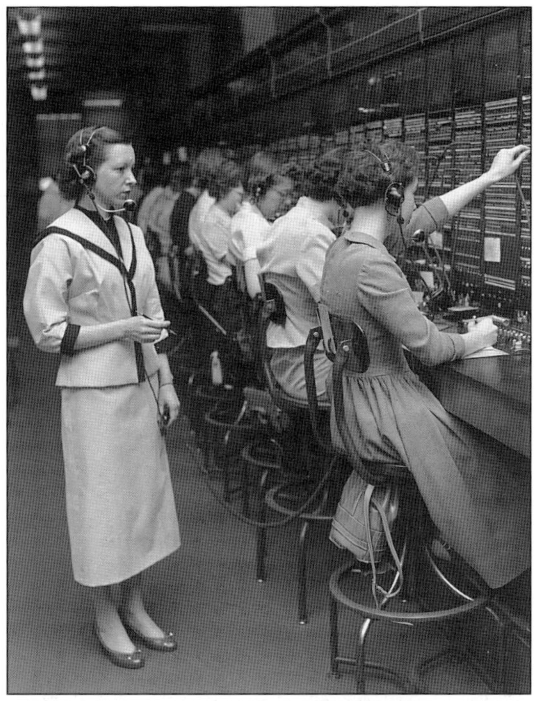

By March 27, 1956, most local users calling long distance would only get a Southern Bell telephone operator's voice. From September 25th, however, long distance calls could be made all the way to Europe, thanks to transatlantic cable operations. Phone ownership had tripled over the prior 20 years; in October 1956, the 50,000th Greensboro phone was installed at the Richard Bernard house at 105 Kimberly Drive. Although most telephones still came in "basic black," colored models were sold as early as 1954. It was with the introduction late in the decade of the "Princess" phone, which came with a lighted dial in five colors, that telephones moved beyond the functional to become stylish accessories. (© Carol W. Martin/Greensboro Historical Museum Collection.)

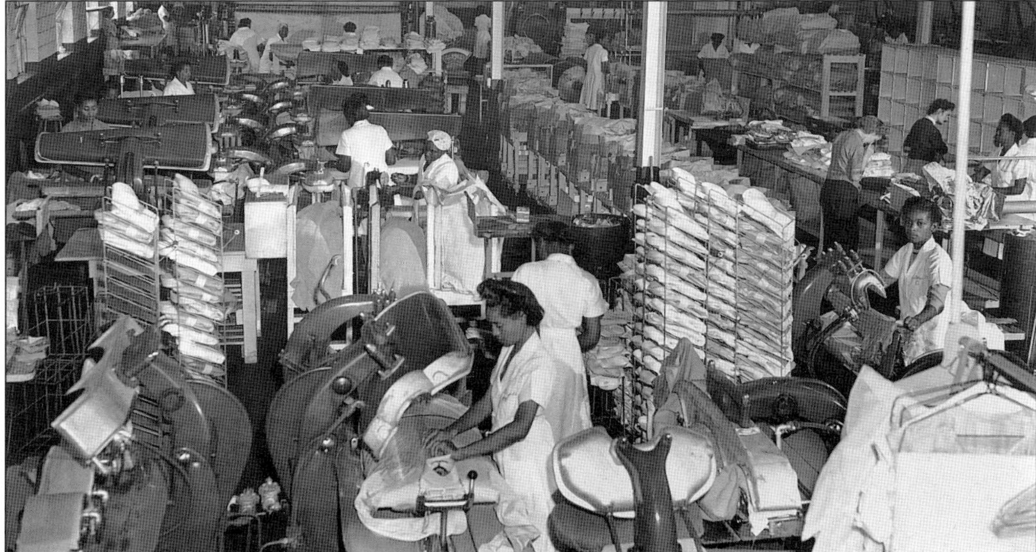

Workers stay busy at Lane's Laundry at 814 W. Market Street on October 22, 1946. Lane's, which is still in business at this location today, joined four other laundries in town when it began operation in the early 1920s. At that time, most cleaning was still done with water and soap, but the new process of "dry cleaning," using chemical solvents instead of water, was offered by all. During WWII, Lane's was taken over for military use when the Army Air Force opened a basic training center camp in Greensboro. (© Carol W. Martin/Greensboro Historical Museum Collection.)

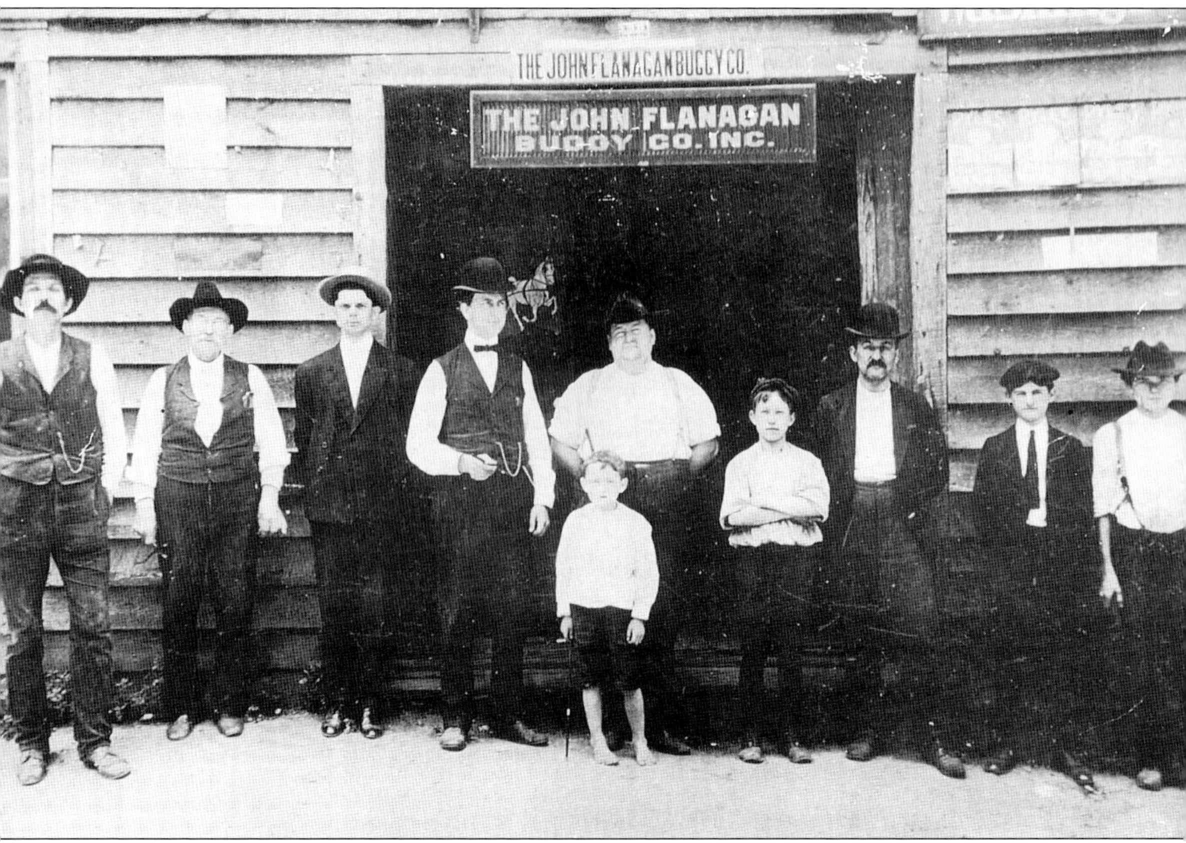

John Flanagan Buggy Company., Inc. Employees in front of the John Flanagan Buggy Co., Inc. on the corner of Fourth and Cotanche Streets in Greenville in 1902. The employees are, from left to right, as follows: Mr. Sutton (Wood Shop), Mr. D.D. Gardner (foreman of the Trimming Room), Mr. W.E. Hoker, Mr. Edward Gaskill Flanagan, Mr. Will Gardner, Lewis Johnson, Bill Smith (Wood Shop), Jimmy Reeves, and Roscoe Jefferson. (Courtesy of East Carolina Manuscript Collection, East Carolina University.)

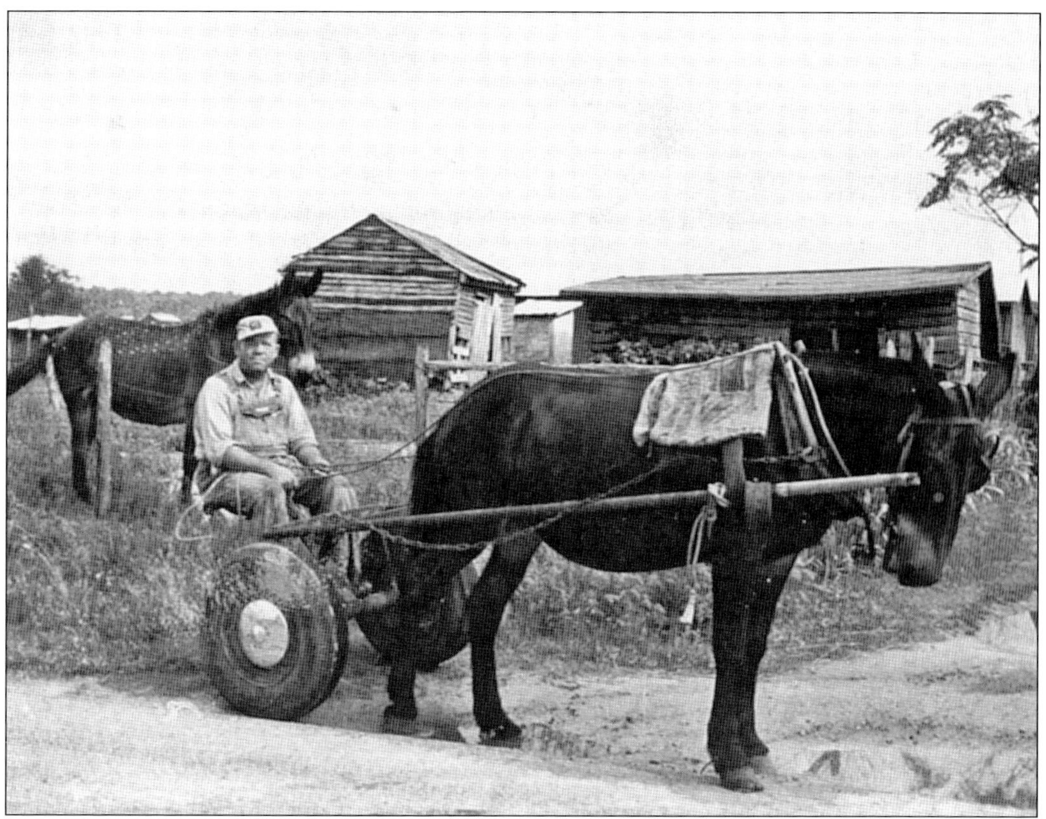

Depression-era Hoover carts had automobile wheels and a shaft which was attached to a mule and a seat. (Courtesy of the May Museum.)

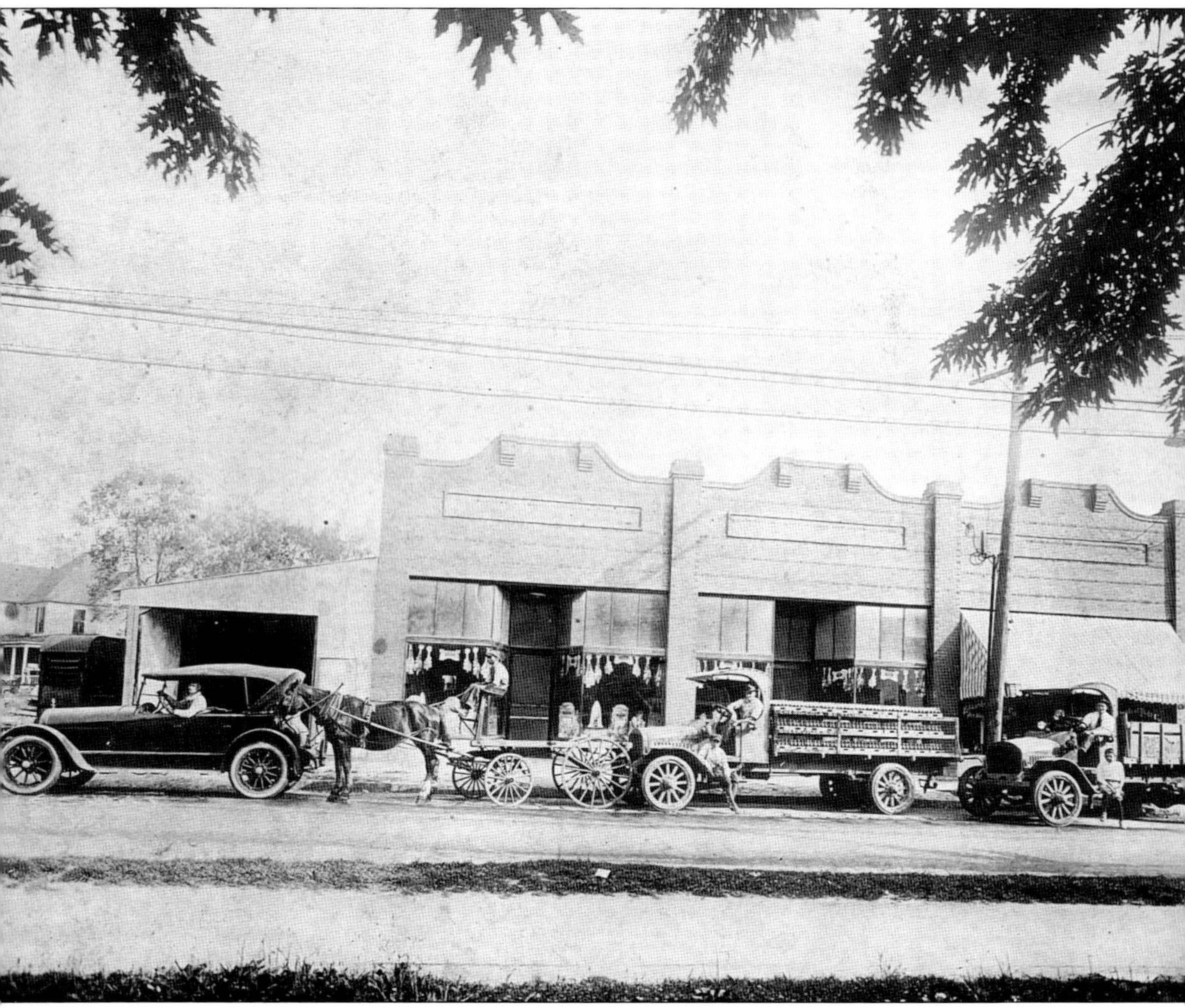

The Chero Cola Plant was located at 706 Dickinson Avenue in Greenville. The 1918 president was W.J. Hardee; vice president, R.T. Cox; secretary/treasurer, C.M. Warren. Coon Williams was the truck driver. (Courtesy of Hazel Eden.)

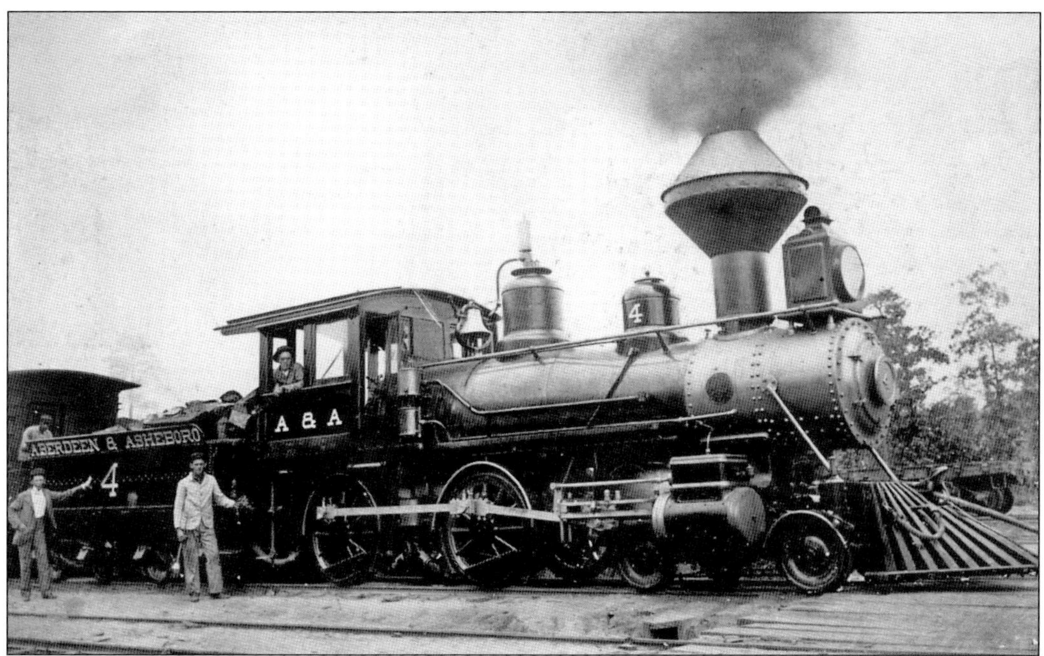

An Aberdeen and Asheboro Railroad locomotive is pictured here in the early twentieth century. The railroad was founded by Allison Page in 1888 as the Aberdeen and West End Railroad and was later sold to the Norfolk Southern Railway in 1912.

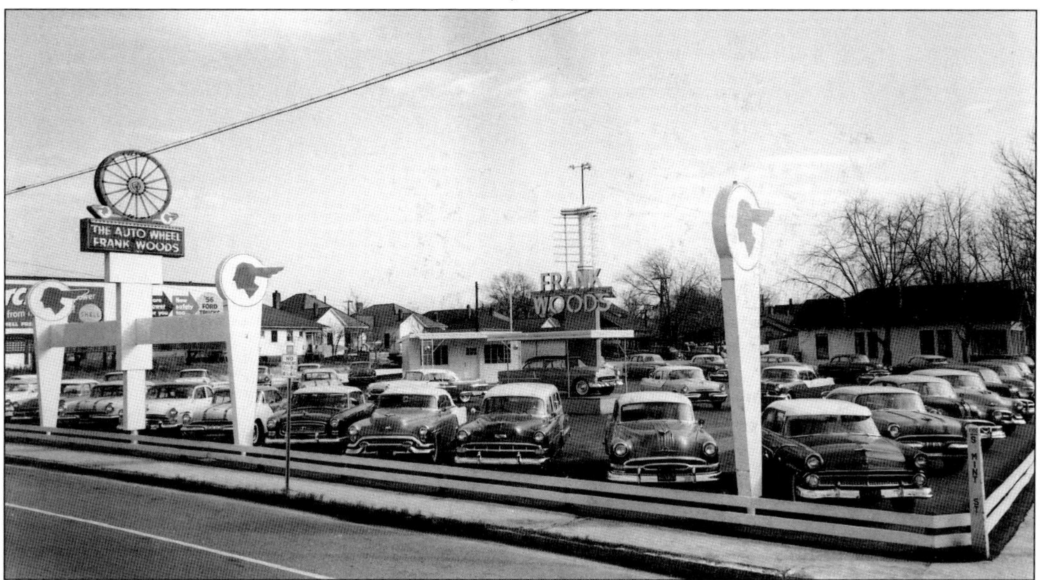

Look at these beauties! It's 1956, and a new car would set you back about $2,000, less for a used car. Take your pick from any of these on display at "The Auto Wheel," Frank Woods' South Mint Street car dealership in Third Ward. The success of this business was due in part to its visibility, as the cars were seen by all who drove or walked along this busy street. Judging from the styles shown in this photograph, two-toned paint was popular. (Kugler's Studio.)

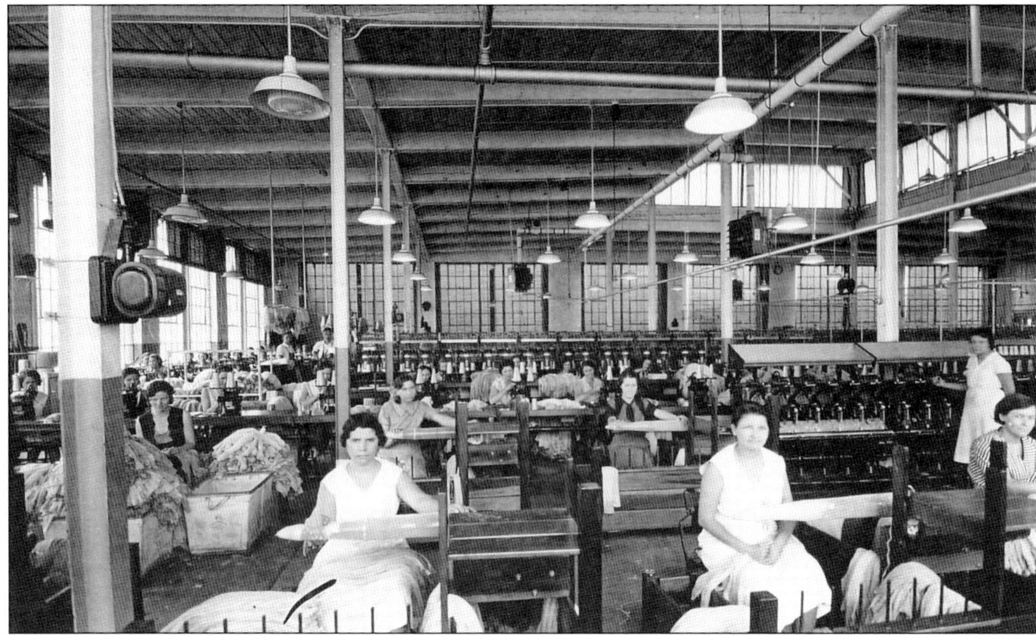

The arrival of the textile mills in Charlotte had an economic impact on the city that would be unrivaled until the explosive growth of the banking industry almost a century later. The mills provided a large employment base and created numerous support industries. One of the results of this rapid development was a boom in neighborhood building as Charlotte's population swelled from just over 7,000 in 1880 to more than 82,000 in 1930, the year this photograph was taken. These women are posing at their machines in the 1893 Atherton Mill, situated between the Dilworth and Wilmore neighborhoods. The factory that employed the workers seen here now serves as the centerpiece of the fashionable South End district, a redevelopment project that features antique shops, restaurants, and offices. (Duke Power Archives.)

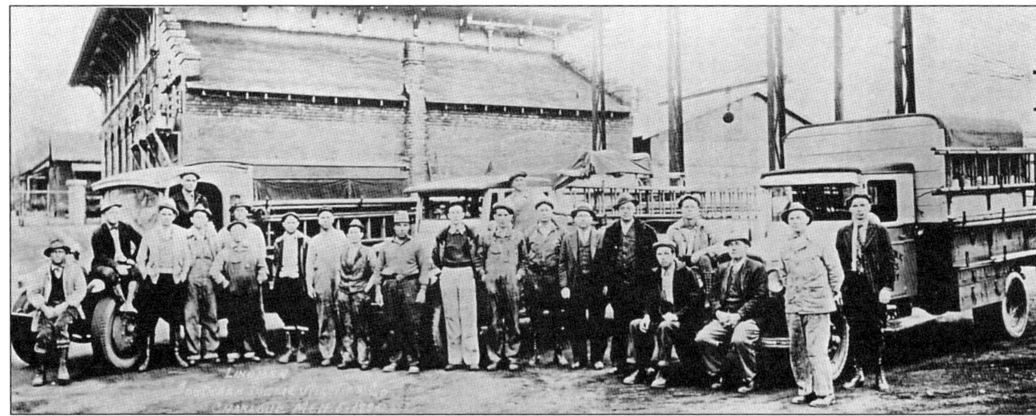

The Southern Public Utilities Company was an early subsidiary of what is now the Duke Power Company. This portrait, taken in March of 1935, shows a group of the company's linemen posing near Dilworth. The electrification of the streetcar system, as well as the new electrical appliances and other conveniences made available through electric companies, helped make Charlotte's early suburbs the great successes that they were. (Duke Power Archives.)

This is the new press at the *Daily Southerner*, the main newspaper in the county since 1826. George Howard moved to Tarboro in that year and set up the weekly paper, then called *The Free Press*. As political and editorial changes occurred, the paper was variously called *The Southerner*, *The Tarborough Southerner*, and finally in the 1890s the *Daily Southerner*. Although the county had three newspapers in the 1890s, in later years only two major papers competed with the Tarboro paper; *The Edgecombe Chronicle* served the county in the 1960s, and the weekly *Tarboro Telegram*, a product of the *Rocky Mount Telegram*, began in the 1990s. (BBH.)

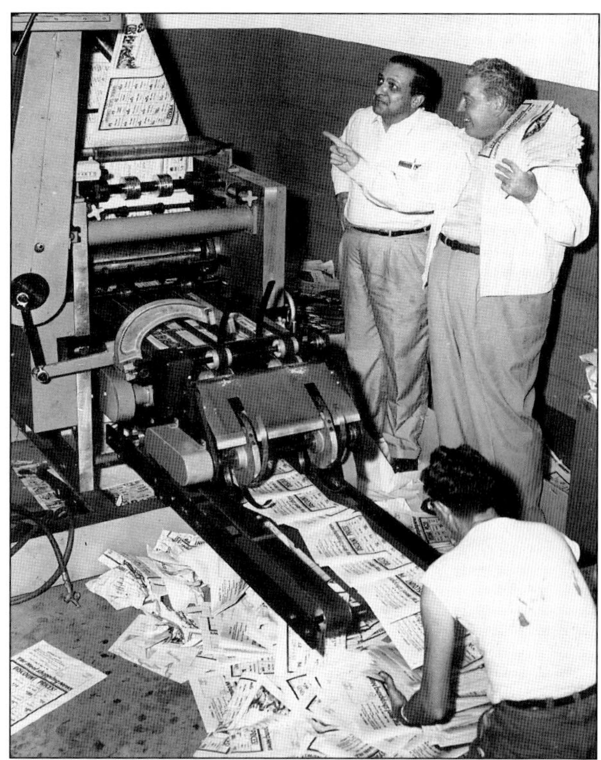

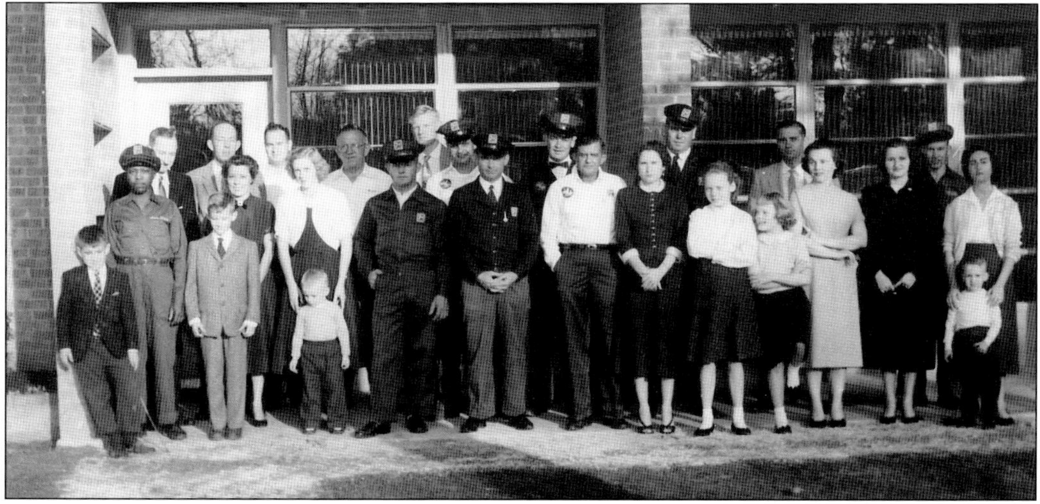

W.D. "Billy" Bryan and J.C. "Ching" Marrow opened a 7-Up plant in the 1950s. Employees and guests include, from left to right, Henry Marrow (young boy); James Glass; Ching Marrow; Jim Marrow; W.D. "Billy" Bryan; Mary Elizabeth Bryan; unidentified man, woman, and little boy; Walter "Goat" Knox, plant manager; four unidentified men; Frank Duncan; Jimmy Harmon; Louise Harmon; Woodrow Edwards; Linda Edwards; Sue Edwards; Lonnie Bullock; Mrs. Edwards; Eula Mae Bullock; Herbert Hopkins Sr.; Mary Elizabeth Hopkins; and Herbert Hopkins Jr. (BBH.)

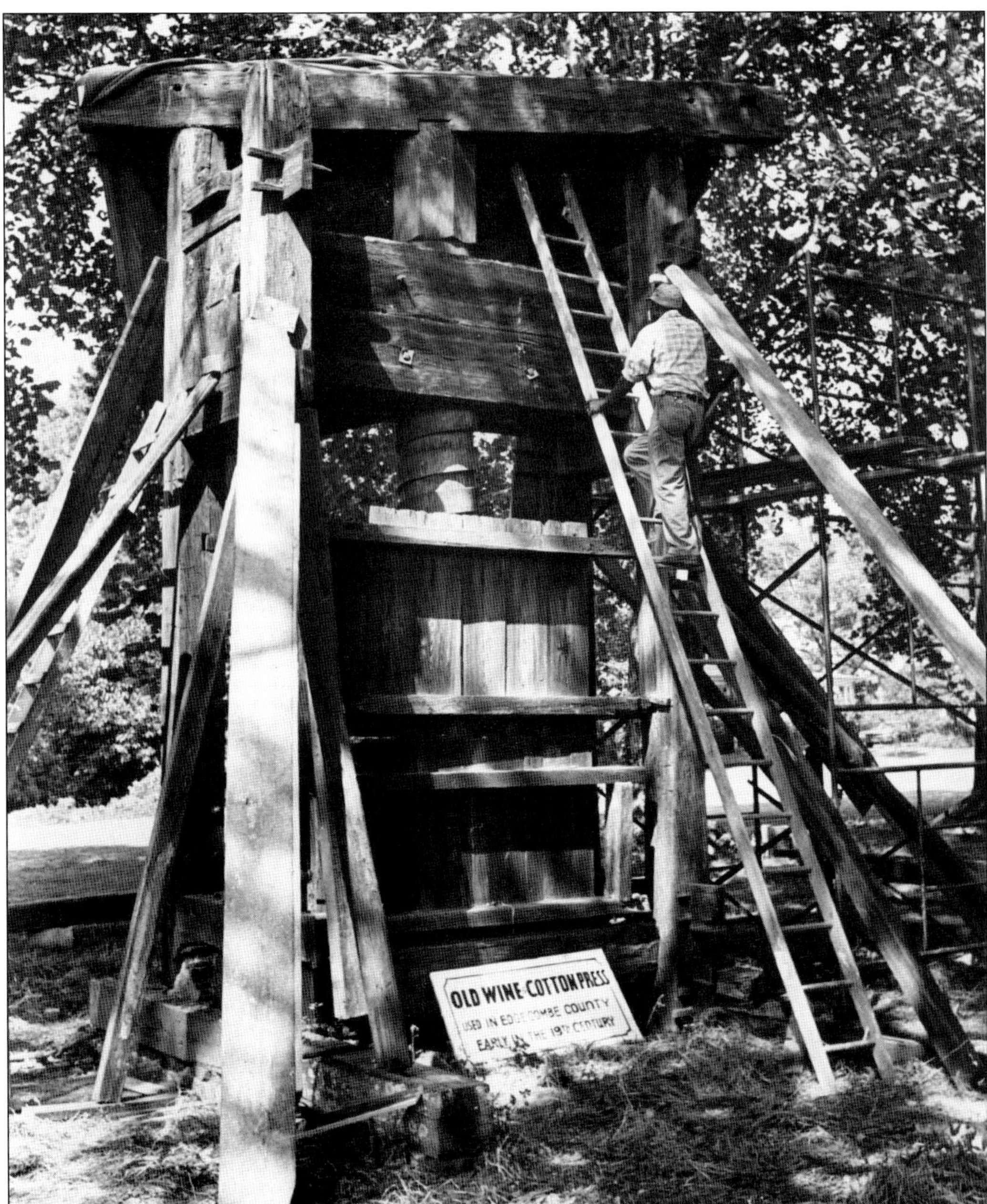

Cotton presses were prevalent in Edgecombe County beginning in 1800. To preserve part of the county's agricultural heritage, this cotton press, built around 1840, was moved from the Norfleet farm to the Town Common in 1960. The press used mule power to turn a large screw carved from a maple tree, to press cotton into 300 or 400-pound bales. When the cotton season was over, the press was also used to press gruit pulp to make cider, wine, and brandy. Edgecombe County was noted for its brandy exports back in the 1770s. (Courtesy of Blount Bridgers' House.)

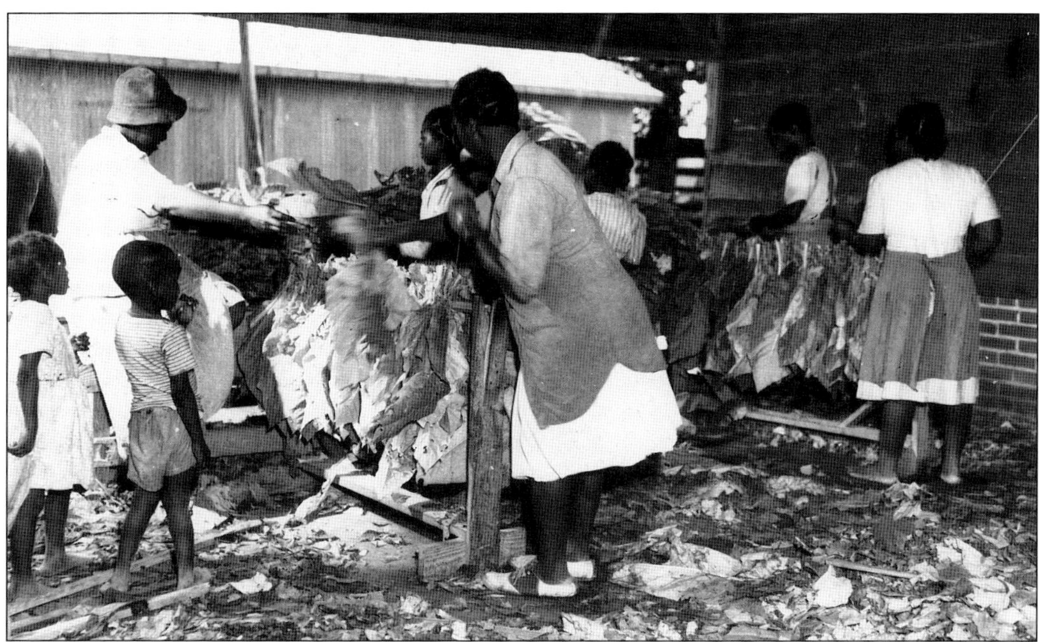

Traditionally, women and older children did the tying, or looping, as it was called in some areas. Men used to work in the fields and lift the baskets of tobacco. Younger children would learn by watching their parents, and they would begin as "handers," which meant handing leaves of tobacco to the loopers, who would tie it to the sticks. Some farms employed children as young as six or seven to hand tobacco to the skilled loopers, working faster than the camera. (NCDAH.)

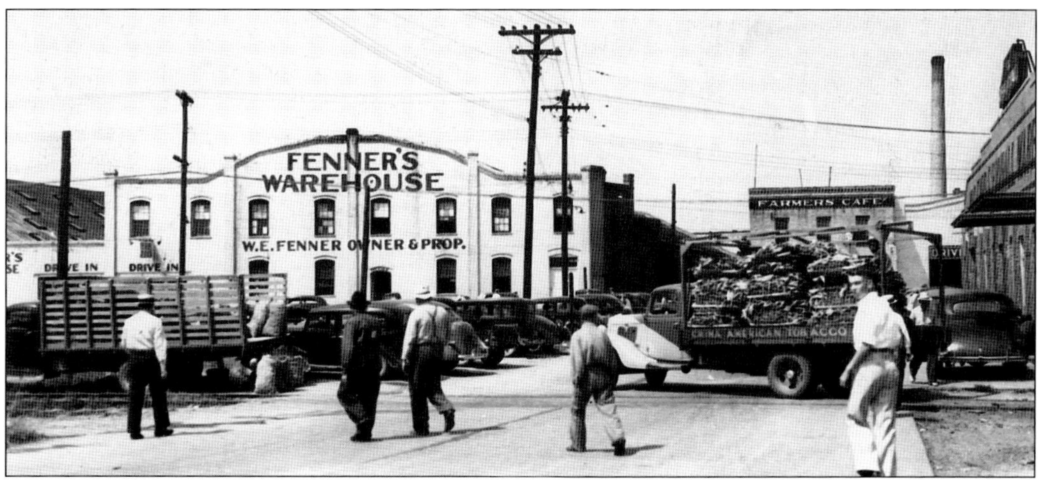

Tobacco became a major commercial crop in northeastern North Carolina in the 1880s. The first warehouse in Nash County was opened in Battleboro by T.P. Braswell in 1885. By 1887, Rocky Mount Warehouse had opened, followed in 1889 by the Nash Warehouse. In 1895, there were four warehouses in Rocky Mount, selling over 7 million pounds of tobacco. Thorpe and Ricks opened a facility to process tobacco, the only such facility in eastern North Carolina. Rocky Mount became the center for tobacco trade. (NCDAH.)

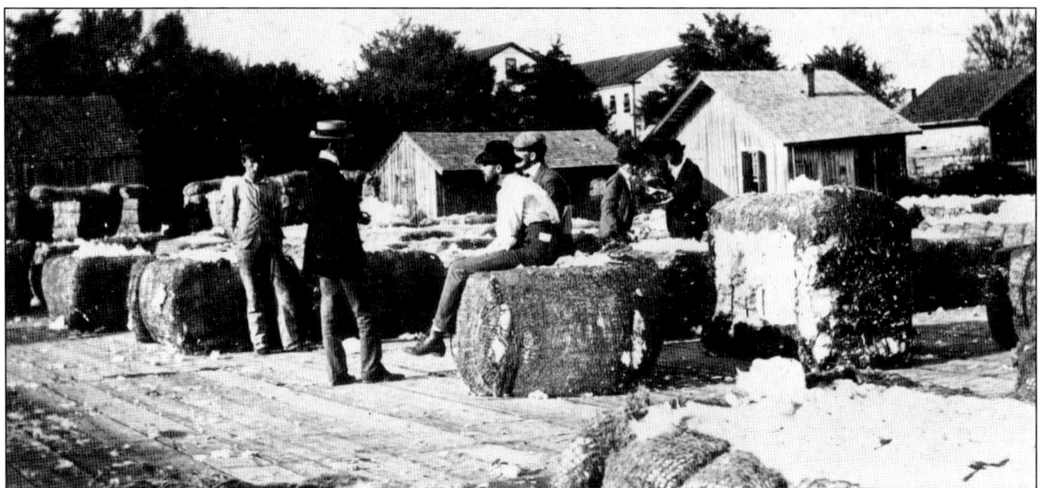

In 1840 Edgecombe County produced 2,445,000 pounds (approximately 6,000 400-pound bales) of seed cotton. In 1858 total cotton production for the county was recorded at 17,608 bales. Although corn, wheat, and sweet potatoes were produced, cotton was clearly the king crop in Edgecombe County prior to 1860. It was raised in great volume even after the War, with production in the 1880s averaging over 25,000 bales a year. Bales were formed at the numerous cotton presses throughout the county and then delivered to either the train depot or the river docks to be shipped to market. (ECML.)

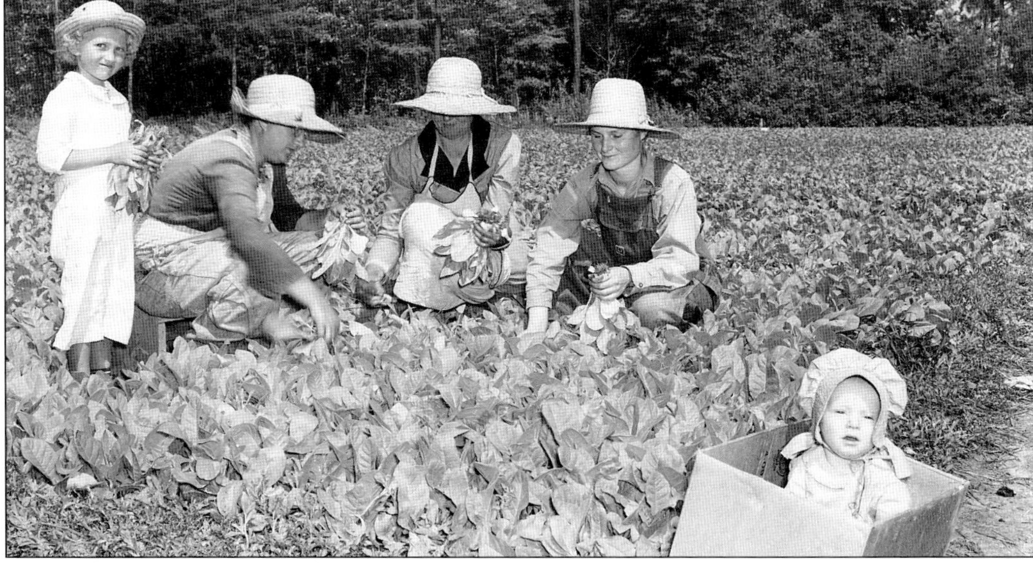

While the profits from tobacco were higher per acre grown than those from cotton, the labor was much more involved, and it kept entire families busy from April until late September. The seed beds were planted in early spring. By late April or May, the bed plants would be pulled and transplanted into a field to grow to maturity. Men usually plowed the fields to prepare them while the women in the family pulled the plants, as shown in this 1930s photograph of a seed bed near the Wilson County line. Daycare for toddlers consisted of a cardboard box or a wooden crate to keep the children out of trouble and away from snakes and other animals. (NA.)

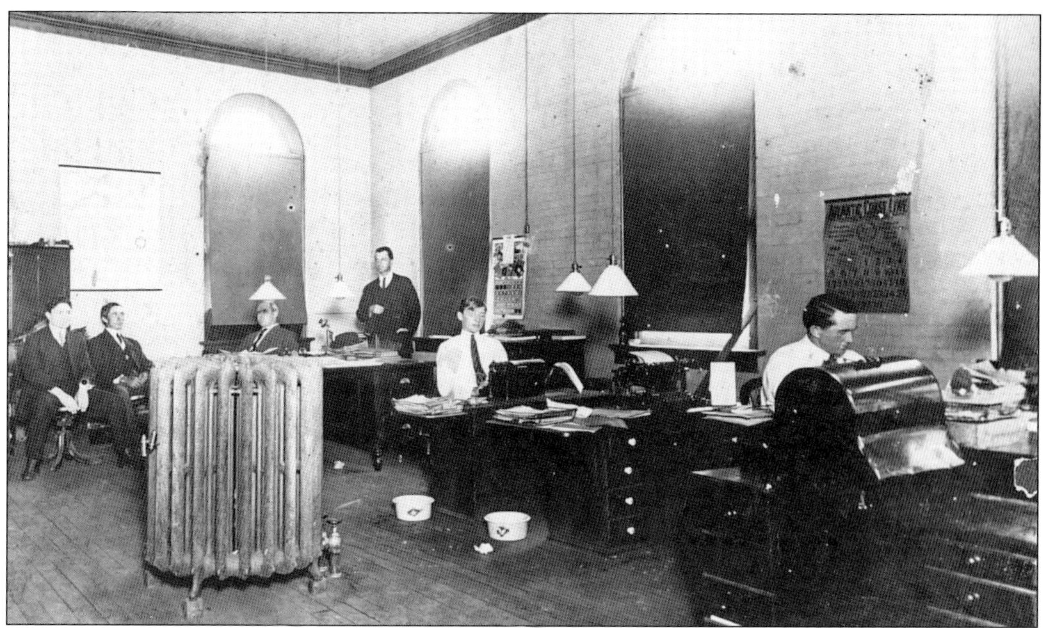

This was a typical Atlantic Coast Line office in 1906. "Inside those buildings, things were not all that glamourous," said a former stenographer. "They were dark and drab. Many of the men chewed tobacco and sometimes in the catwalk they didn't bother with a spittoon. The exhaust from all the steam engines added to the smell. . .There were more pleasant places to work in Wilmington, but no one could match the salaries the coast line paid."

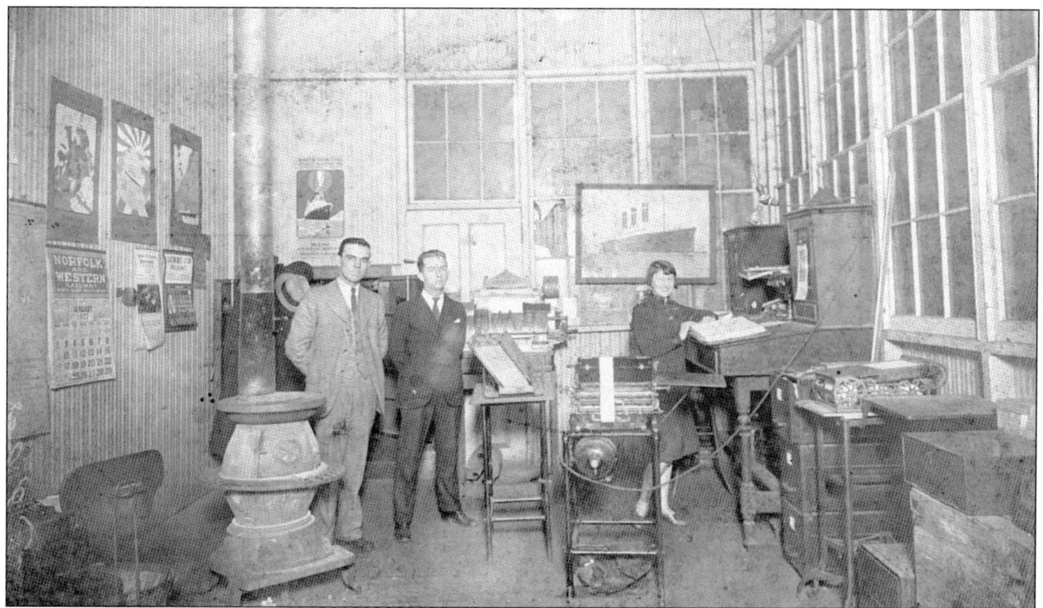

W.H. McEachern, a wholesale vegetable and fruit distributor, has been supplying produce to Wilmington for 100 years. Pictured are, from left to right, W.H. McEachern Jr., Sug Powell, and Lina McEachern McCarley in the Water Street office they occupied in the 1920s.

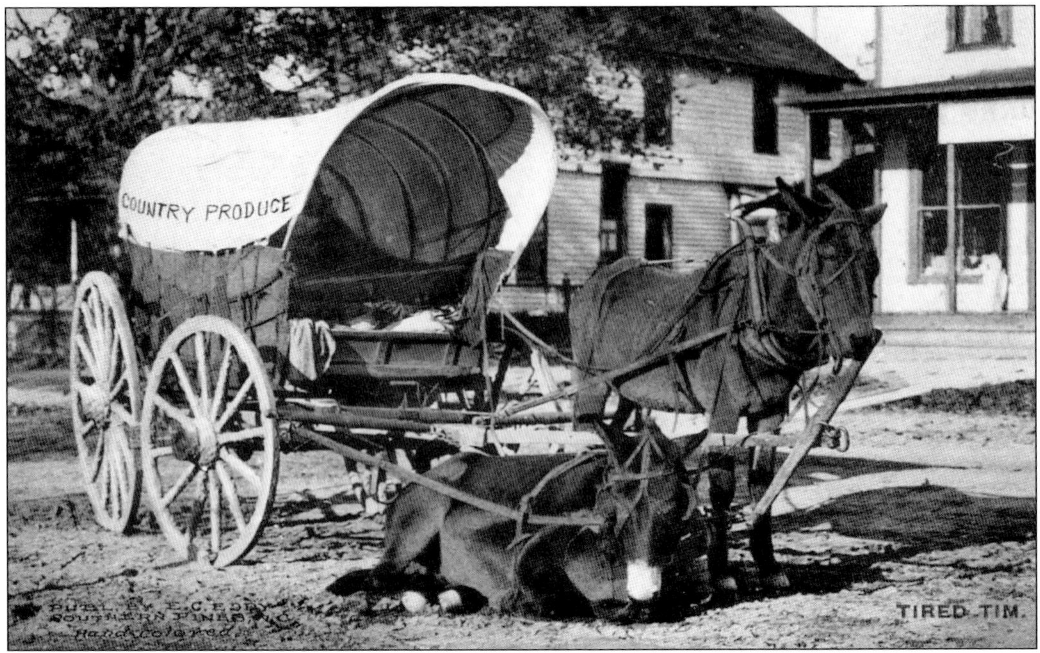

A pair of mules harnessed to a schooner wagon awaits the return trip to the farm. One of the animals, identified as "Tired Tim," takes full advantage of the rest on Broad Street in Southern Pines about 1915. (From Stephen E. Massengill Collection.)

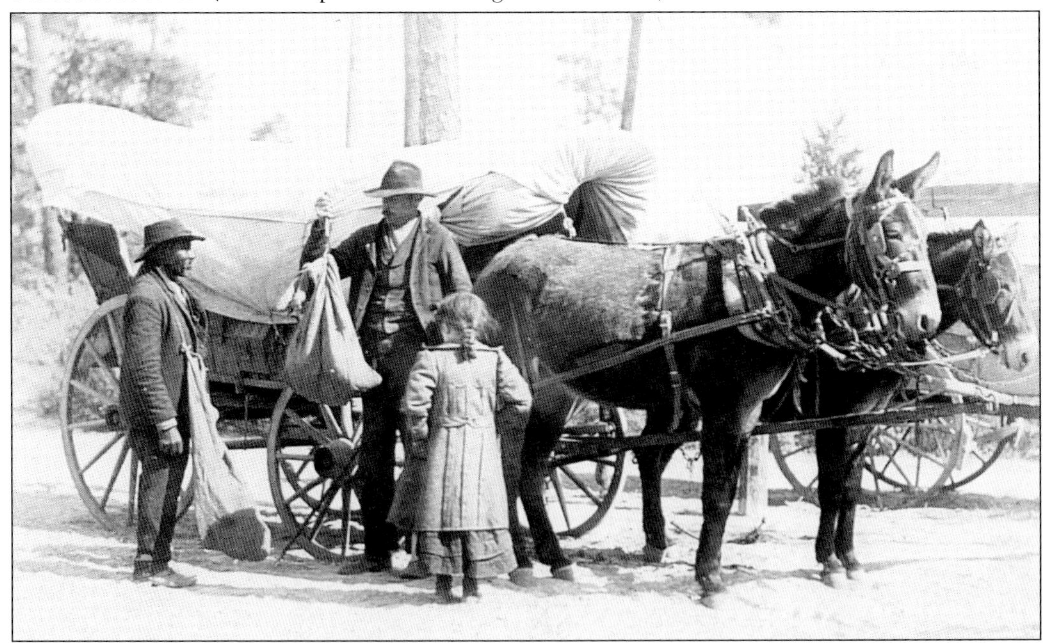

These farmers have arrived by wagon at Southern Pines with produce and farm products to barter and sell at the local market. Eddy observed that many of the natives were still riding into town in schooner wagons and oxcarts before 1920. (Courtesy of Sarah M. Pope.)

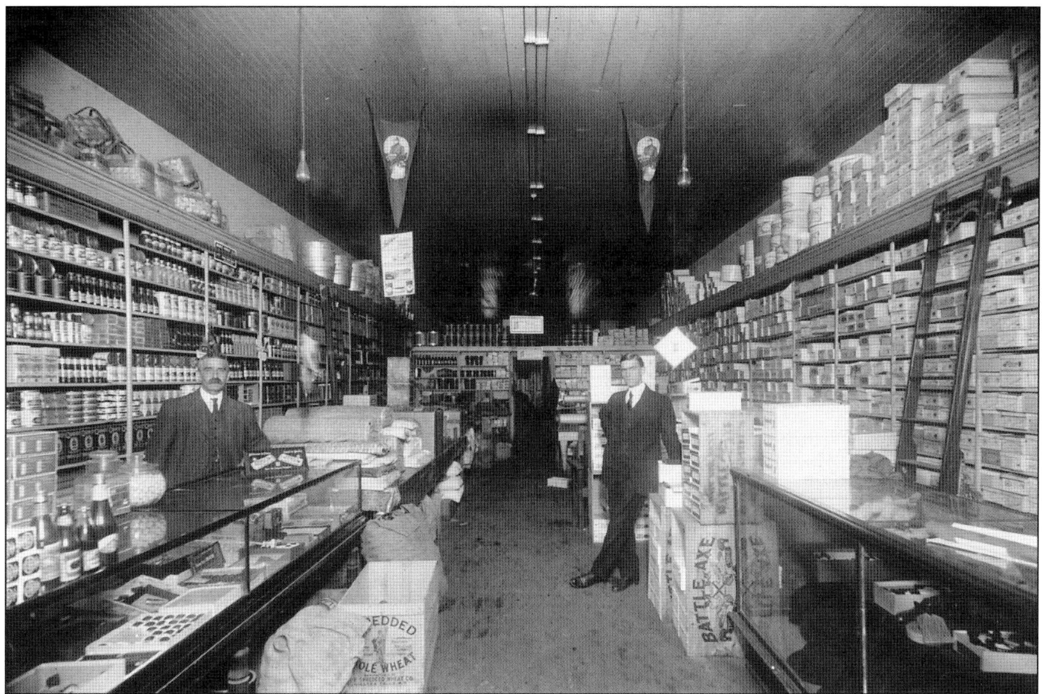

Hubbard's Store, one of Reidsville's early merchandise outlets, specialized in quality and service. (Courtesy of the Jimmy Waynick Collection, Reidsville.)

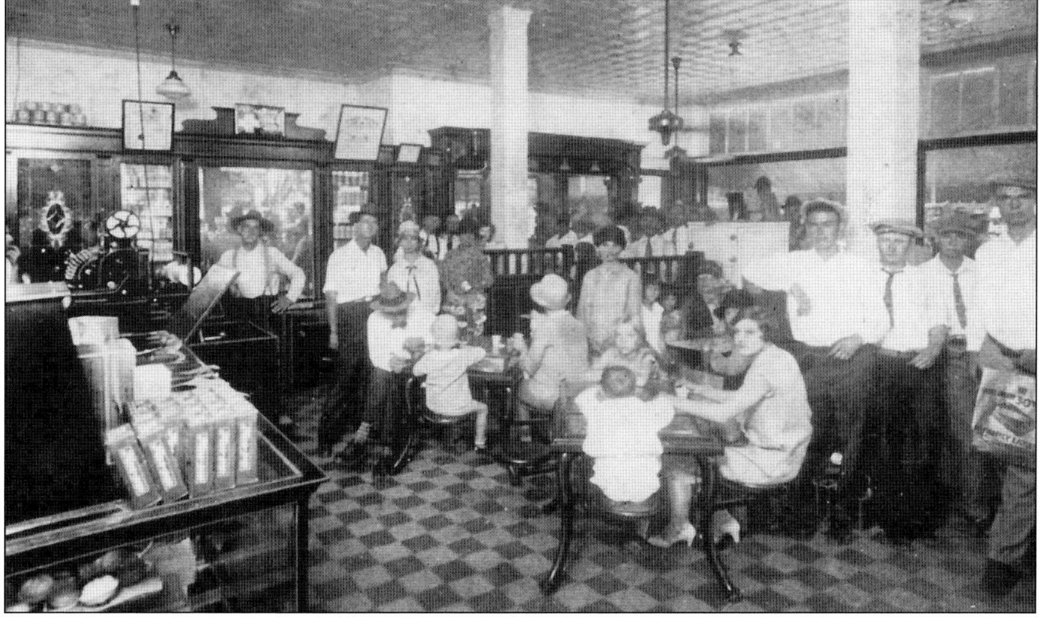

This postcard is an interior view of the Piedmont Drug Company. Dating from around the 1930s, the image shows friendly townspeople enjoying the soda shop. (Courtesy of the Jerri B. Griffin Collection, Madison, NC.)

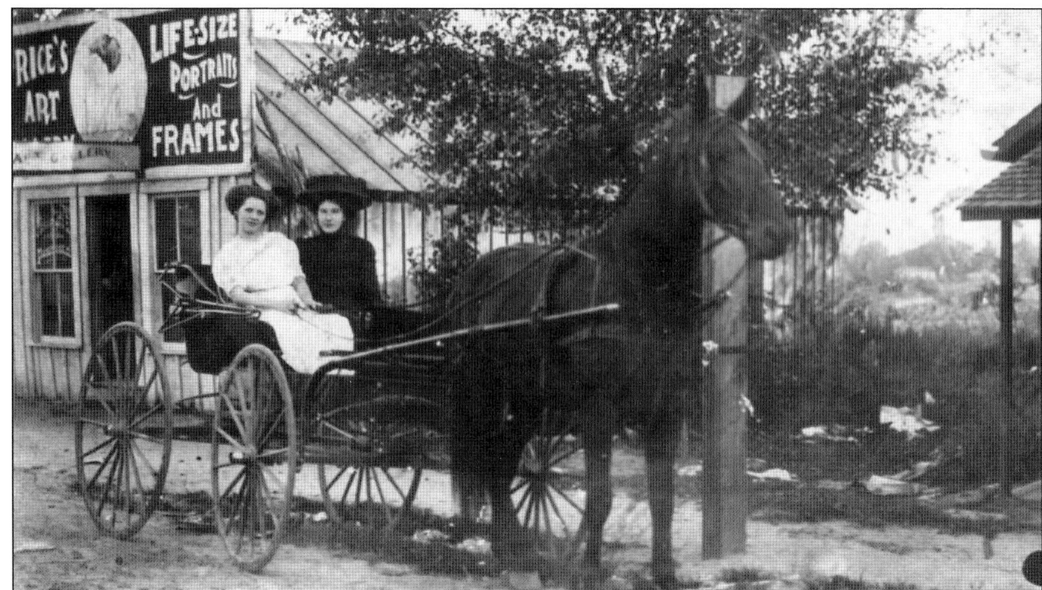

Commercial photographers of Eden unknowingly captured much history on glass plates (film negatives came later). Above is the studio of "Picture" Price, one of the more well-known photographers from East Rockingham County. Behind the ladies and their buggy is his studio, which was located on the Boulevard in Spray in the early 1900s. (Courtesy of Roscoe Hankins Collection, Eden, NC.)

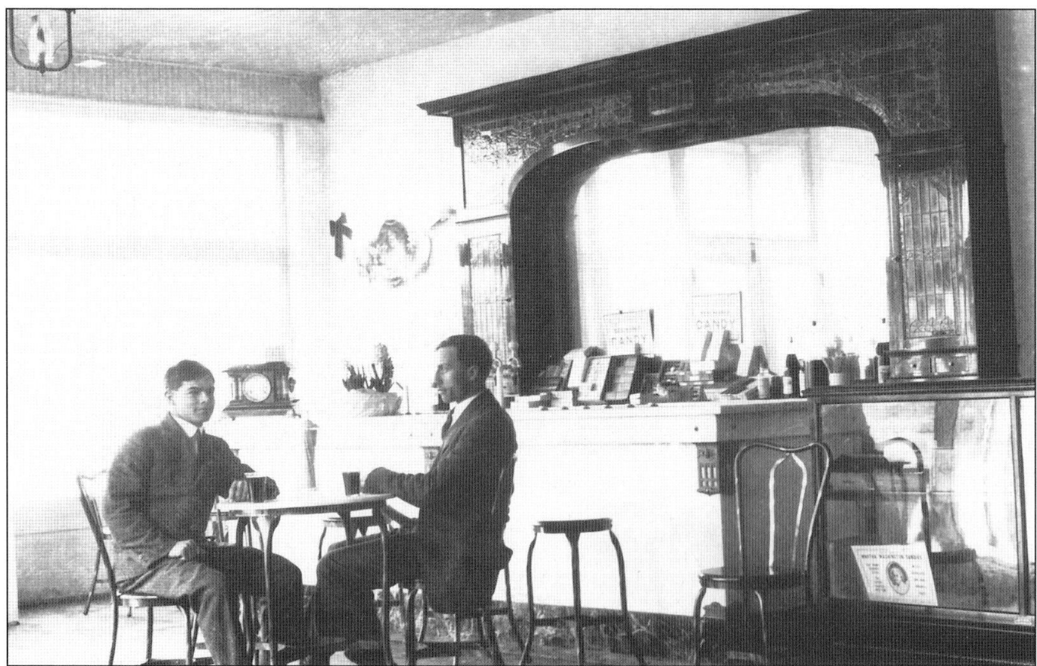

The soda shop at Red Lauten's was a wonderful meeting place for people like Roy Farmer (left) and his friends. (Courtesy of the Jeff Bullins Collection, Mayodan, NC.)

Four

TO SERVE AND PROTECT:
PUBLIC SERVANTS

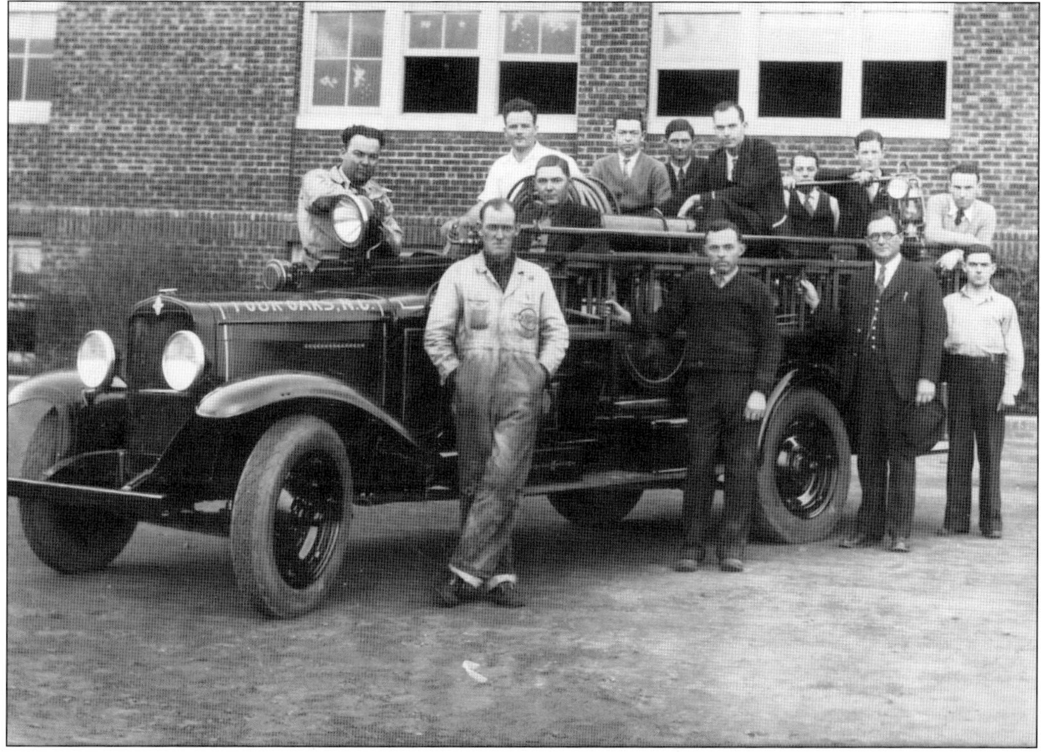

This was Four Oaks' first firetruck—a 1930 Chevrolet. The backdrop is the high school building. Shown here are town leaders and members of the first fire department, which was organized in 1930. (Courtesy of Johnston County Room.)

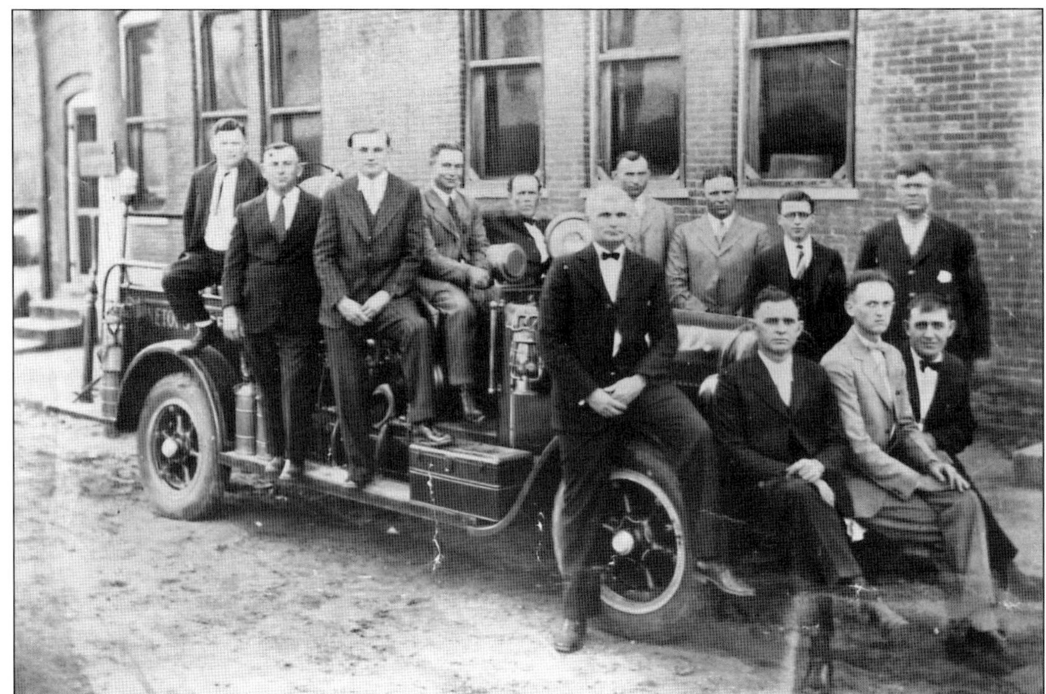

Pinetops Fire Department in 1927 comprises, from left to right: (front row) Herbert Kemp, George Phillips, Fred H. Phillips, C.M. Clark, Sam L. Parker, B.A. Stedman, Sam Moore, and J.I. Gatlin; (back row) Joe Harper, Fred Phillips, Eddie Fulghum, Jonas Owens, Jim Parker, and their new 1927 Dodge truck. (PC-Fuller.)

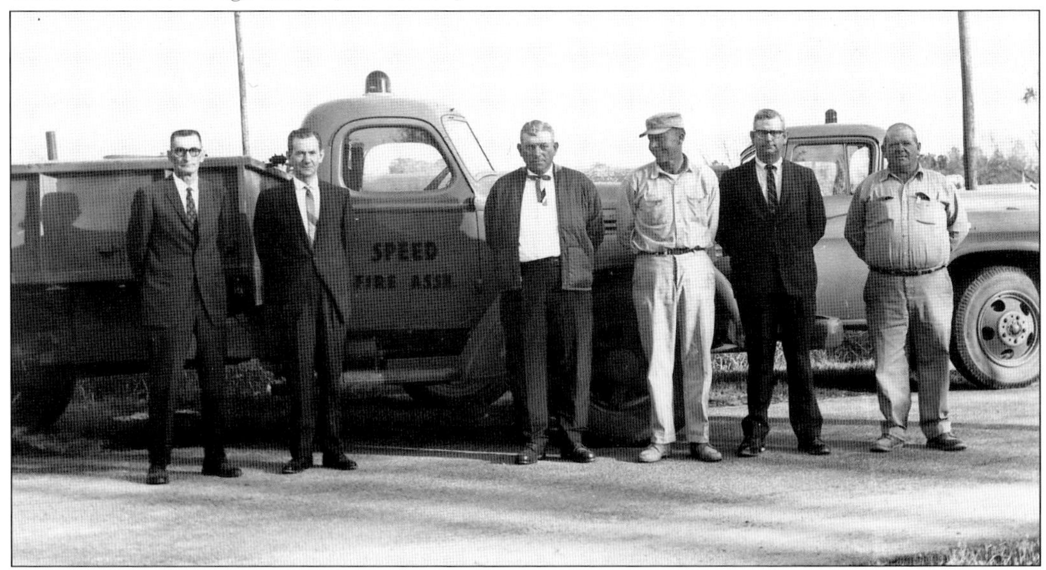

The Speed Fire Department had two units and ten members, including, from left to right, Chief Hugh Shelton, Powell Satterthwaite, Jim Satterthwaite, Billy Edmondson, Sam Satterthwaite, and Josh Satterthwaite. (ECML.)

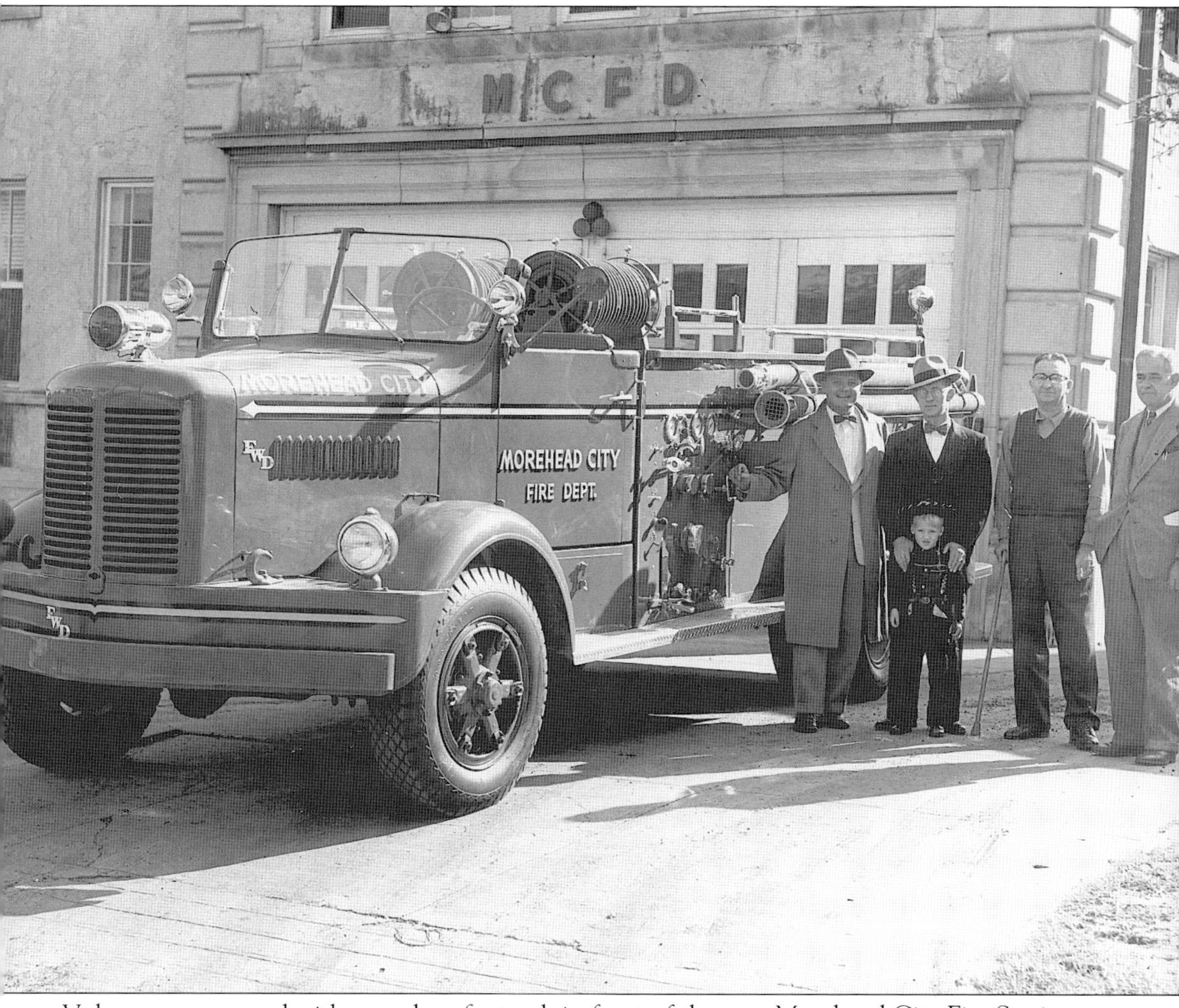

Volunteers are posed with a modern firetruck in front of the new Morehead City Fire Station, which was built in 1927 and is still in use today. A municipal building was built with the fire station that opened onto Evans Street. Pictured from left to right are the following: Bud Dixon, George Dill, and George Dill Jr. (in front). (Courtesy Carteret County Historical Society.)

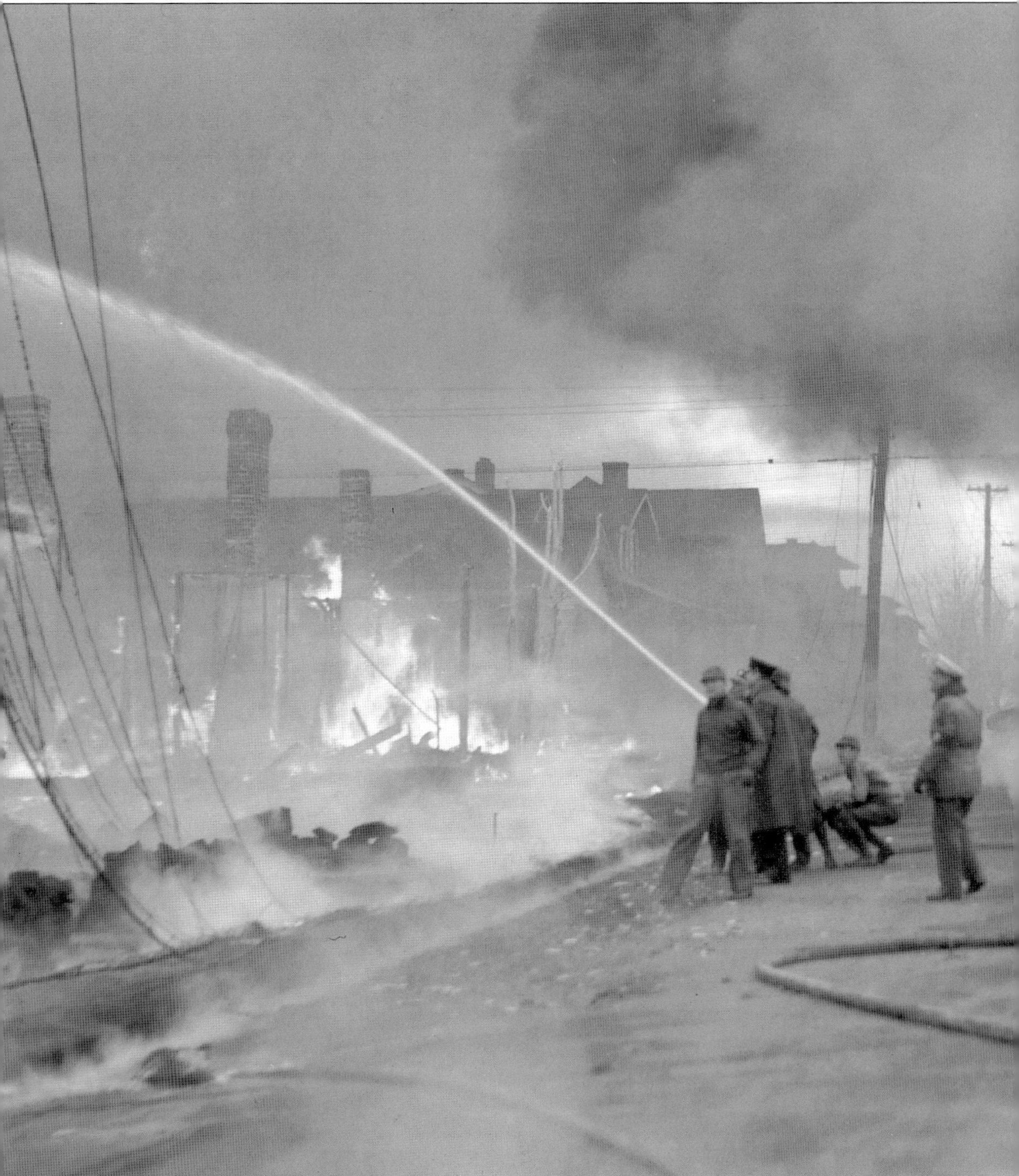

On January 14, 1944, four houses were destroyed in the 1000 block of Gorrell Street when a gasoline tanker truck's axle broke, causing the trailer to drag and produce sparks that set off an explosion. The flames spread 300 feet, burning through fire hose lines with heat so intense

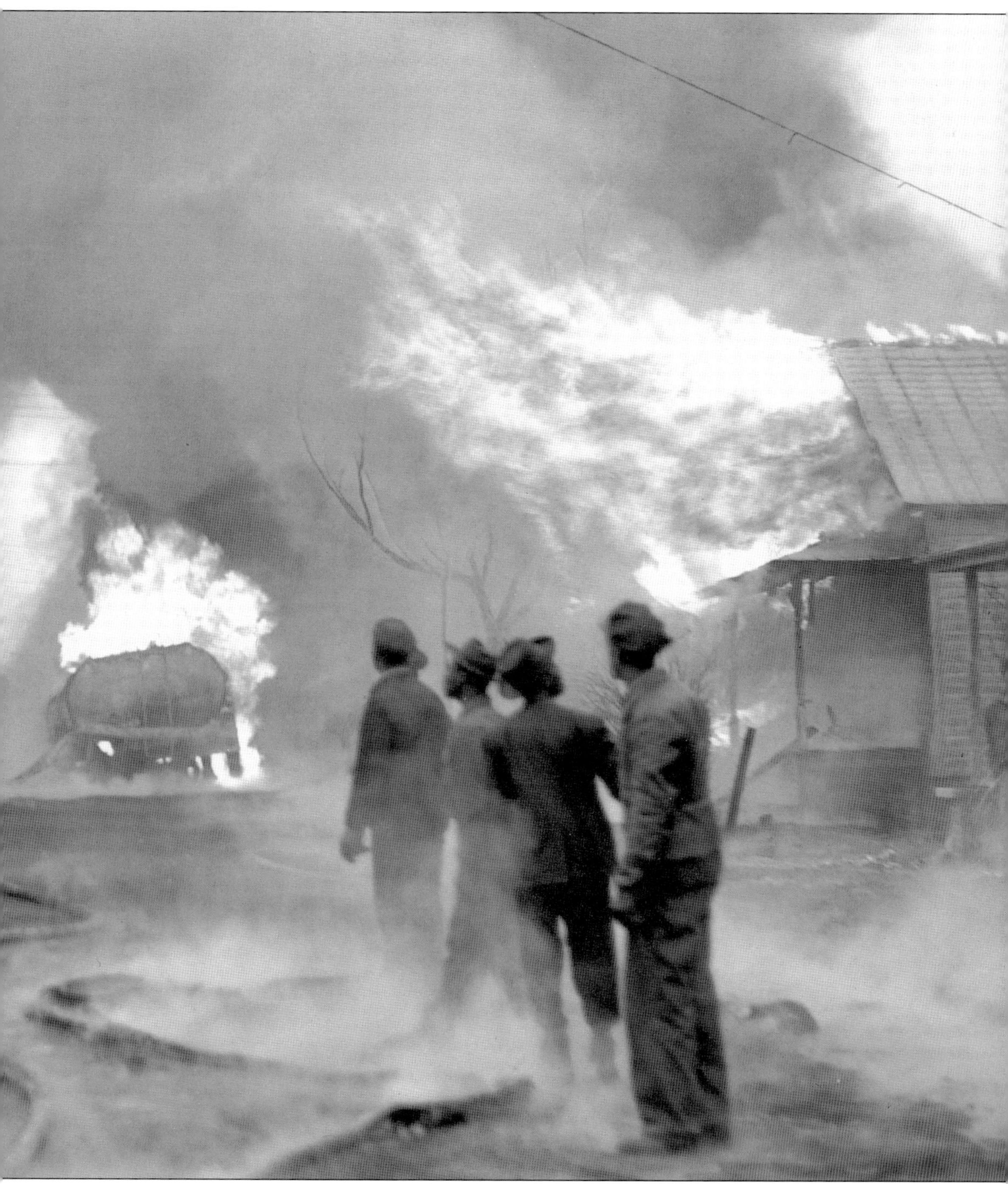

it could be felt two blocks away. Luckily, no one was seriously injured. (© Carol W. Martin/ Greensboro Historical Museum Collection.)

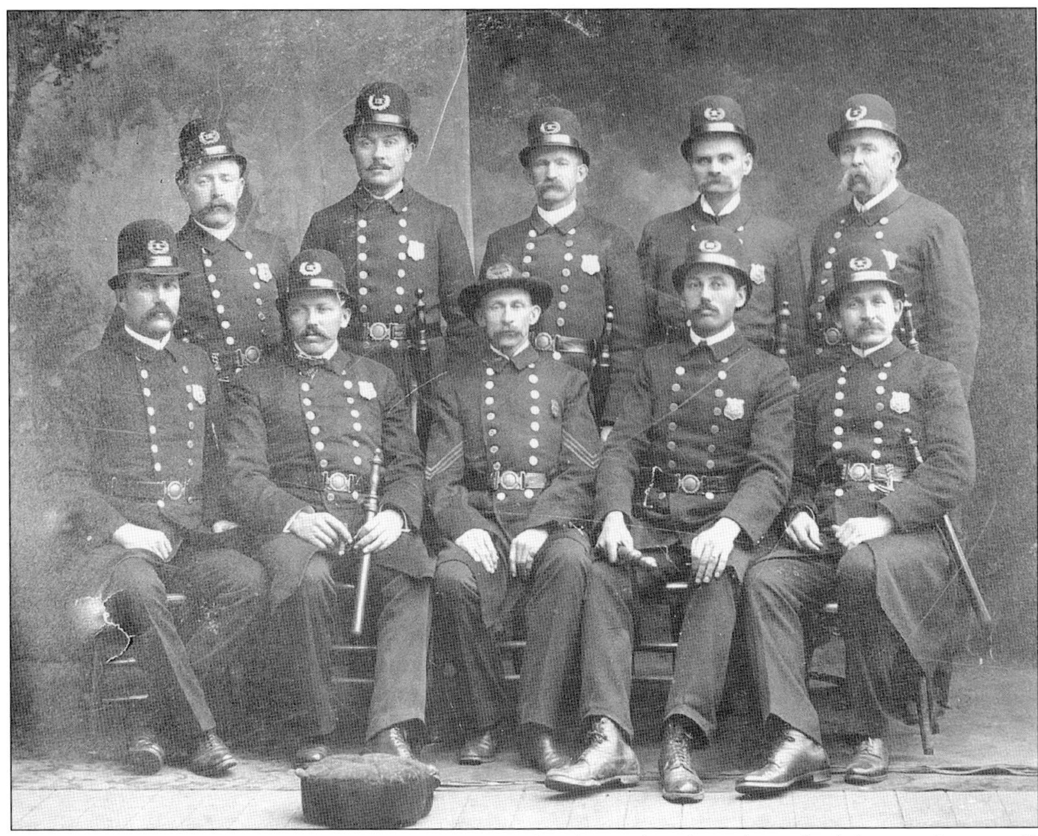

Throughout Charlotte's history the people who have lived and worked here—from mill workers and bankers to teachers and families—have given the city its unique character. Even when growth and the influence of new citizens have altered Charlotte's physical appearance, the city has always retained its central characteristic as a Southern town that values its social traditions.

This group portrait of Charlotte's police officers, taken around 1910, shows a group of civil servants that appear as if they would fit as easily into a neighborhood in the industrial Northeast as in a Carolina Piedmont town. Yet the underlying personality of Charlotte has remained constant. Even as the city attracted famous visitors and acquired the trappings of a major metropolis, Charlotte's people have been its timeless asset. (Robinson-Spangler Carolina Room, Public Library of Charlotte and Mecklenburg County.)

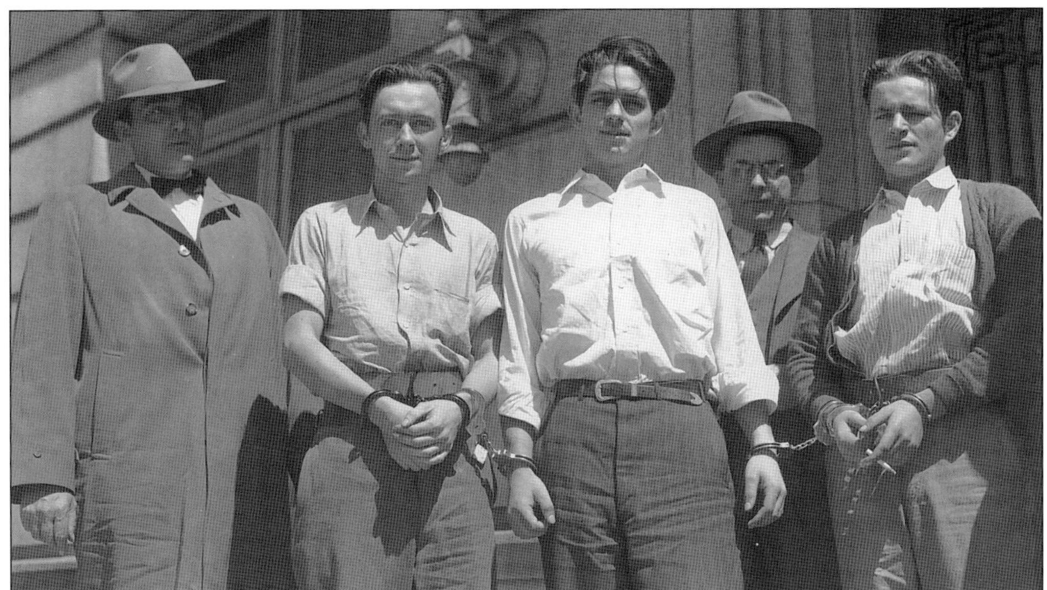

Shown here in February 1944 are Sheriff John Story and a deputy guarding William Dalton Biggs, his brother Elmer Hardie Biggs, and John Edgar Messer. All three were given the death sentence for the 1943 pistol slaying of E.J. Swanson, and were executed in Raleigh on March 9, 1945. (© Carol W. Martin/Greensboro Historical Museum Collection.)

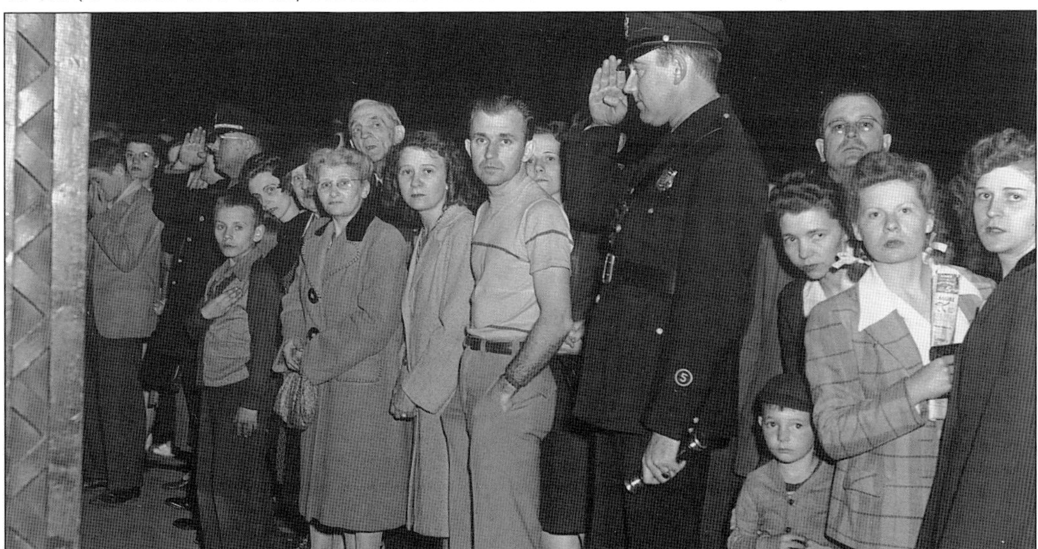

An officer salutes as President Roosevelt's funeral train passes through Greensboro shortly before 1 a.m. on April 14, 1945. Thousands of citizens stood along the tracks, including honor guards from ORD, Fort Bragg, and Camp Butner. Two green and gold Southern Railway engines pulled the train, its last car fully illuminated with the raised bronze casket flanked at each corner by a serviceman in full dress uniform. When asked about this historic moment in 1995, Carol Martin told a reporter, "Not a word was spoken as the train rolled by . . . the atmosphere was very heavy." (© Carol W. Martin/Greensboro Historical Museum Collection.)

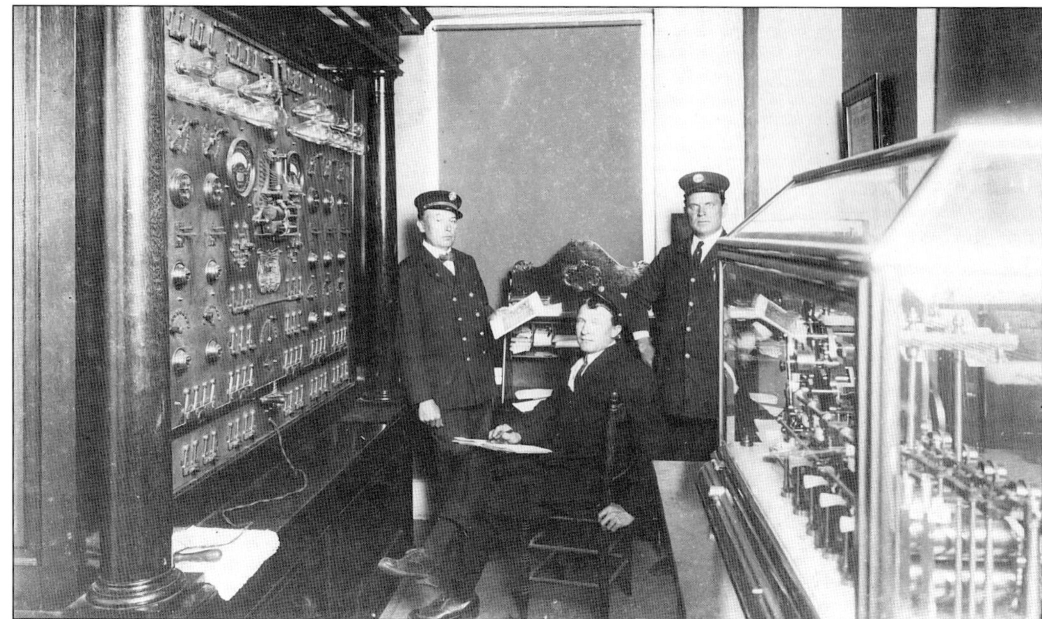

Appearing to have no patience with false alarms, Chief Charles Schnibben, George T. Williamson, and Assistant Chief William P. Monroe man the station at 20 South Fourth Street, about 1899. The building pictured had accommodated horse-drawn engines and was demolished just after the turn of the century to construct a new station with wider doors and updated alarm systems on the same site. The bell on display at Fourth and Dock is all that is left from the old building.

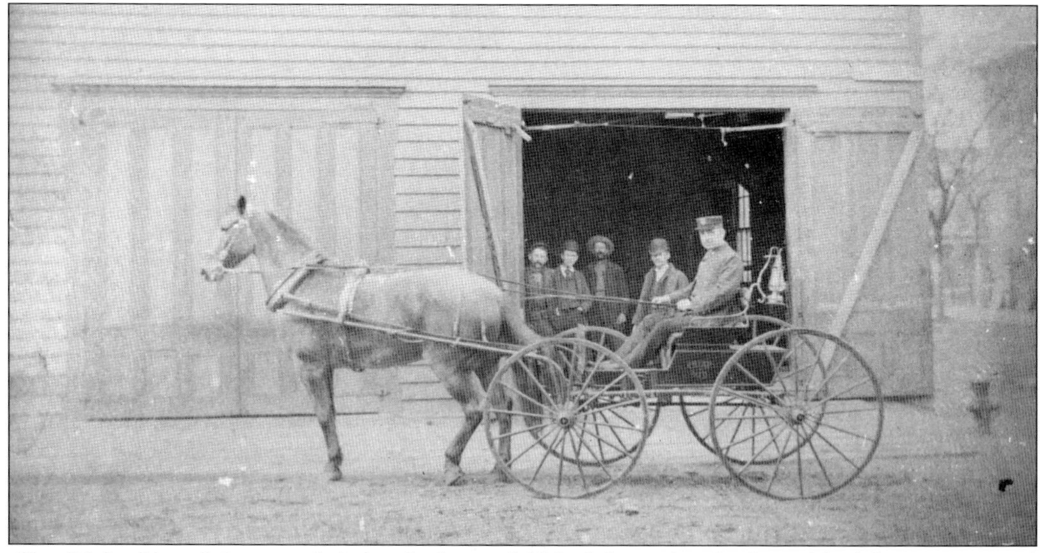

Chief Schnibben "always rode behind a beautiful black horse hitched to a black buggy trimmed with red that ran smartly down the street, whether to and from a fire or on a simple jaunt during the dinner hour," said Henry Bacon McKoy. Chief Schnibben and Assistant Chief Monroe both died in accidents that occurred en route to a fire.

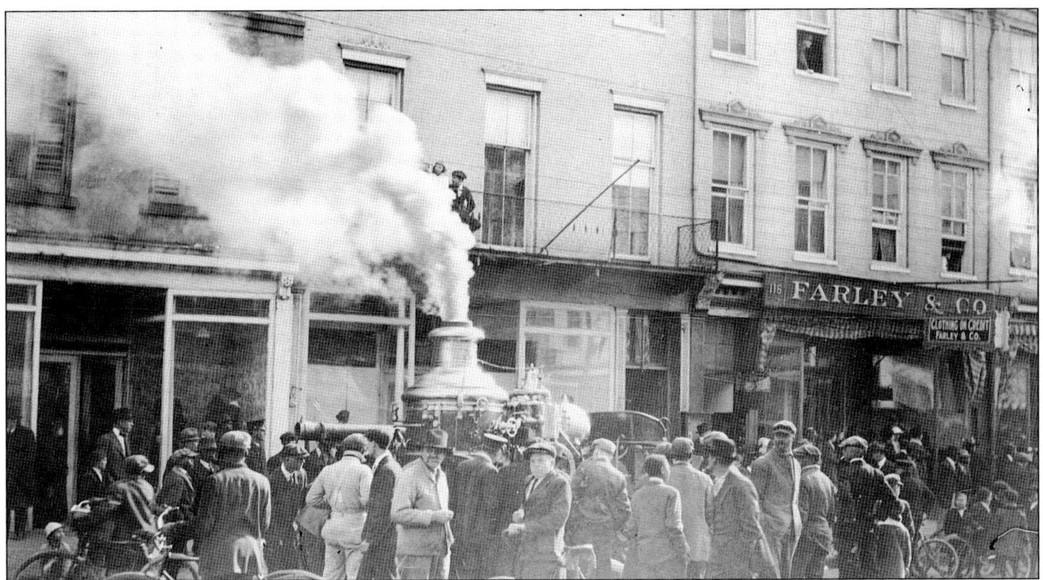

An iron balcony afforded a great view of progress, 1910-style. "But the fire engine was the thing to see and watch for. On each was a tall upright brass or nickel boiler . . . the pumps gleamed with brass and nickel and were always kept immaculately clean and brightly polished," wrote contractor and author Henry Bacon McKoy, who never forgot that he once wanted to be a fireman.

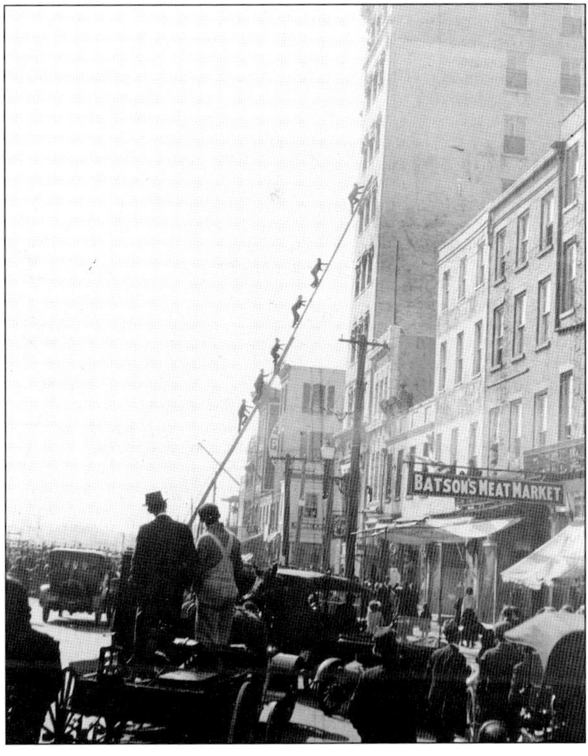

Firemen scramble to the sixth floor of the Atlantic Trust and Banking Company building at Front and Market Streets in 1918, possibly as participants in a statewide firemen's tournament. "The town turned out en masse," wrote Henry Bacon McKoy of such events. "Men stopped all work, nurses grabbed up the little babies and lined the streets to see them go by or to follow after them."

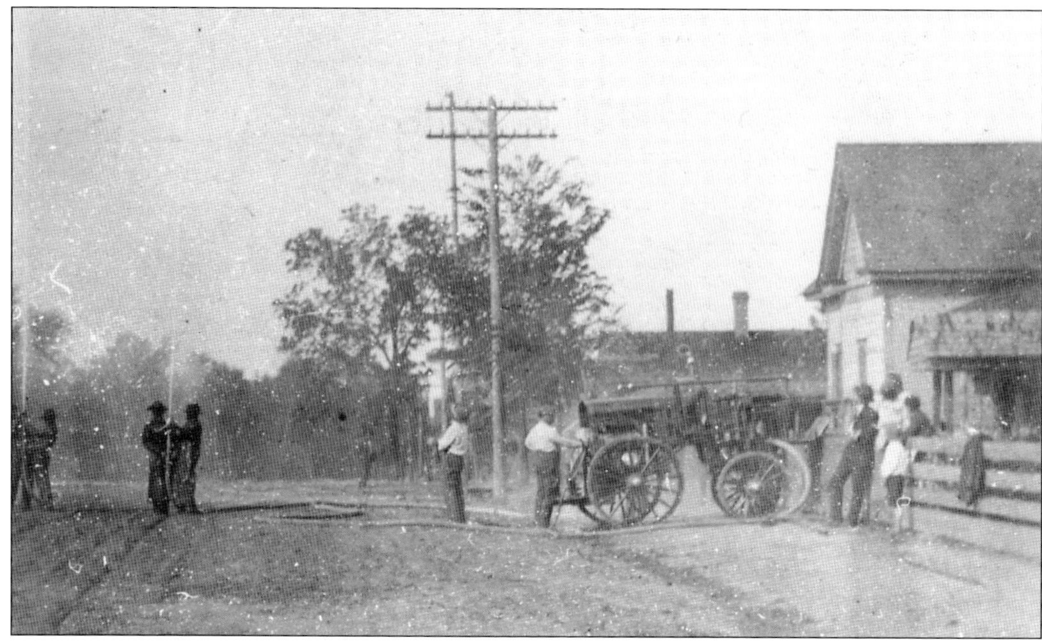

Benson firemen tested their first pumper around 1907. It was horse drawn, and the pump was powered by gasoline. The town purchased this equipment in 1907 and still owns it. The equipment is said to have been the first of its kind in North Carolina. The water was pumped from cisterns at four or five sites around town. (Courtesy of Harold Medlin.)

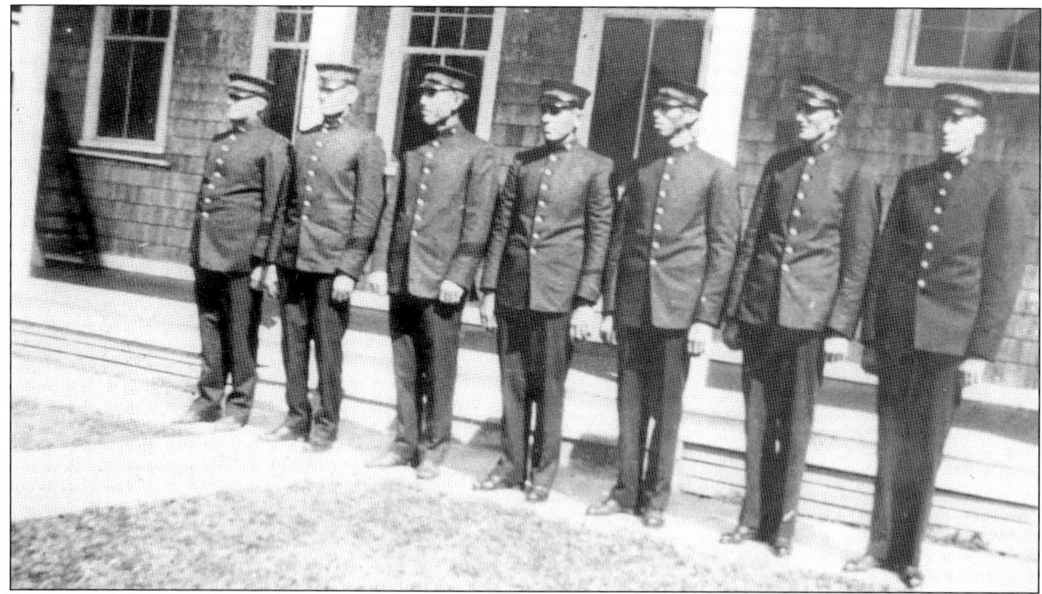

Members of the Lifesaving Service stand at attention on the porch of the Portsmouth Lifesaving Station. The station was completed on June 24, 1894, and was in charge of Watchman A.J. Styron. The men drilled, patrolled the coast, and ultimately saved lives from boats in distress. (Courtesy Dorothy Louise S. Pospisil, private collection.)

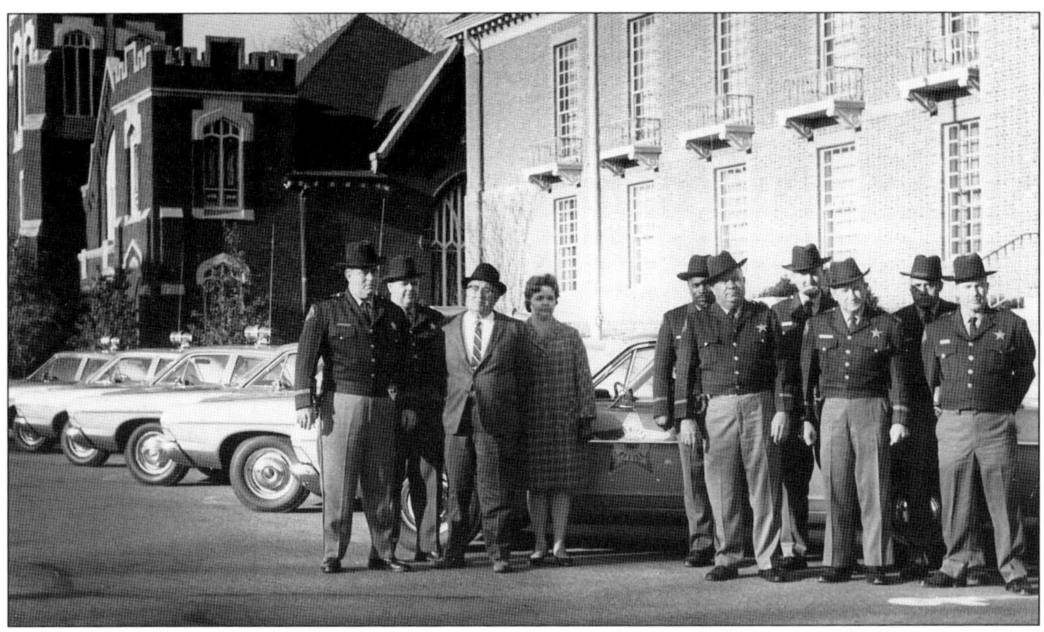

In the late 1960s, the sheriff's department received new cars. Officers include Enoch Sawyer Jr., Clarence Price, Sheriff Tom Bardin, Joe Boyd, Milton McLin, Jack Harrell, Horace Ward, Chris Knight, Thomas Moore, and dispatcher Bettie Godfrey. Sheriff Bardin served in that position for over forty years. Chris Knight was the first African-American deputy sheriff in Edgecombe County in the twentieth century. Knight was retired from the Army with twenty-two years of service as a master paratrooper in the 82nd Airborne. (BBH.)

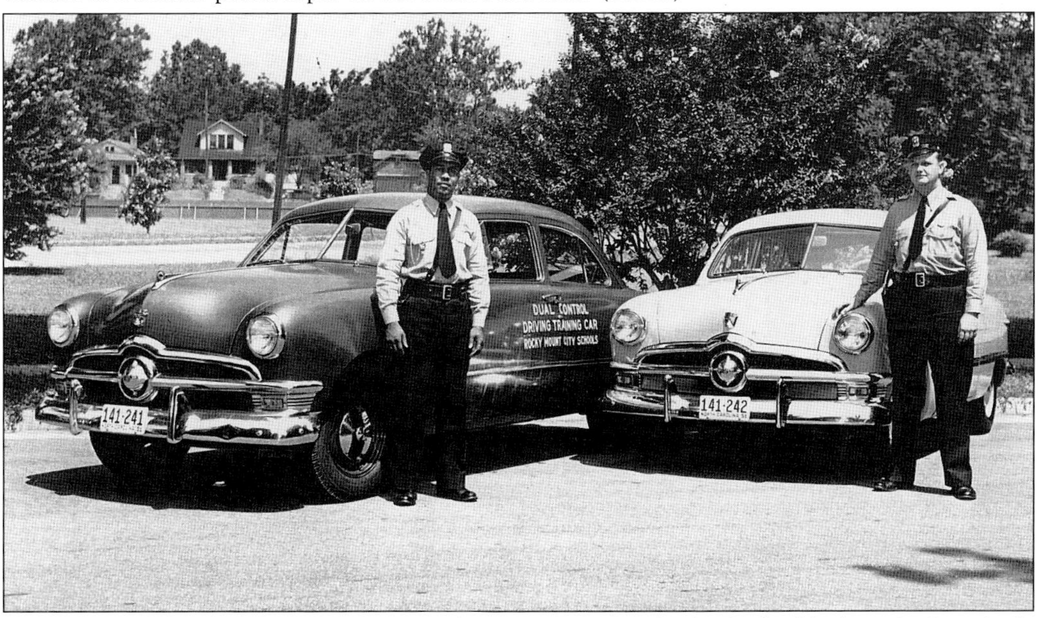

Rocky Mount schools provided driver education training for both the black and white high schools in the 1950s. (NRMS.)

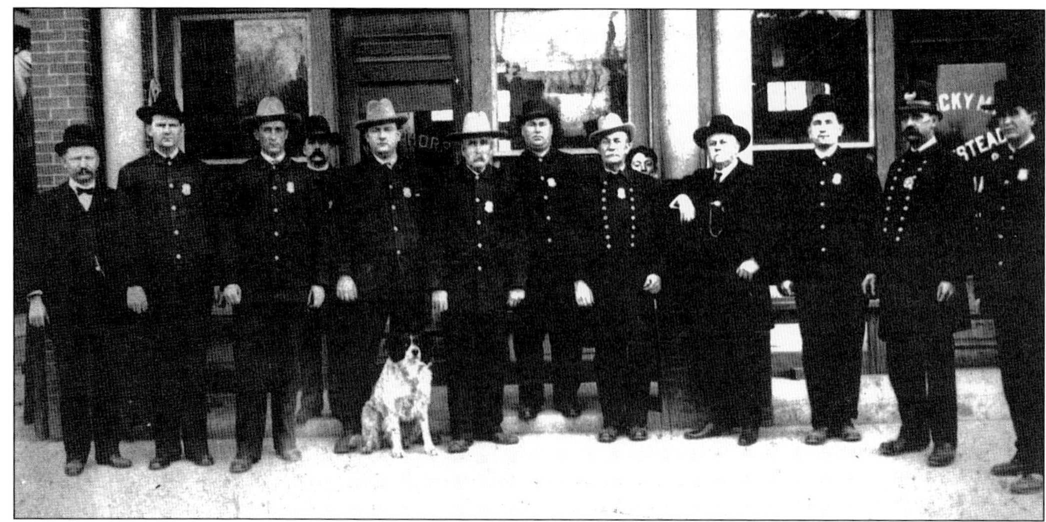

By 1915, the Rocky Mount Police Department had a paddy wagon, one bicycle, and a dog. Members of the force included Bud Harris, Oliver Wheeless, A.A. Parrish, Sid Taylor, Eli Stephenson, Jimmie Reams, George Denny, Sid Davis, W.L. Thorp, Henry Hedgepeth, and Police Chief Oliver Hedgepeth. (Courtesy Barringer.)

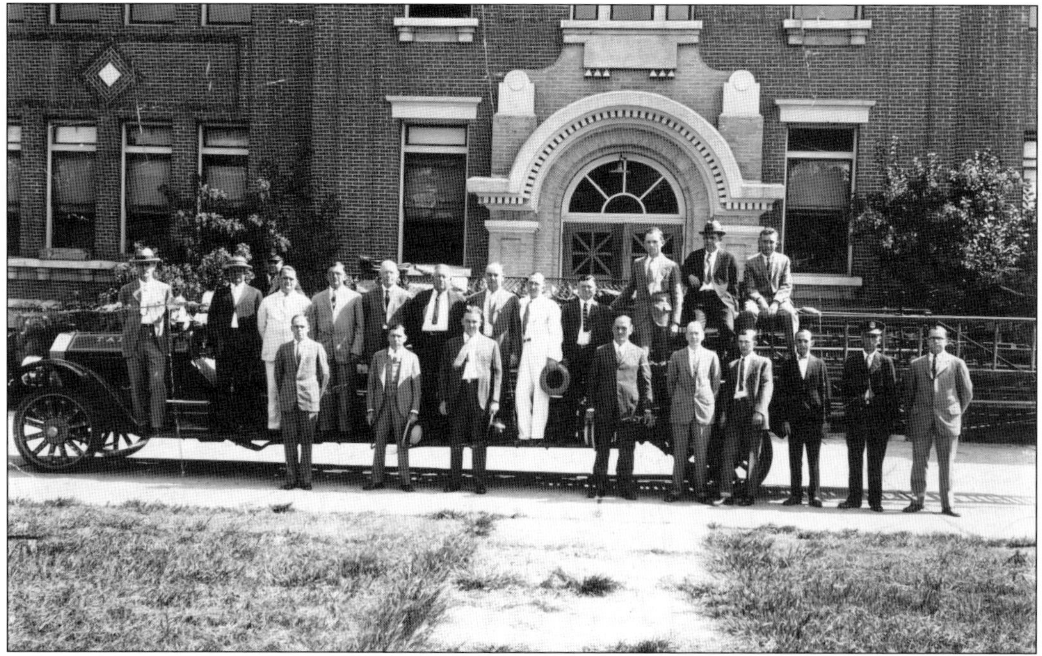

A new ladder truck was purchased for the fire department in 1925. The men in this photograph, taken on the occasion of the purchase, include Carl Rosenbaum, Tom Bardin, Isaac Brown, and John A. Weddell. All of the men were volunteers except for the fire chief. (Courtesy PC Cherry.)

This is an early photograph of Durham's first black police officers, who were hired as a result of a request by C.C. Spaulding for black police officers in Hayti to help diffuse racial tensions between black citizens and white police officers. (Courtesy of Durham County Public Library.)

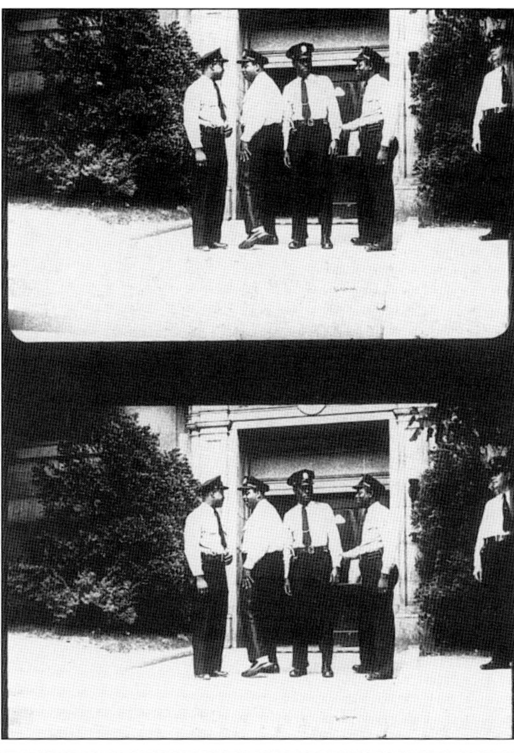

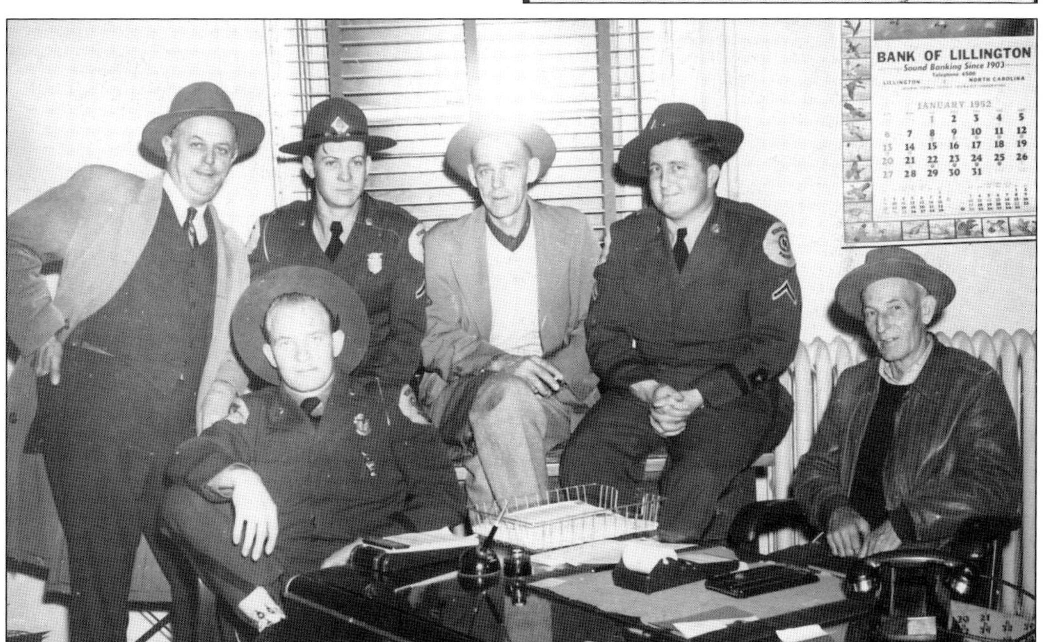

Law Enforcement Officers in the Courthouse in Lillington, 1952. Pictured are Herman Word, Bill Grady, Wade Stewart, B. Leonard, and Kirkland Stewart. (Courtesy N.C. Department of Archives and History.)

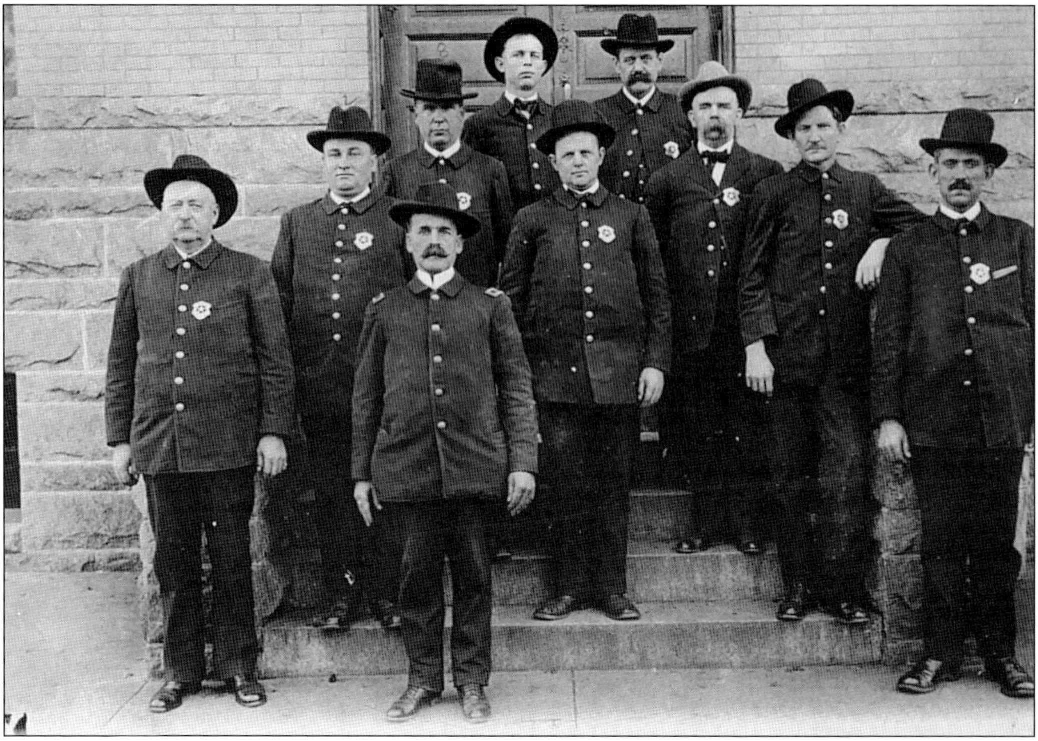

The members are, from left to right, as follows: (first row) Luther Kimball, formerly chief of the Salem force; Chief James A. Thomas; and Columbus A. Wall; (second row) E. Frank Apple; Robert W. Bryant; and Robert Young; (third row) Robert L. Blackburn and John T. Thomas; (fourth row) Norman B. Williams and sanitary inspector Charles A. Pratt. (FCL.)

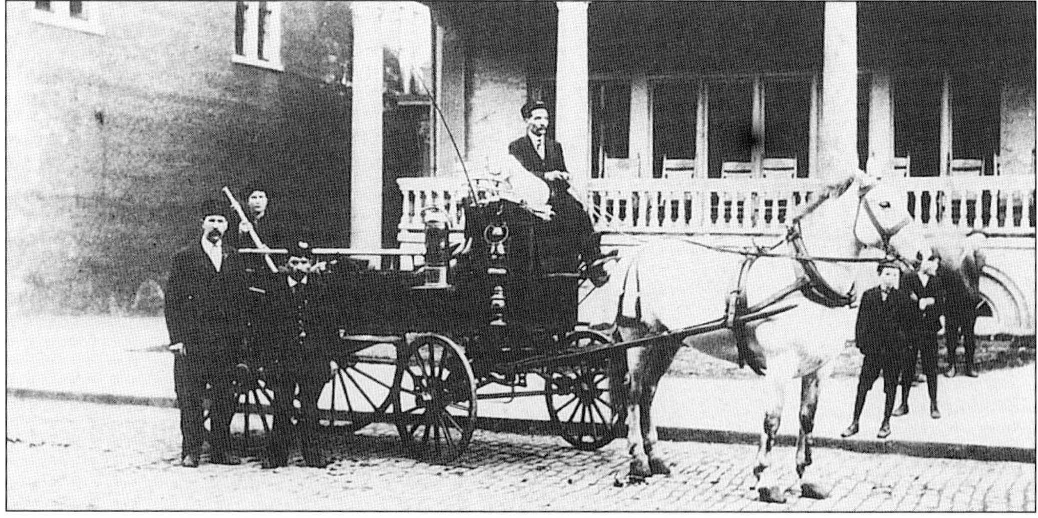

Tom Keith holds the nozzle at the rear of wagon; standing at the far left is Bob Shelton and next to him is Winston's first paid fireman, John H. Holmes. In the driver's seat is Watt Knight. The boy under the horse's head is Red Powell. (FCL.)

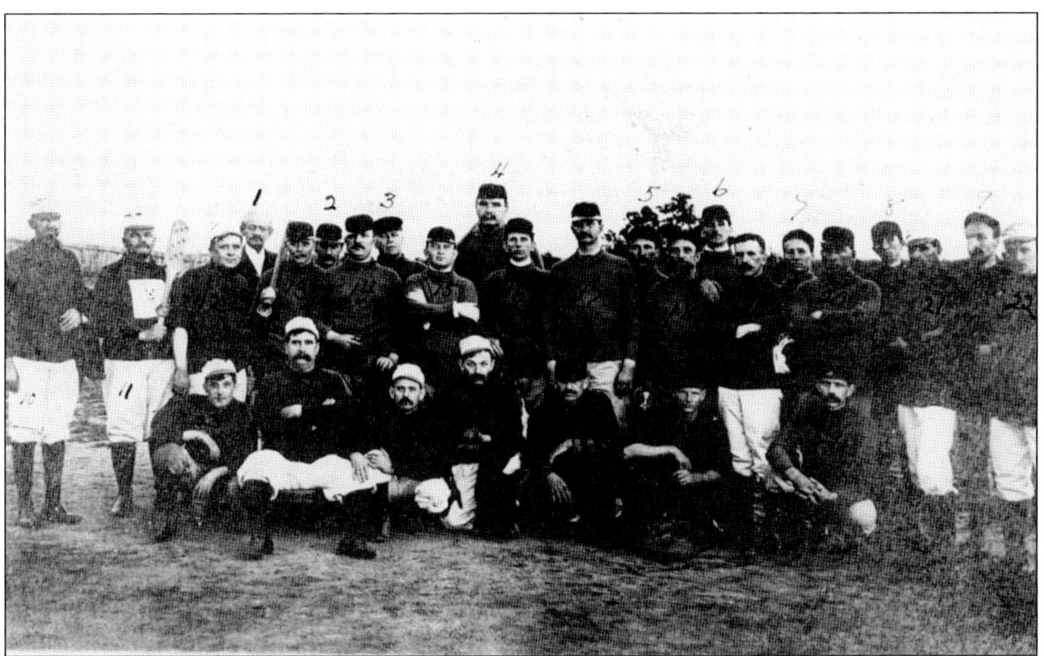

The members, from left to right, are as follows: O.W. Hanner, Frank Martin, J.J. Cofer, W.M. Sugg, Henry Valentine, and John T. Thompson; (seated at left) Chief J.W. Bradford and Jesse C. Bessent. (FCL.)

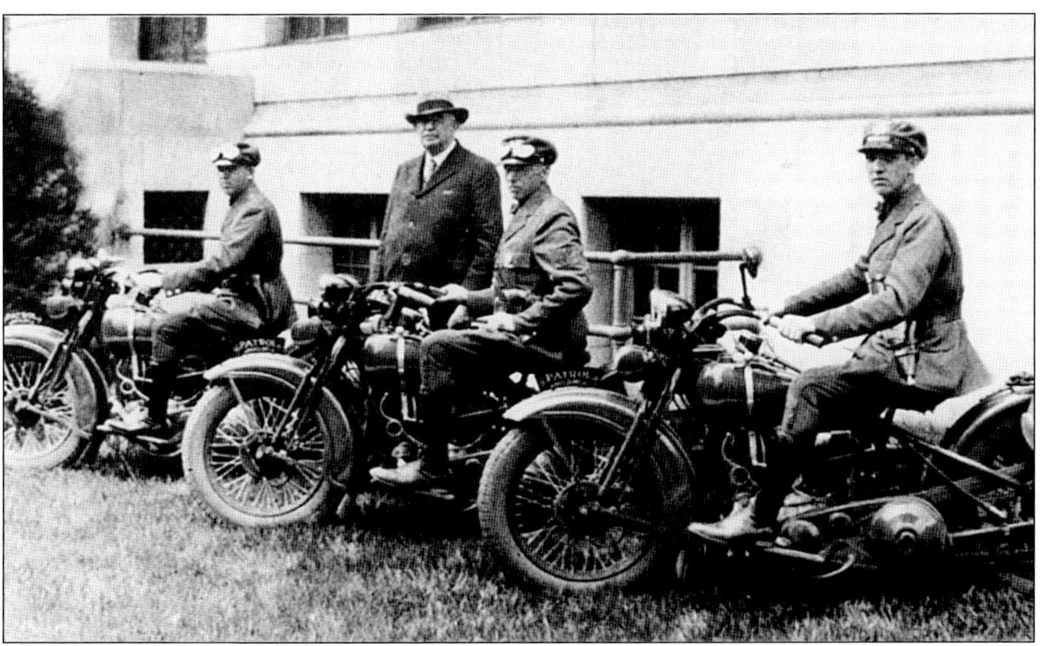

The officers are, from left to right, as follows: Ken Pfaff, Mack Spainhour, A.C. Bovender, and J.B. McCreary, sheriff (standing). (FCL.)

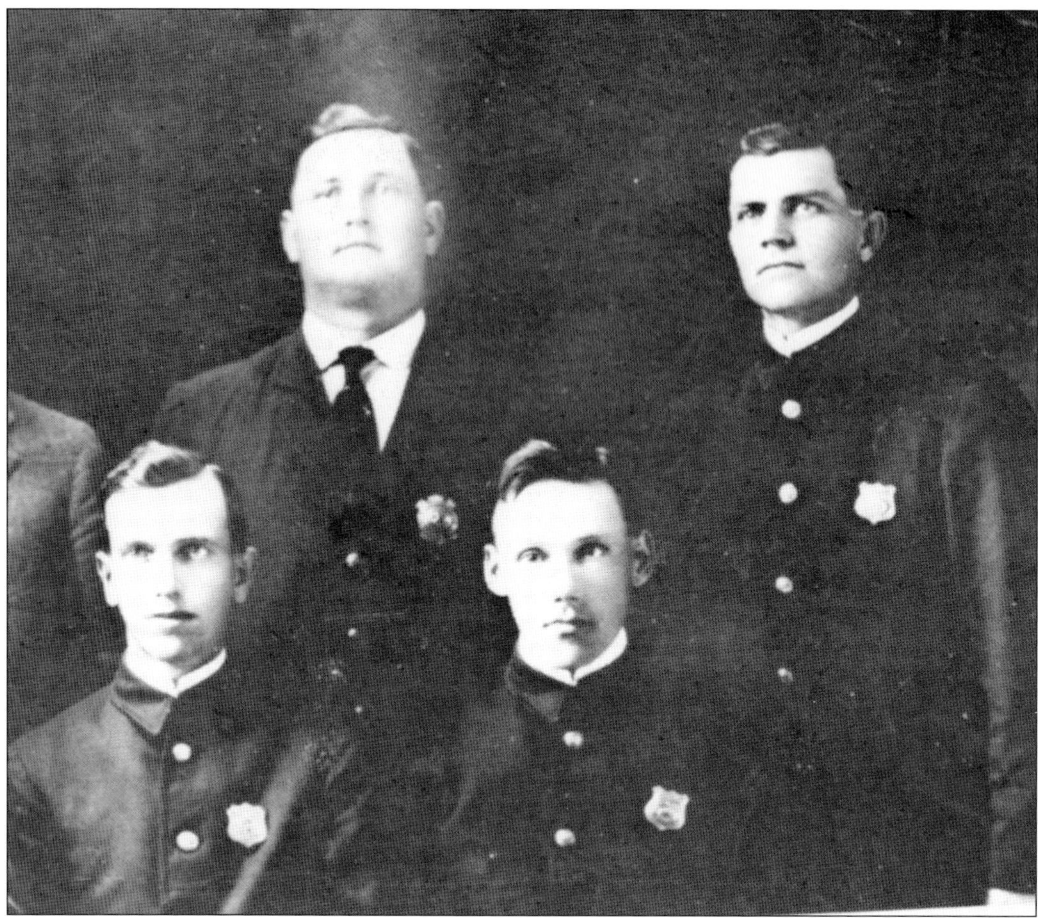

Tarboro has had a police department since the early nineteenth century. Until the early twentieth century, the regular duties of law officers involved arresting offenders, watching the jail, and escorting prisoners to court (or in some cases to a public hanging). In 1917, however, two officers were killed in the line of duty while attempting to arrest a bootlegger. Officers Matt R. Gwatney (top right) and Plummer Ray Riggin (front left) are buried in Greenwood Cemetery under a single headstone. (BBH.)

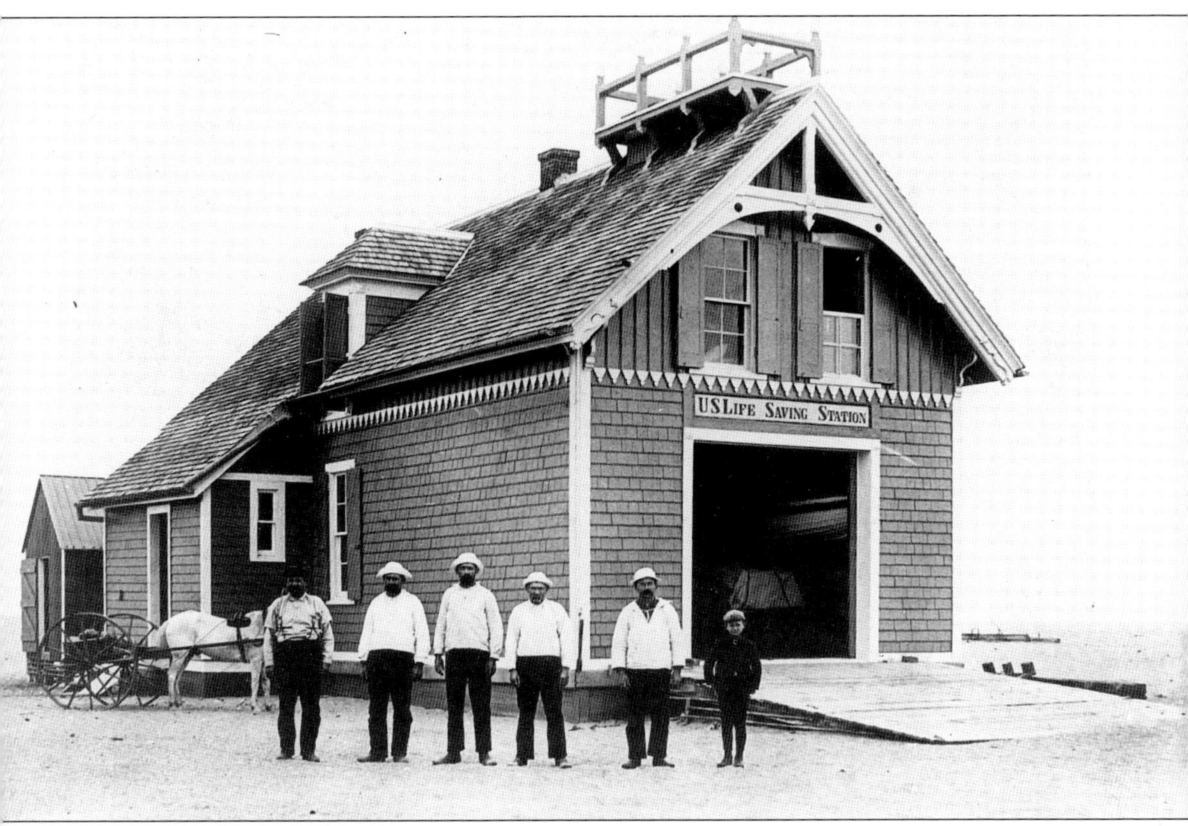

The Little Kinnakeet Lifesaving Station appears in this *c.* 1895 photograph. The original station at this site was erected in 1874. (U.S. Coast Guard.)

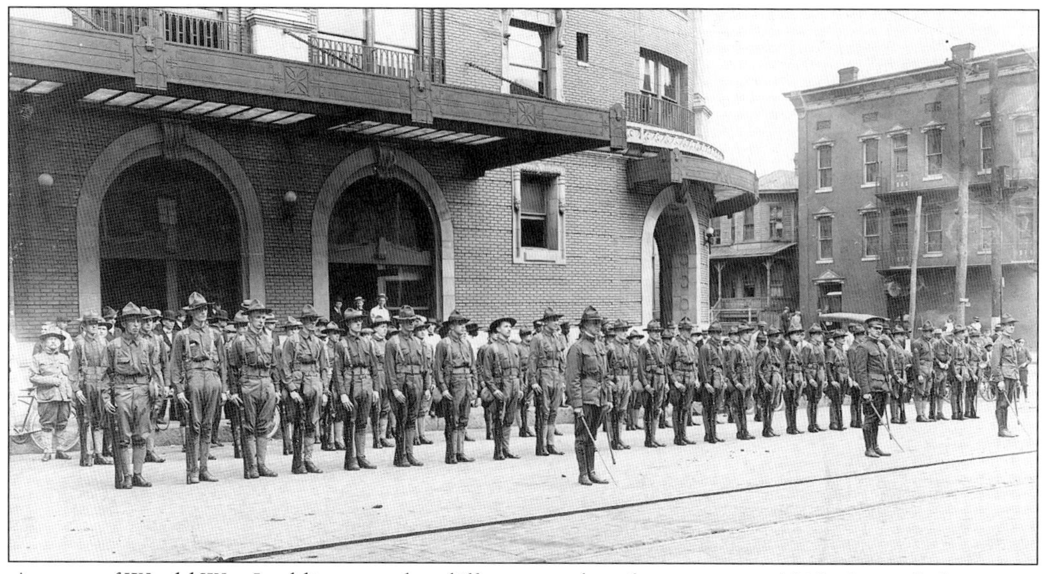

A troop of World War I soldiers stood at different grades of attention in 1918. A gnarled veteran of the Spanish-American War, possibly Thomas Cowan James, joined them. The officer on the far left (foreground, with sword) is Capt. Edward P. Bailey. In the background is Union Station, the Atlantic Coast Line terminal and executive office building that was located on the northeast corner of Front and Red Cross. On an average day, 18 trains arrived and departed from Wilmington.

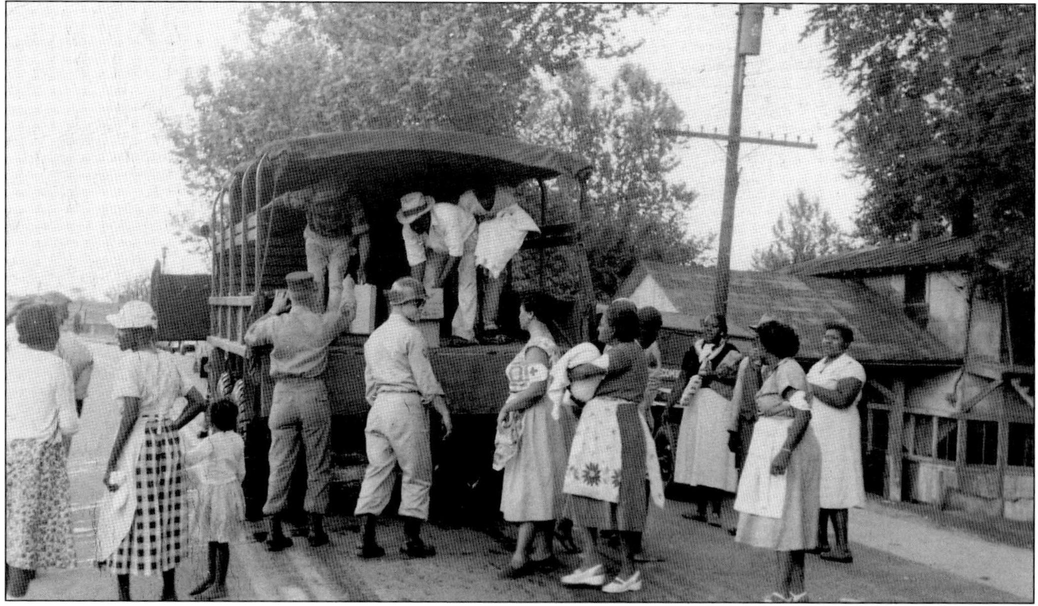

Company F of 119th Infantry of the National Guard brought aid to victims of the May 1958 flood in Princeville and Tarboro. The Red Cross used the Princeville School as an emergency shelter, but even that had to be evacuated because of rising water which was damaging water and sewage lines. Over 150 families were resettled at Pattillo School. (Courtesy PC-Cherry.)

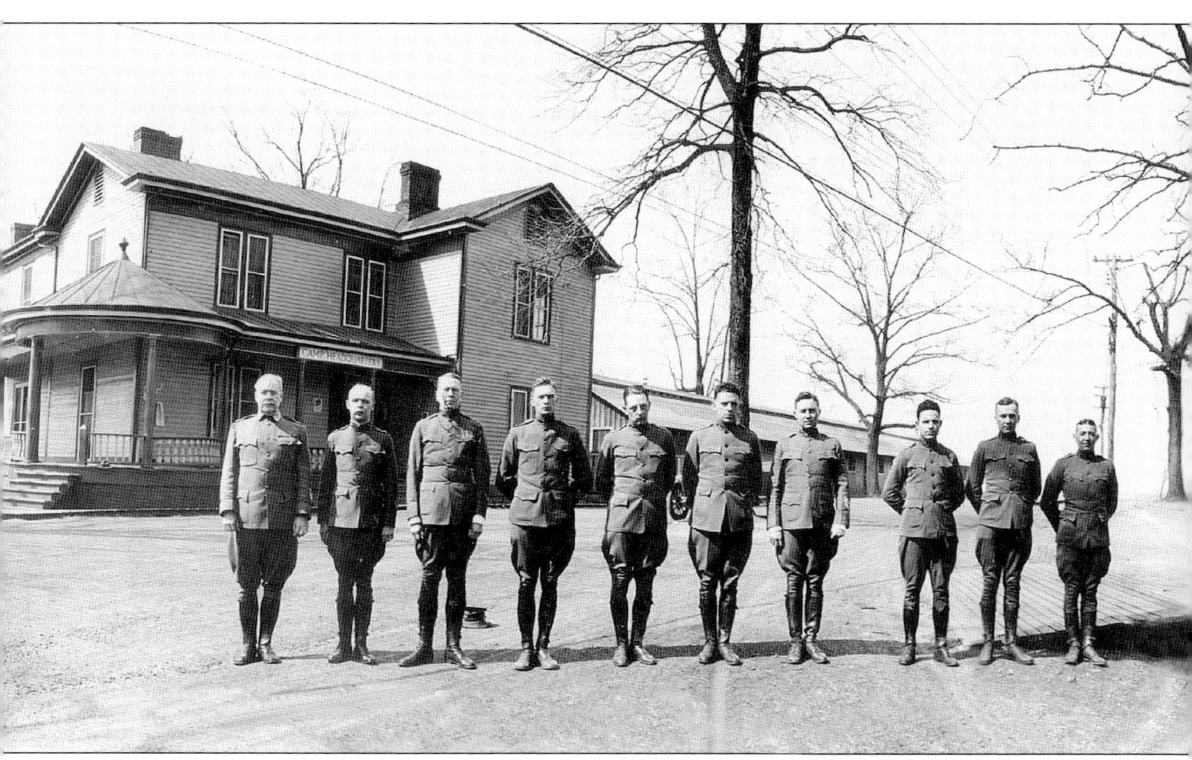

When the United States entered World War I, a U.S. Army training facility was quickly established on Charlotte's west side. Nearly sixty thousand men came through Camp Greene during its brief life, which ended soon after the armistice in November of 1919. Here, Colonel Macomb and his staff pose in March of that same year outside the camp headquarters at the old Dowd farmhouse. The house still stands today on Monument Avenue. (Robinson-Spangler Carolina Room, Public Library of Charlotte and Mecklenburg County.)

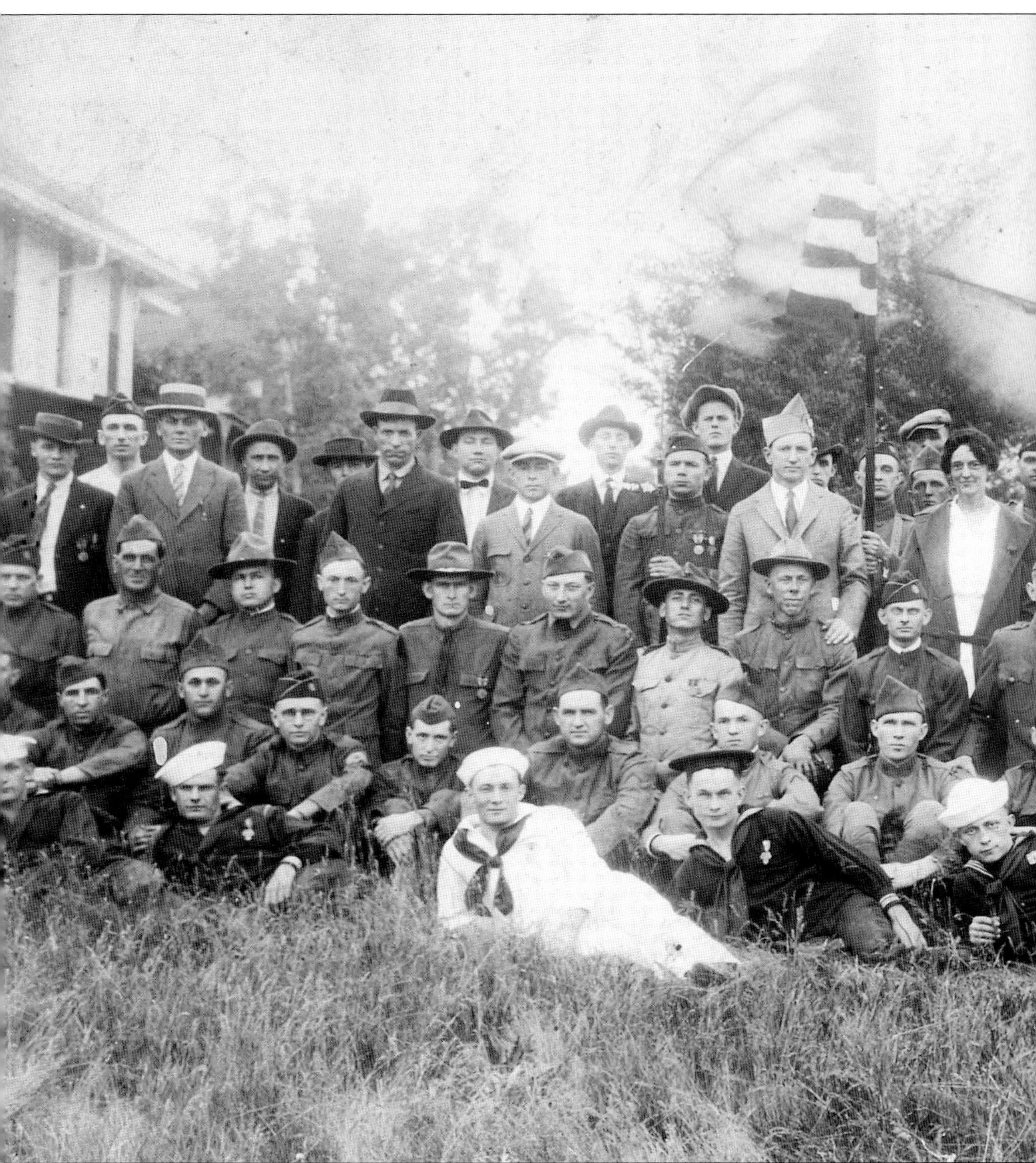

Here is a portrait of World War I veterans from the tri-city area—the common name given to Leaksville, Spray, and Draper prior to the towns' consolidation into the City of Eden in 1967. Some of the men are identified, but the list is out of order. Among them are Melvin Tucker Sr., Bill Hopper, Allen Hancock, Mr. Morgan, Mr. Matthews, G.D. Scott, Judson Hall, George Bateman, Luther H. Hodges, Tom C. Stanley, Ernest I. Hankins, Will Vernon,

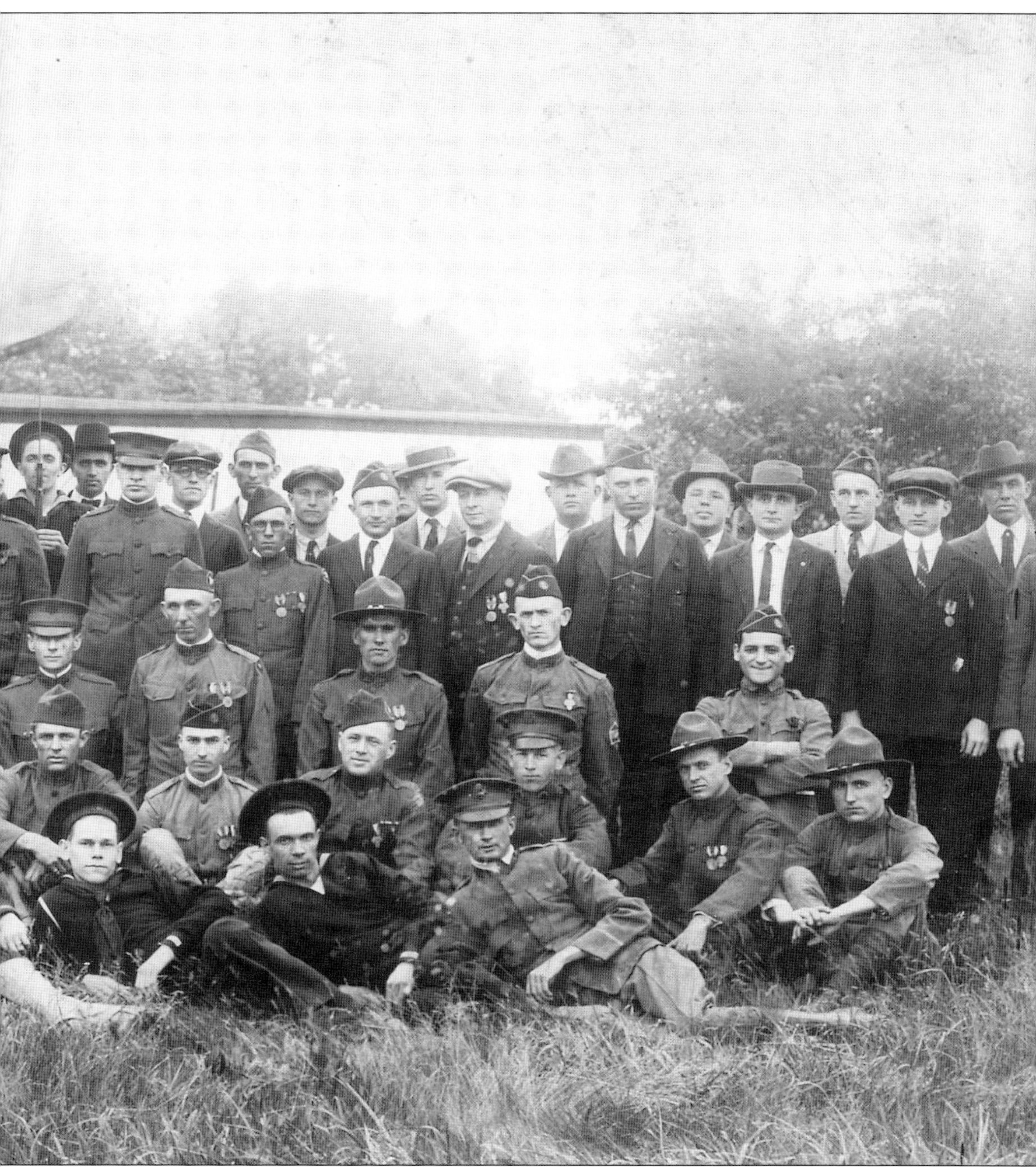

Dan Lashly, Bremy Vernon, Cornelious Purdy, Mr. Brown, Curt Moore, and Fred Hundley. Dan Aheron is the second individual from the left in the first row, wearing Navy blues. (Courtesy of Bertha Vestal Aheron and the Aheron family. Courtesy of the Roscoe Hankins Collection, Eden, NC.)

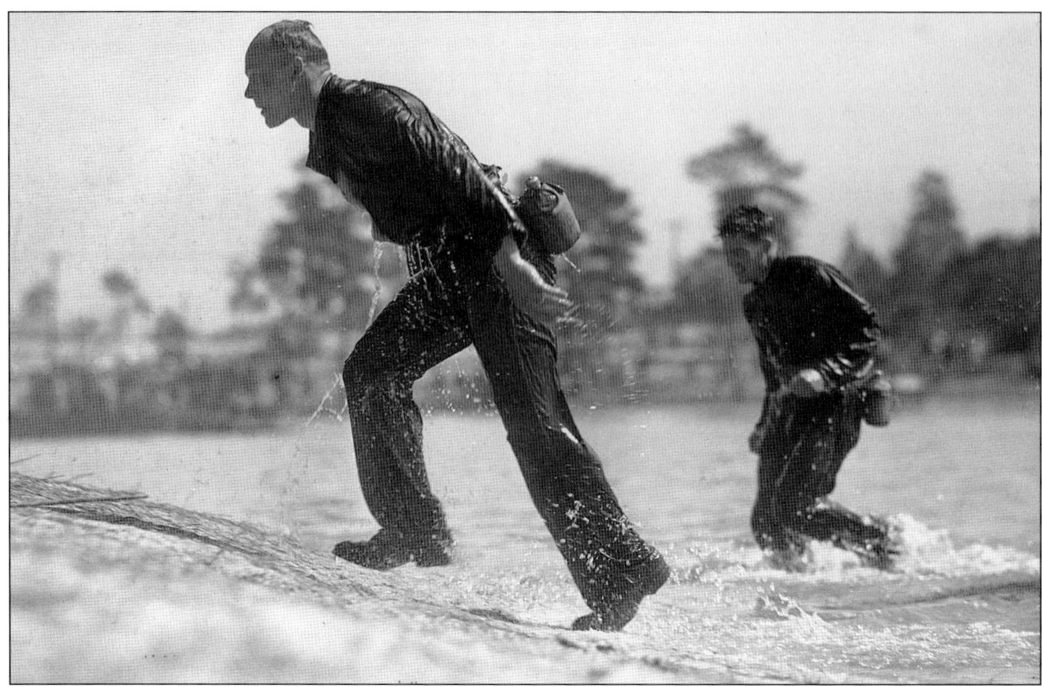

Fort Bragg was the largest artillery post in the world during World War II, covering 122,000 acres, with 3,135 buildings. Carol Martin captured these soldiers in action during Army Day on April 6, 1942. Fort Bragg, which was one of 21 military installations in North Carolina, mushroomed from a 1940 capacity of 5,400 men to over 100,000 by war's end. (© Carol W. Martin/Greensboro Historical Museum Collection.)

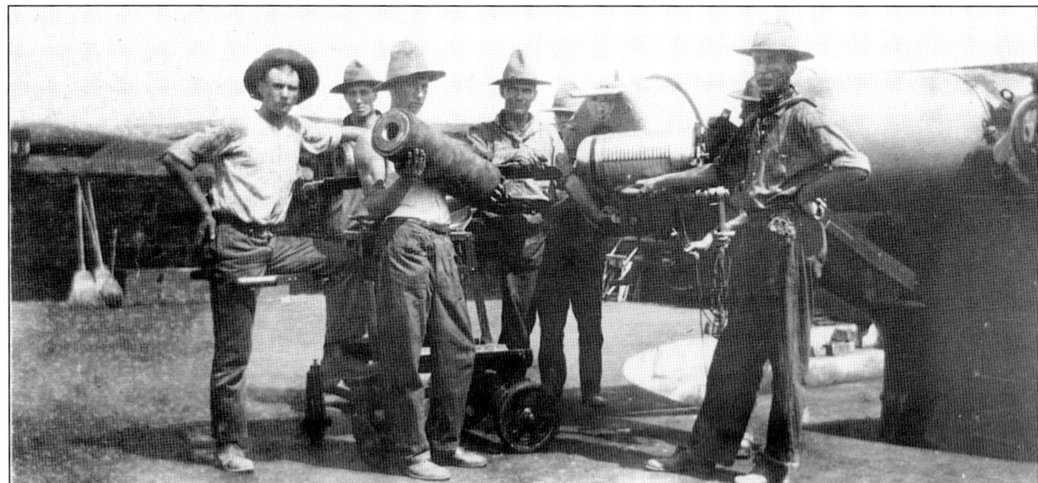

Fort Caswell, at the mouth of the Cape Fear, is a massive masonry post which was built as a federal garrison, 1826–1838. Commandeered by the Confederacy and later captured by the Union, it was deemed by U.S. Rear Admiral D.D. Porter, "almost impervious to shot and shell . . . in many respects stronger than Fort Fisher, and harder to take by assault." Here, World War I soldiers load the big guns.

Five

The Good Old Days:
Snapshots

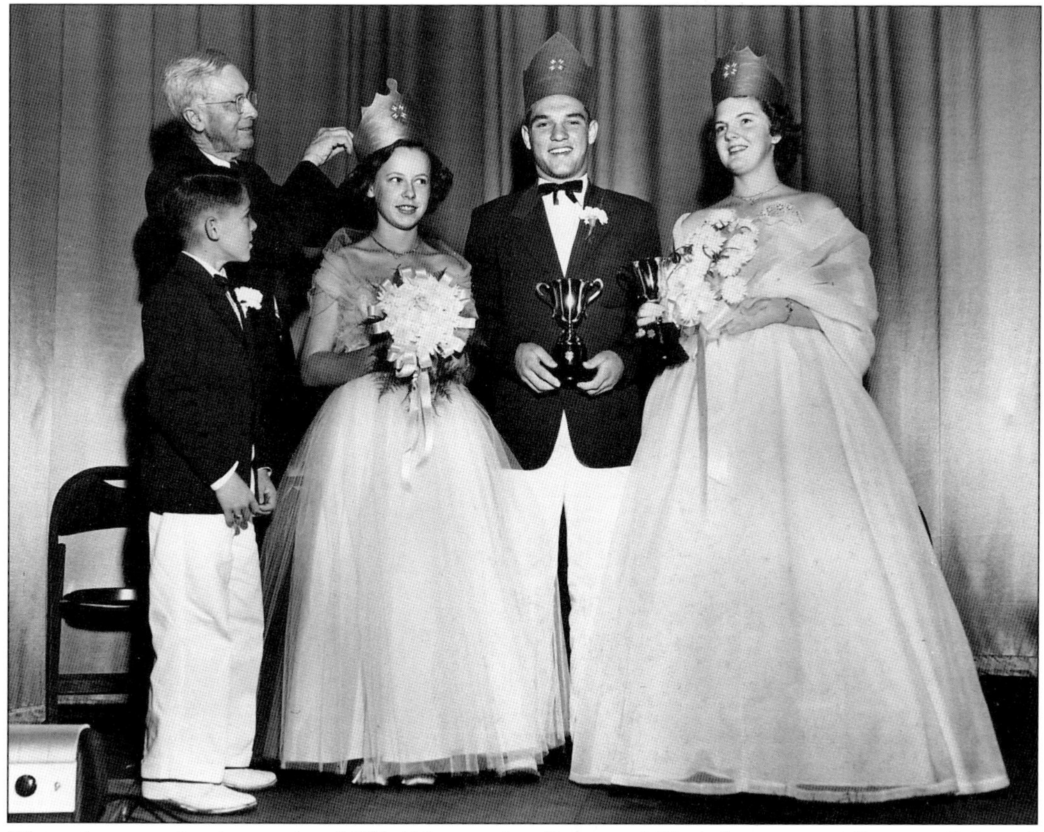

This photograph shows the 1952 Edgecombe County 4-H Achievement Day at Colonial Theater in downtown Tarboro. The Junior and Senior Health Improvement Kings and Queens are, from left to right, Jerry Bullock, Otis Bullock, unidentified, and Sara Lawrence. (Courtesy PC-Dupree.)

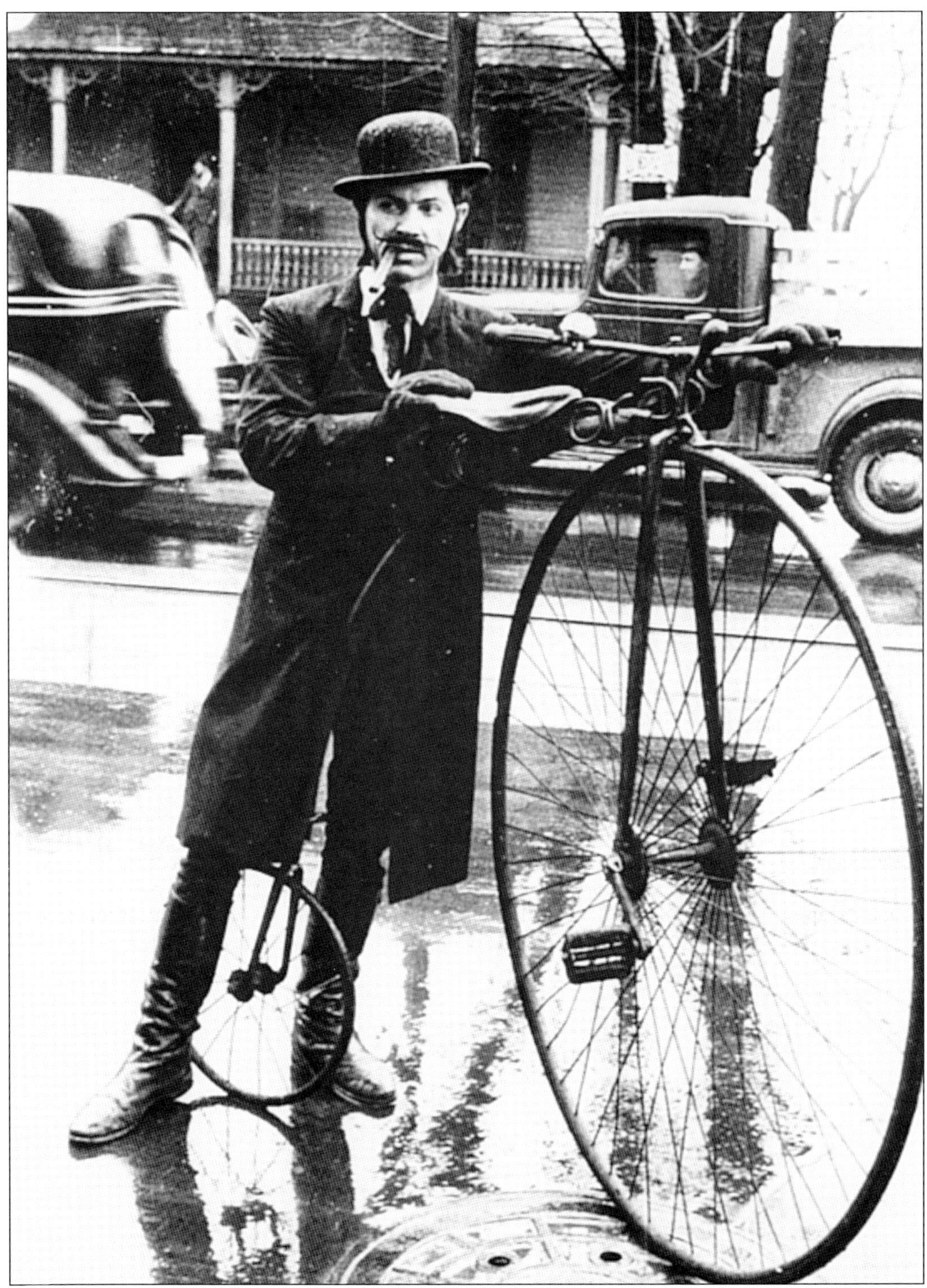

An unidentified cyclist takes on damp weather for this sophisticated pose. (FCL.)

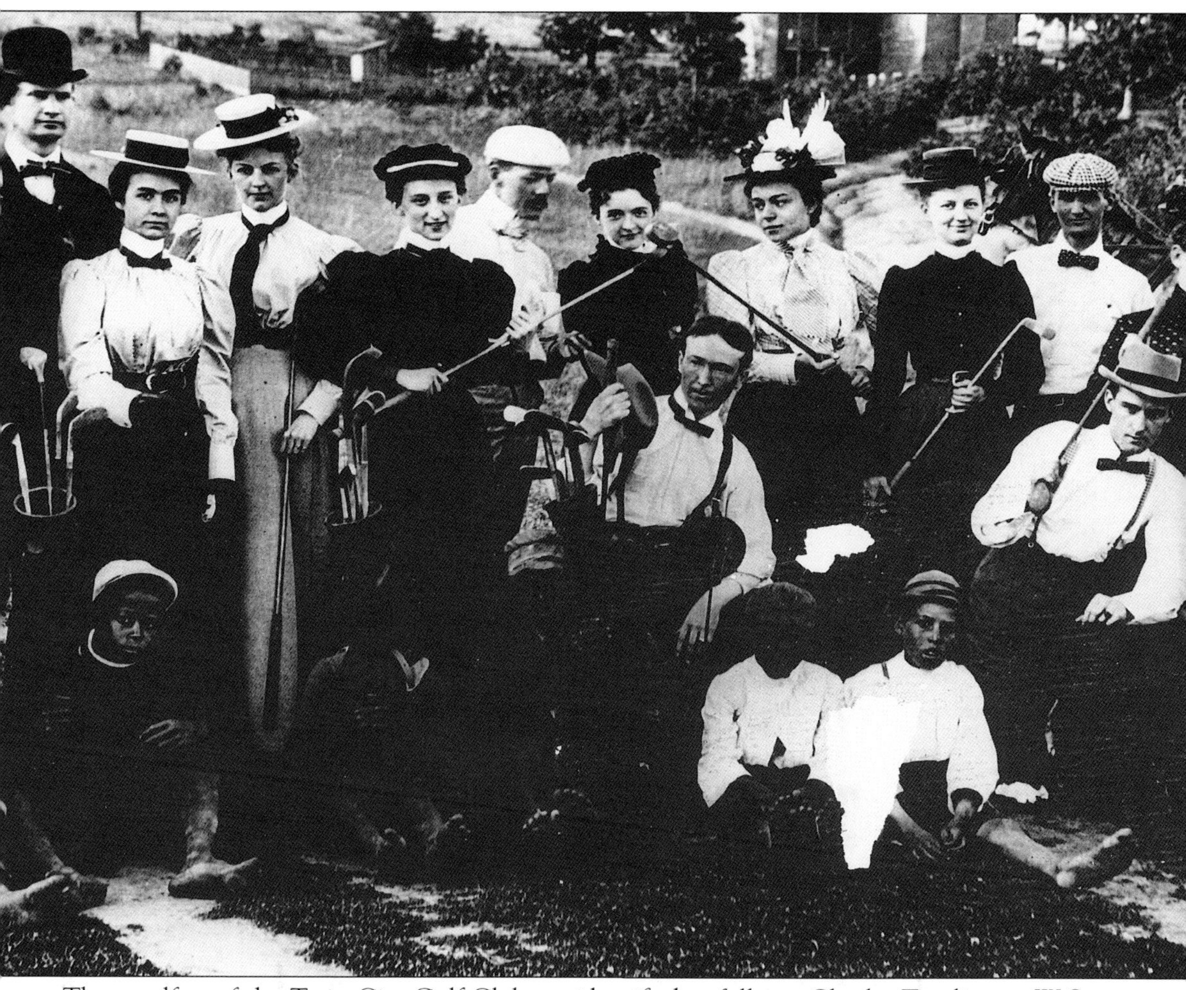

These golfers of the Twin City Golf Club are identified as follows: Charles Tomlinson, W.S. Snipes, Daisey Vaughn Gilmer, Lou Gorrel Farris, Eleanor Follin, George Gibbs, Mamie Gray Galloway, A.H. Galloway, Edna Maslin, Adelaide Fries, Alfred Belo Jr., Marion Follin, and Lottie Tomlinson Morrison. (FCL.)

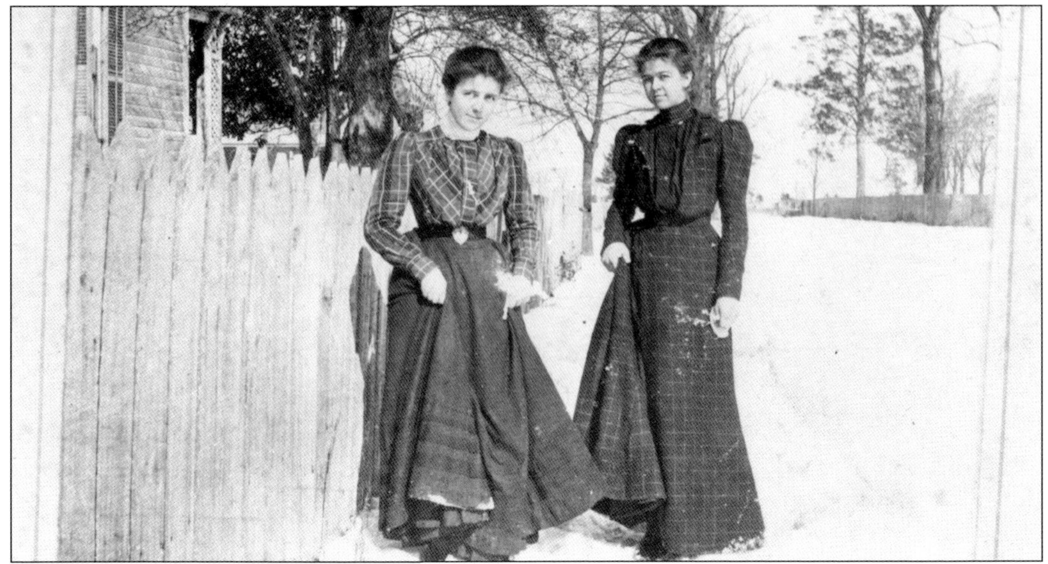

Two Tarboro ladies enjoy a stroll through the snow in 1899. This was one of many memorable snowstorms in the late 1890s. (BBH.)

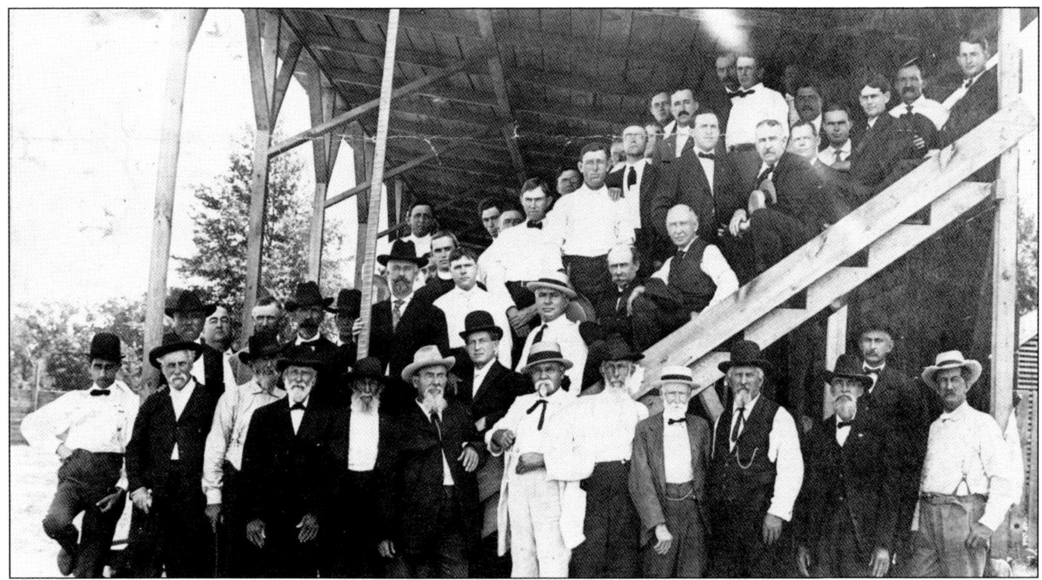

Civic and fraternal groups have been present in Tarboro since the town was established. One of the first Masonic lodges in North Carolina was built in Tarboro. Some of the other groups active prior to World War II were the Woodmen of the World, the Moose, the Kiwanis Club, the Rotary Club, and the American Legion. Women belonged to the Daughters of the American Revolution and the United Daughters of the Confederacy. In the 1870s there was an active temperance society which led to the founding of the Temperance Hall community. The civic group pictured here is gathered on the old fairgrounds. The front row includes veterans of the Civil War. Two people identified in the group are George Howard (fourth from the left) and Dr. Keech (at the very top). (ECML.)

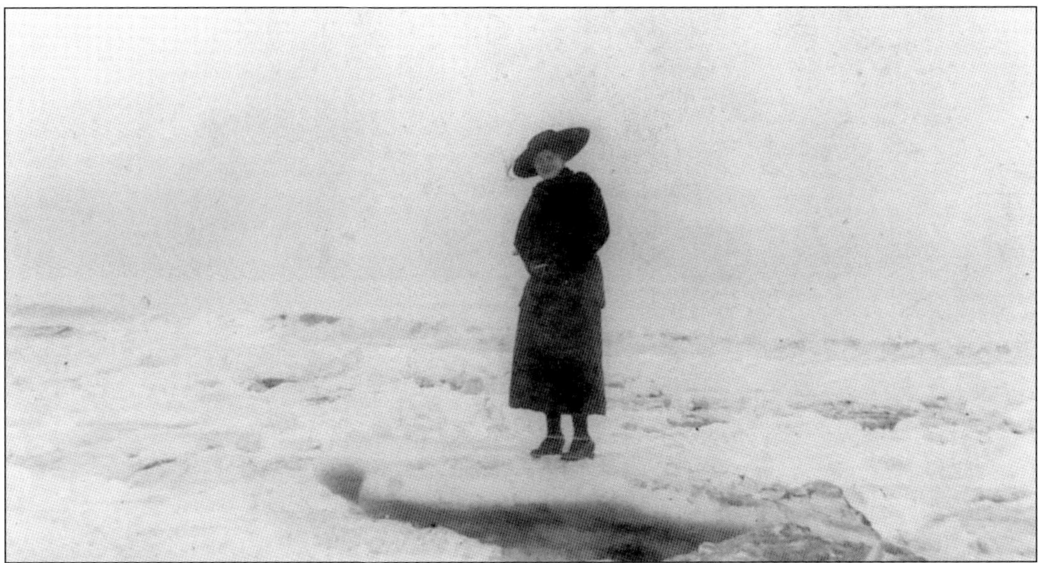

When the temperature plunged in December of 1917, no one could imagine that it would stay below freezing for 17 days in a row. The Sound froze solid and many residents reported walking across it to find supplies. Frances Sibert was photographed on January 6, 1918, standing on the frozen surf of the Atlantic Ocean. (Courtesy North Carolina Department of Archives and History.)

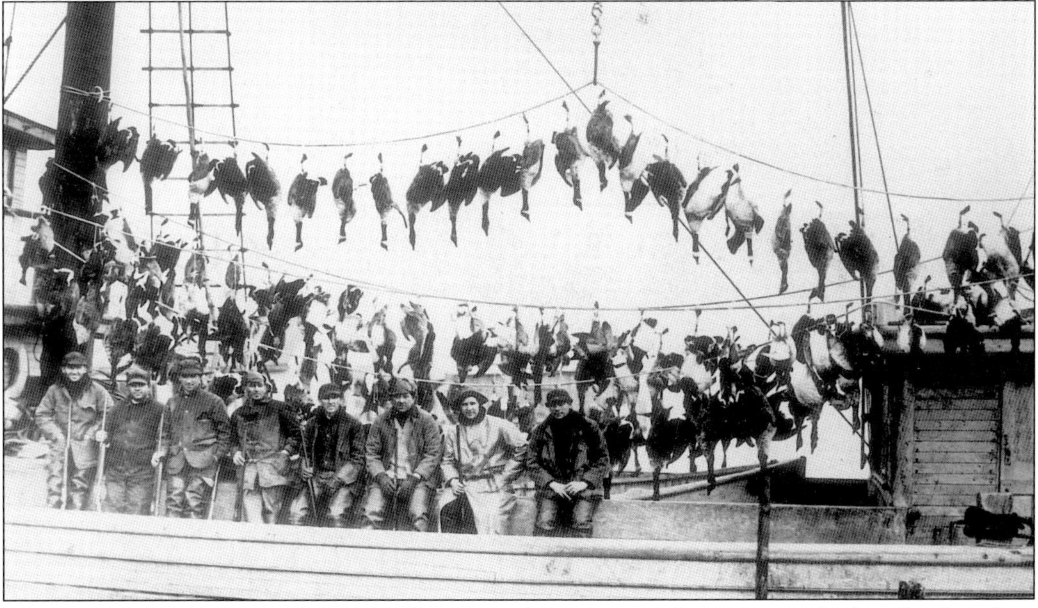

This picture from the early 1900s illustrates the great number of waterfowl to be found in Carteret County. Hunters came from great distances to engage hunting guides. These hunters are pictured on an early menhaden boat with over 100 ducks from a day's shoot. In addition to the meat from the fowl, the feathers would be used for bedding. (Courtesy Core Sound Waterfowl Museum.)

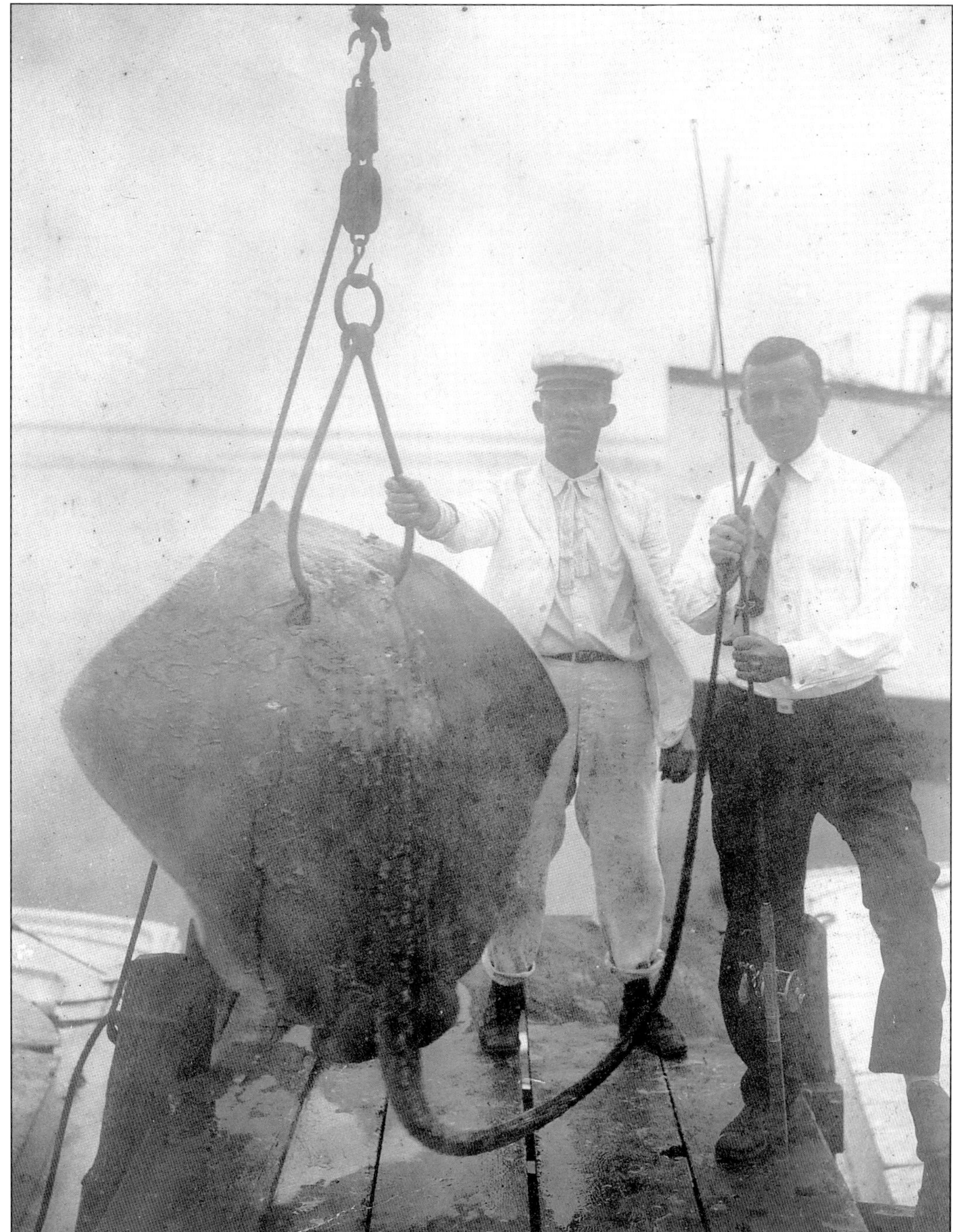

John Motley Morehead II is shown with Captain Gib Willis and their "catch-of-the-day," a giant ray. Captain Gib was Mr. Morehead's captain most of his adult life and was known for his outstanding sailing skills. In the winter months he was a hunting guide for the Morehead family and their guests. (Courtesy Nettie Murrill, private collection.)

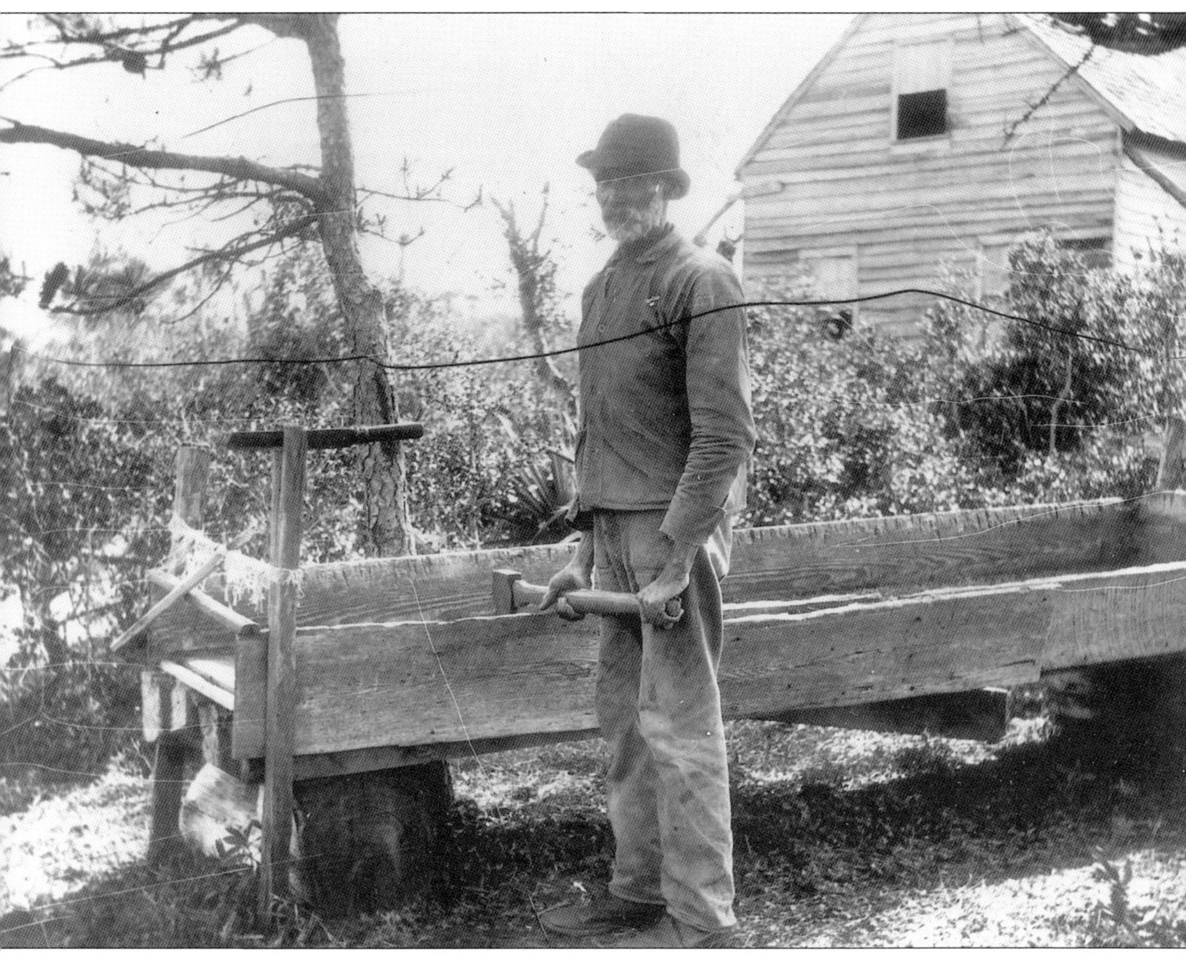

Yaupon tea was a beverage once widely used among the inhabitants of the Outer Banks. During the process of making the tea, twigs from the yaupon with leaves attached were put into a trough and chopped down to approximately an inch long. H.H. Brimley photographed the trough shown above in 1903. (Courtesy North Carolina Division of Archives and History.)

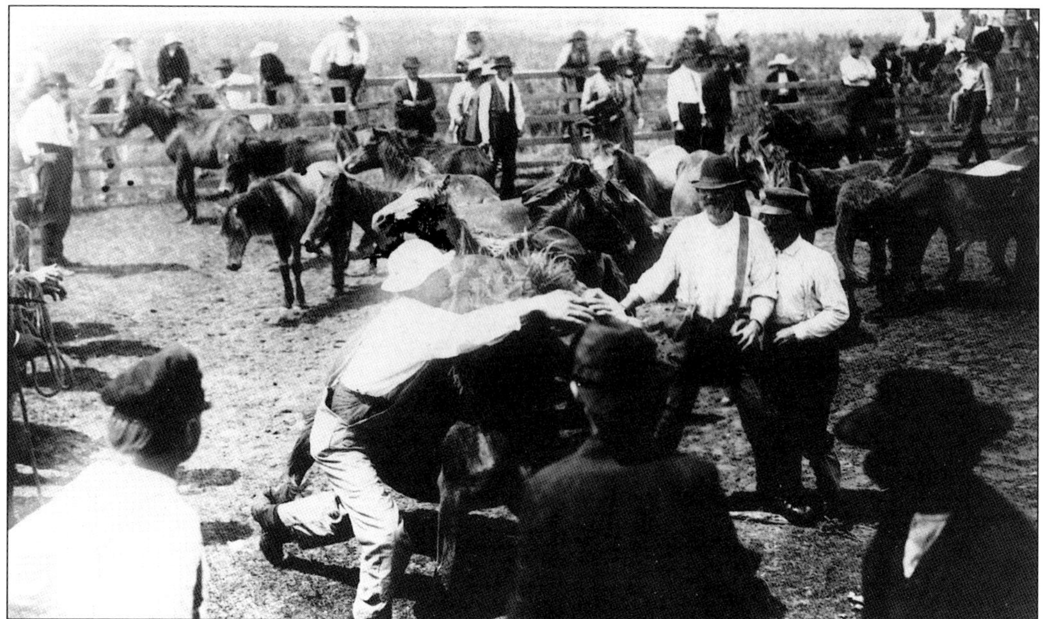

These wild ponies are being rounded up on the Core Banks in 1907. (Courtesy North Carolina Division of Archives and History.)

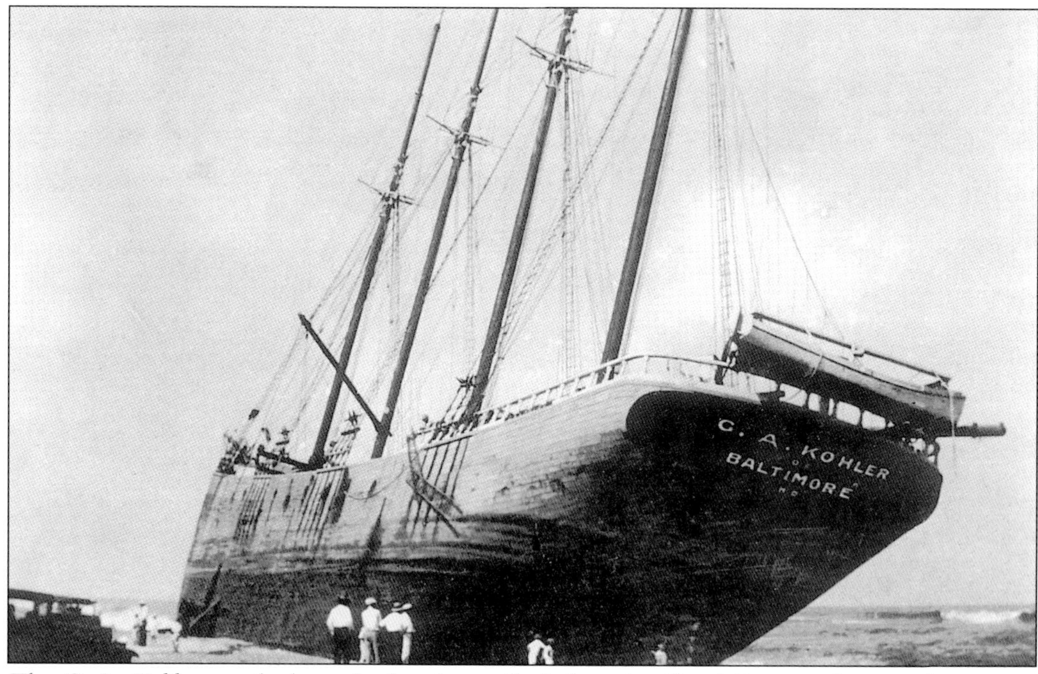

The G.A. *Kohler* wrecked on the beach a mile below the Shoal Station during a hurricane on August 2, 1933. Everyone on board was rescued, but the ship was stranded high up on the beach, where it became a tourist attraction of sorts. The ship was destroyed in the early 1940s for scrap iron. (Courtesy Museum of the Albemarle.)

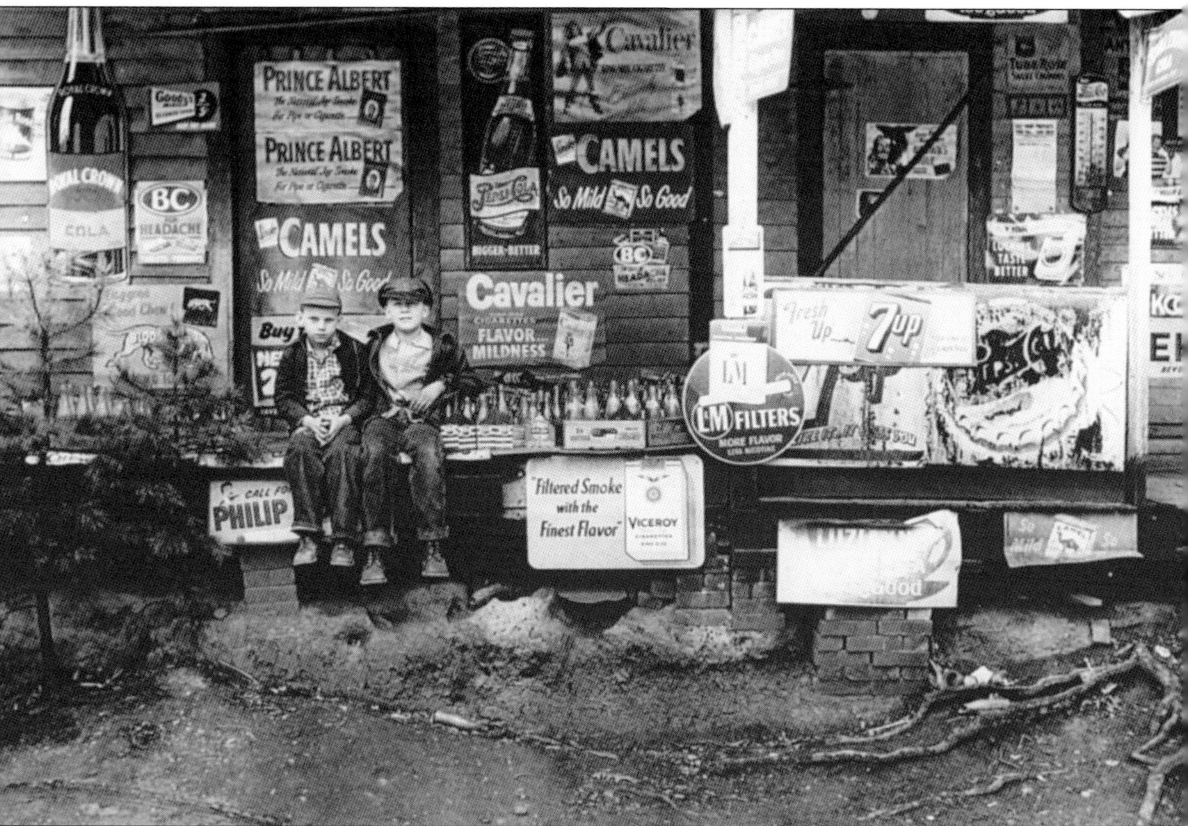

The E.G. Davis Store on Old 421-Yadkinville Highway is still standing, but no longer in use. (FCL.)

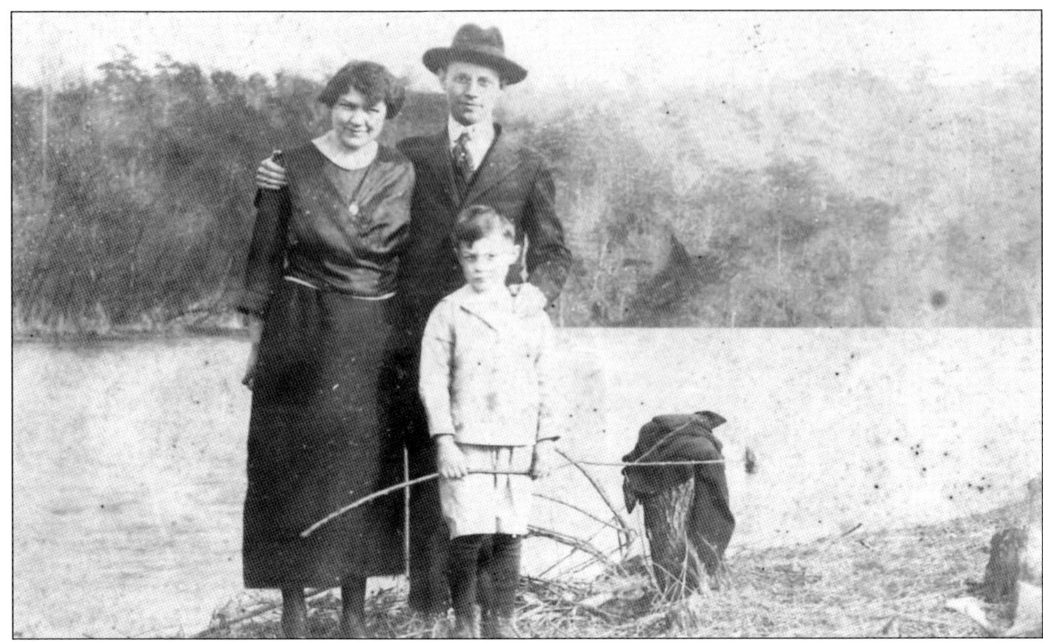

This early 1900s postcard depicts a family outing along the Mayo River two miles south of Avalon, a village that existed on the cartographer's map for approximately ten years. One dismal day in 1911 everything changed, and all that remained in Avalon was the river itself. (Courtesy of the Jeff Bullins Collection, Mayodan, NC.)

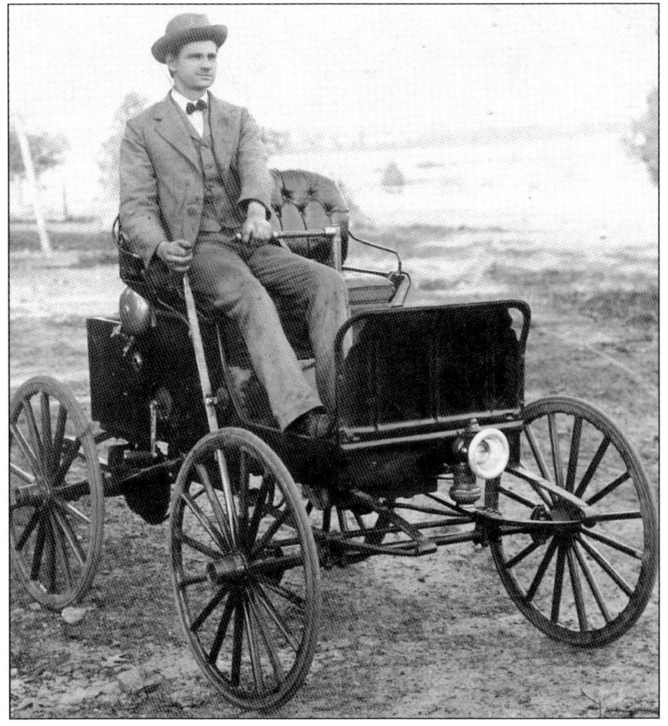

Fletcher Waynick is most recognizable to historians in this portrait. Fletcher, a blacksmith, liked inventions. He put together all the parts of this car—from the commode tank (in the rear) to the kerosene lantern on the front of the carriage. This photograph was taken in 1902, and since Fletcher appears in some postcards, this helps collectors to date their images even when no postmark is clear. (Courtesy of the Jimmy Waynick Collection, Reidsville.)

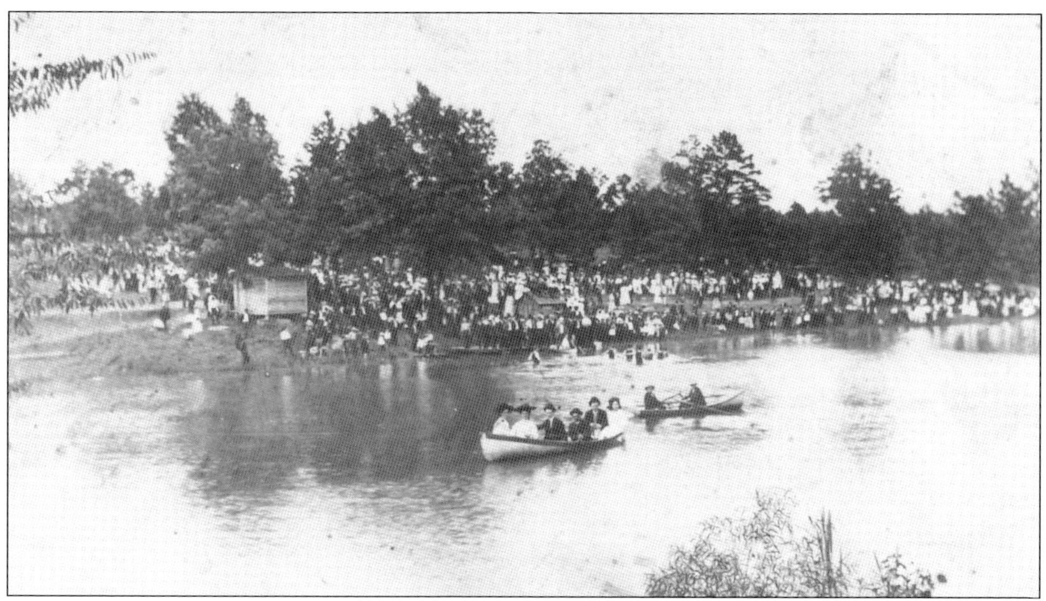

Spray Park (now in the vicinity of Lake Drive and DeHart Ballpark) was the only recreational area in the city at the time this photo was made on July 4, 1908. The park was the site of plenty of baptismal services. "Picture" Price took the picture. (Courtesy of the Roscoe Hankins Collection, Eden, NC.)

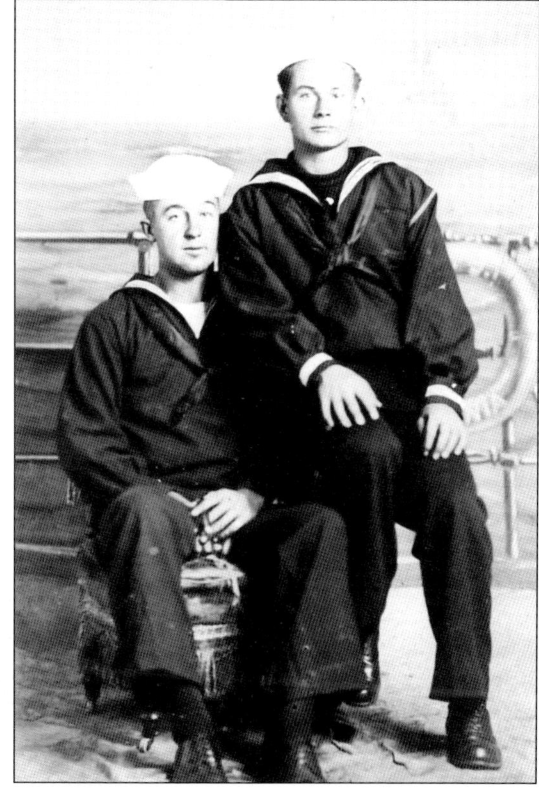

This postcard features World War I sailors Charles Clark (left) and his friend, Dan Aheron. They served on the *USS Mississippi*. Bertha Aheron used this postcard by Price to announce her husband's safe return from overseas. (Courtesy of Bertha Vestal Aheron and the Aheron family, Eden, NC.)

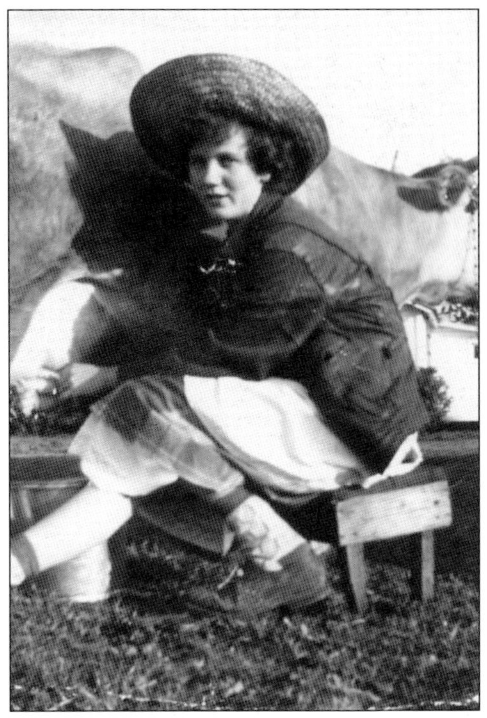

Milking was a common chore on farms throughout the region well into the mid-20th century. Shirley Strickland of Erwin is shown here milking the cow on her family's farm in 1950.

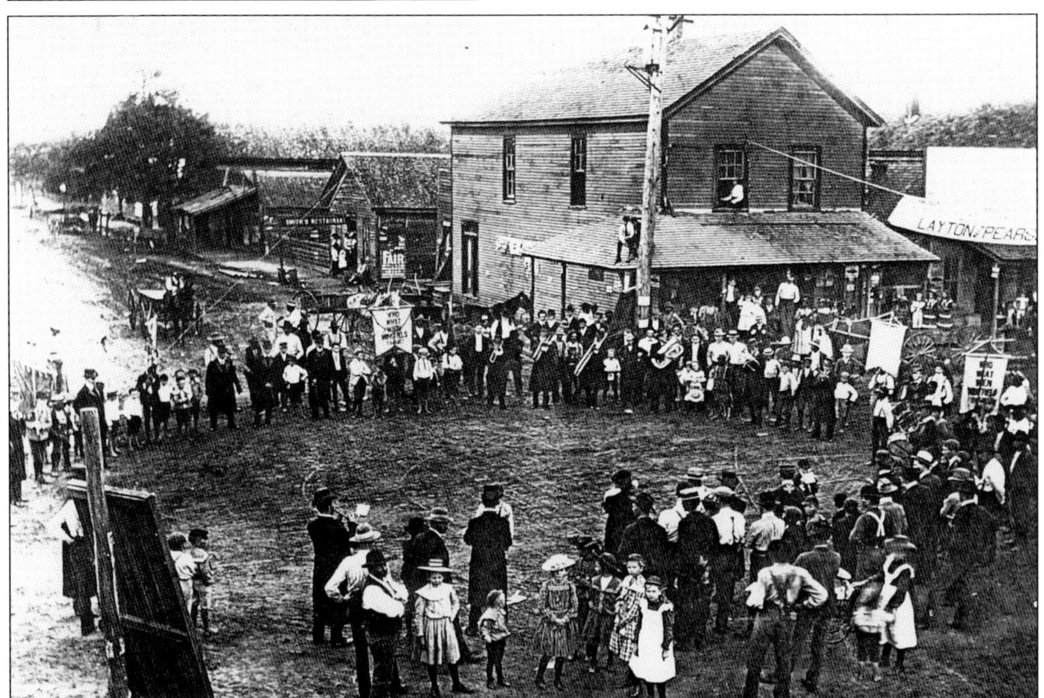

This crowd gathered *c.* 1895 at the corner of Wilson Avenue and Broad Street to enjoy the sounds of the *Who, What, When Minstrels*.

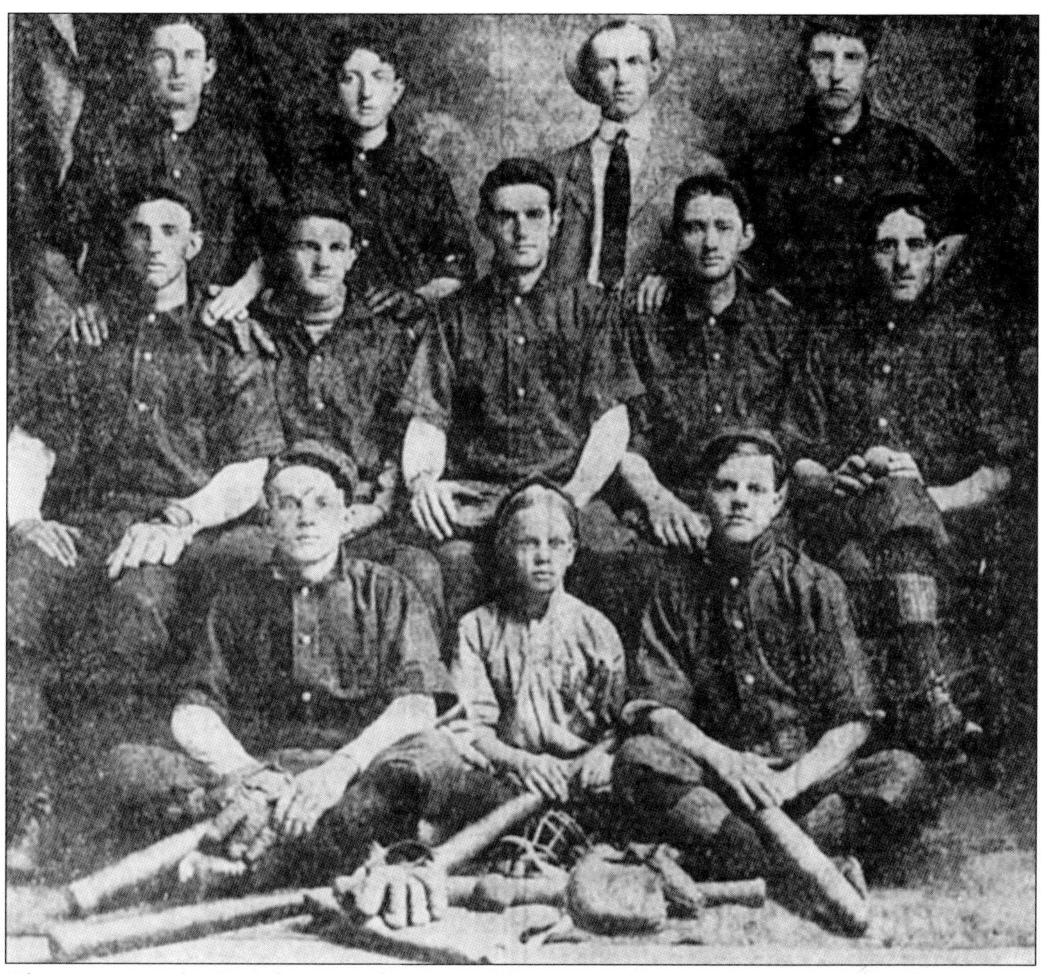

The team members of the Waughtown Wildcats of 1907, from left to right, are as follows: (front row) Sid Teague, shortstop; Bernie Teague, bat boy; and Bill Vogler, right field; (middle row) Fate McGee, third baseman; Carl Nissen, pitcher; Hank Nissen, catcher; Tip Crowder, first baseman; and Harvey Cook, utility man; (back row) John Brown, center field; Jim Cofer, second baseman; K.E. (Ned) Shore, utility man; and Charlie Elliott, left field.

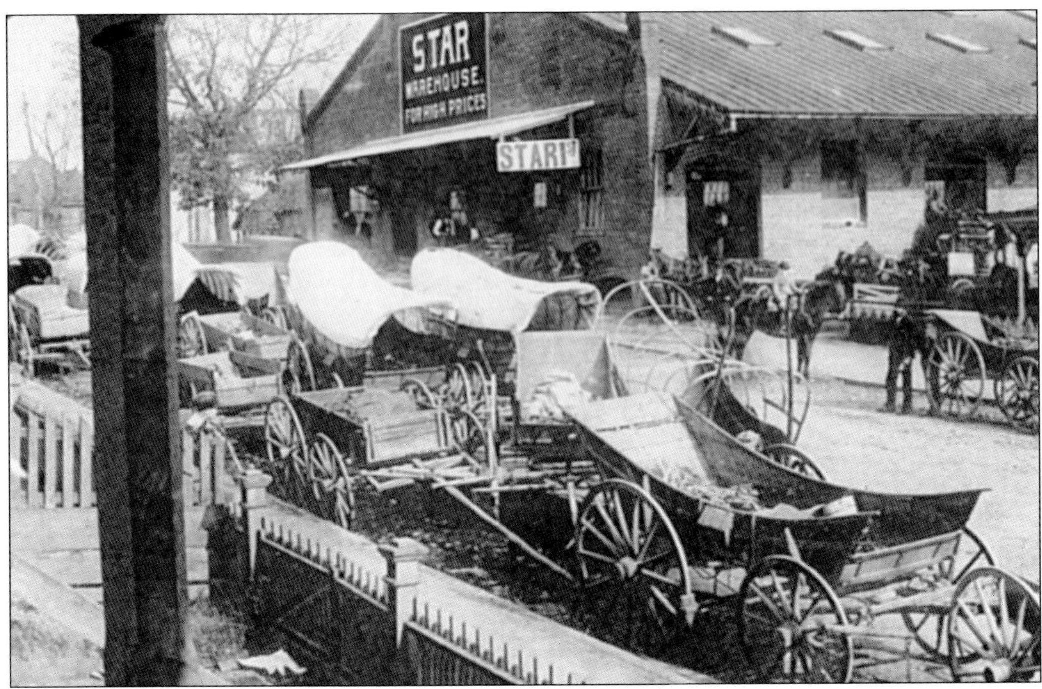

Star Tobacco Warehouse, located at 541–545 Main-Street in Winston-Salem. (FCL.)

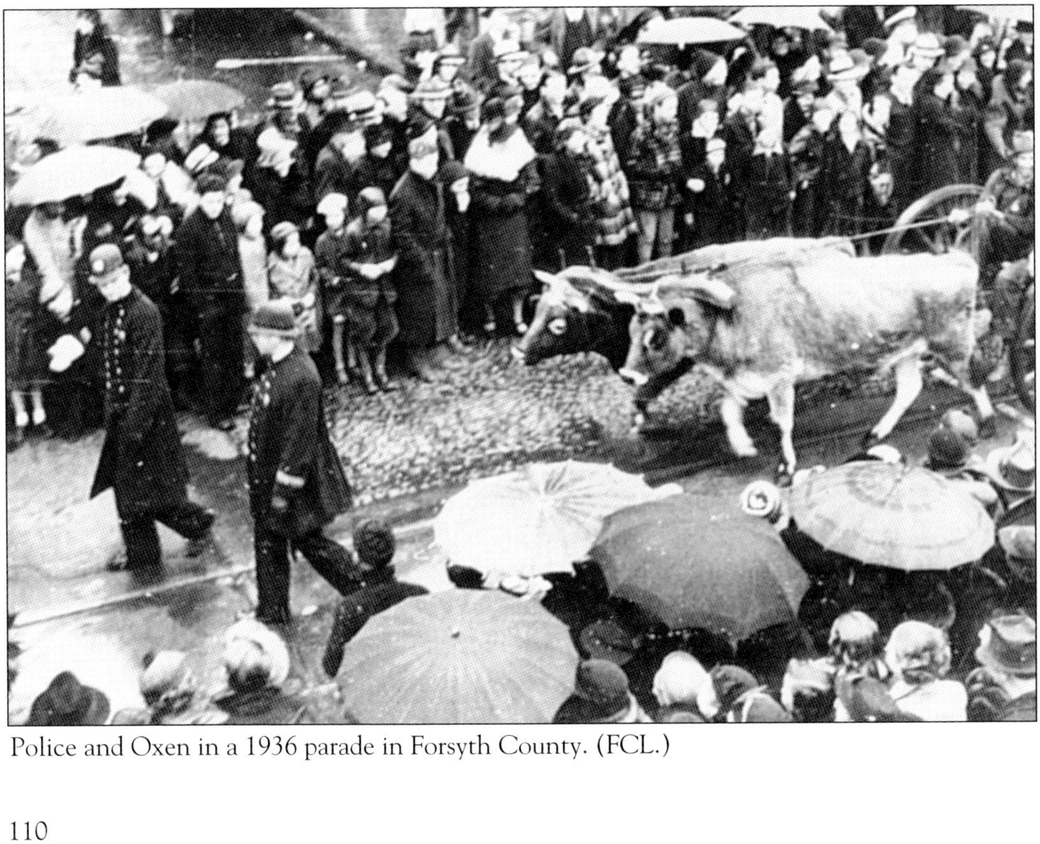

Police and Oxen in a 1936 parade in Forsyth County. (FCL.)

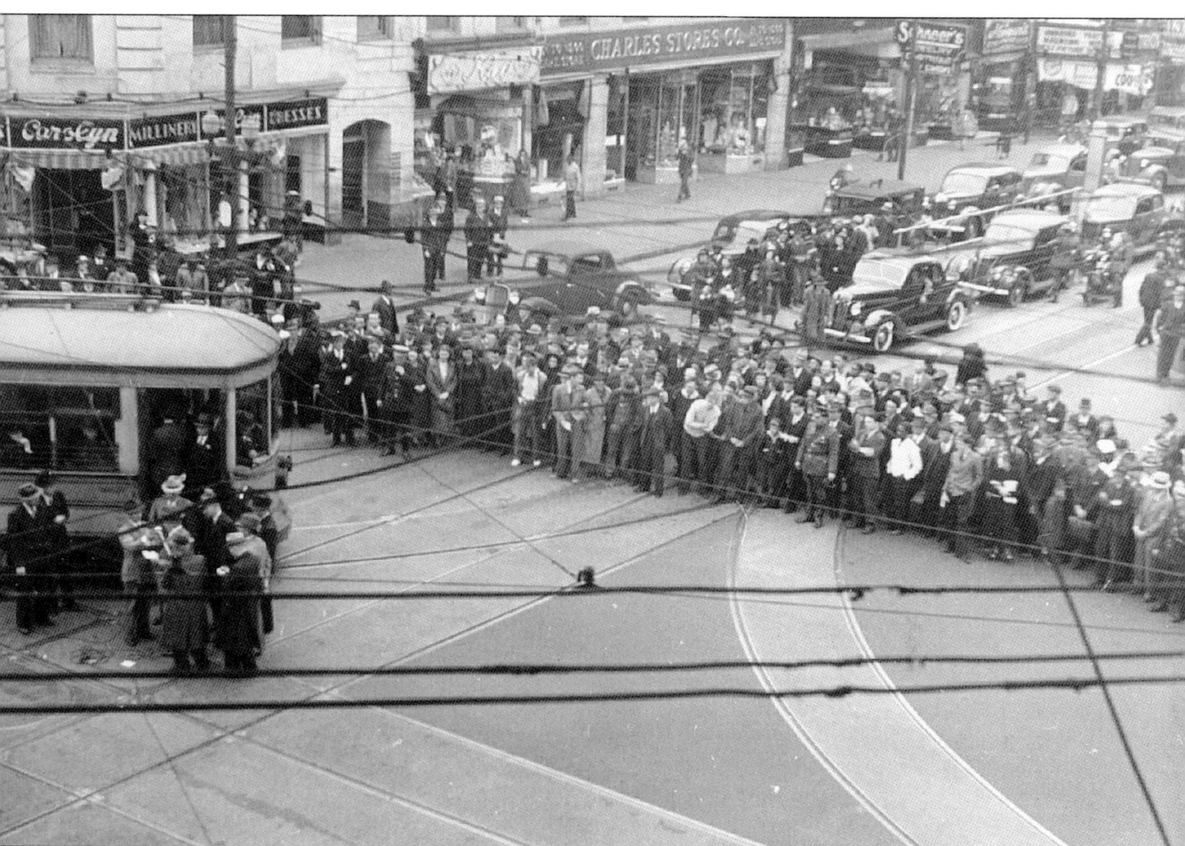

Charlotte's last trolley ran on March 14, 1938. During the 1930s, the Duke Power Company had successfully petitioned the State Utilities Commission and the Charlotte City Council to allow the replacement of the city's street railroads with a bus system that would be phased in throughout town. This memorable image shows the crowd of citizens and dignitaries that turned out to meet the last trolley at the Square. For more than four decades, the trolley was a part of daily life in Charlotte. The farewell event marked the end of an era, and a shift in the character of the city. (Robinson-Spangler Carolina Room, Public Library of Charlotte and Mecklenburg County.)

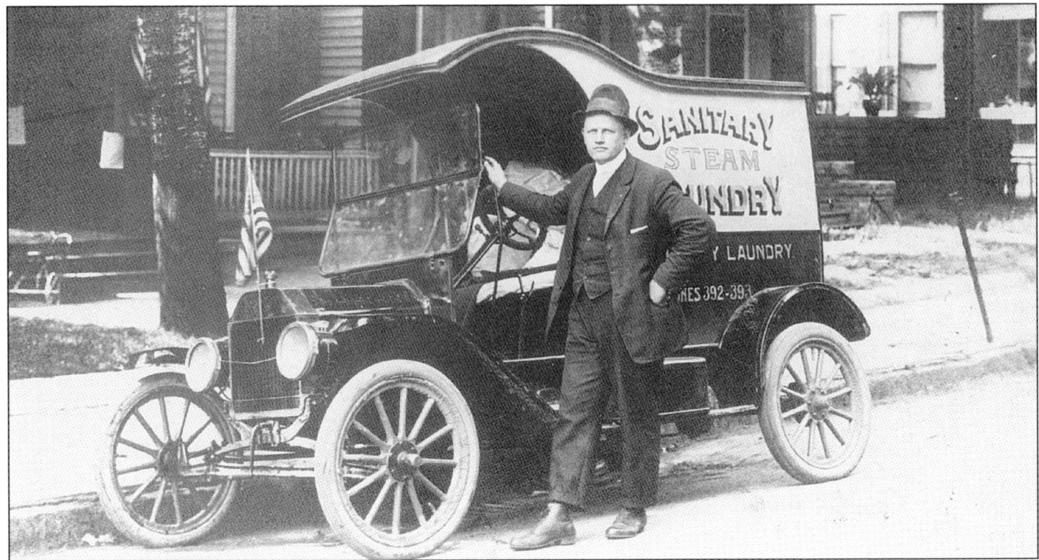

What a luxury it was to have laundry pick-up and delivery! Roland S. Ferguson, shown here around 1920, operated the Sanitary Steam Laundry, which is believed to have been located on North Cecil Street near the Elizabeth neighborhood. The prosperous business boasted two telephone numbers. (Robinson-Spangler Carolina Room, Public Library of Charlotte and Mecklenburg County.)

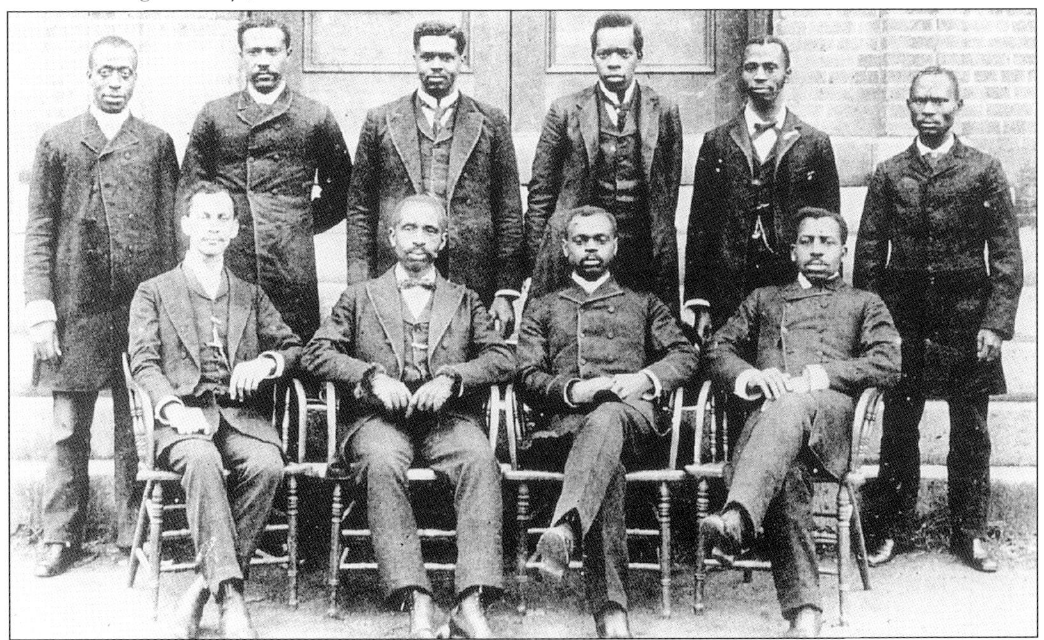

These gentlemen, gathered on the steps of Biddle Hall, are the students and graduates of the class of 1892. They attended the theological program at Biddle Institute. Today, the school is known as Johnson C. Smith University. (Robinson-Spangler Carolina Room, Public Library of Charlotte and Mecklenburg County.)

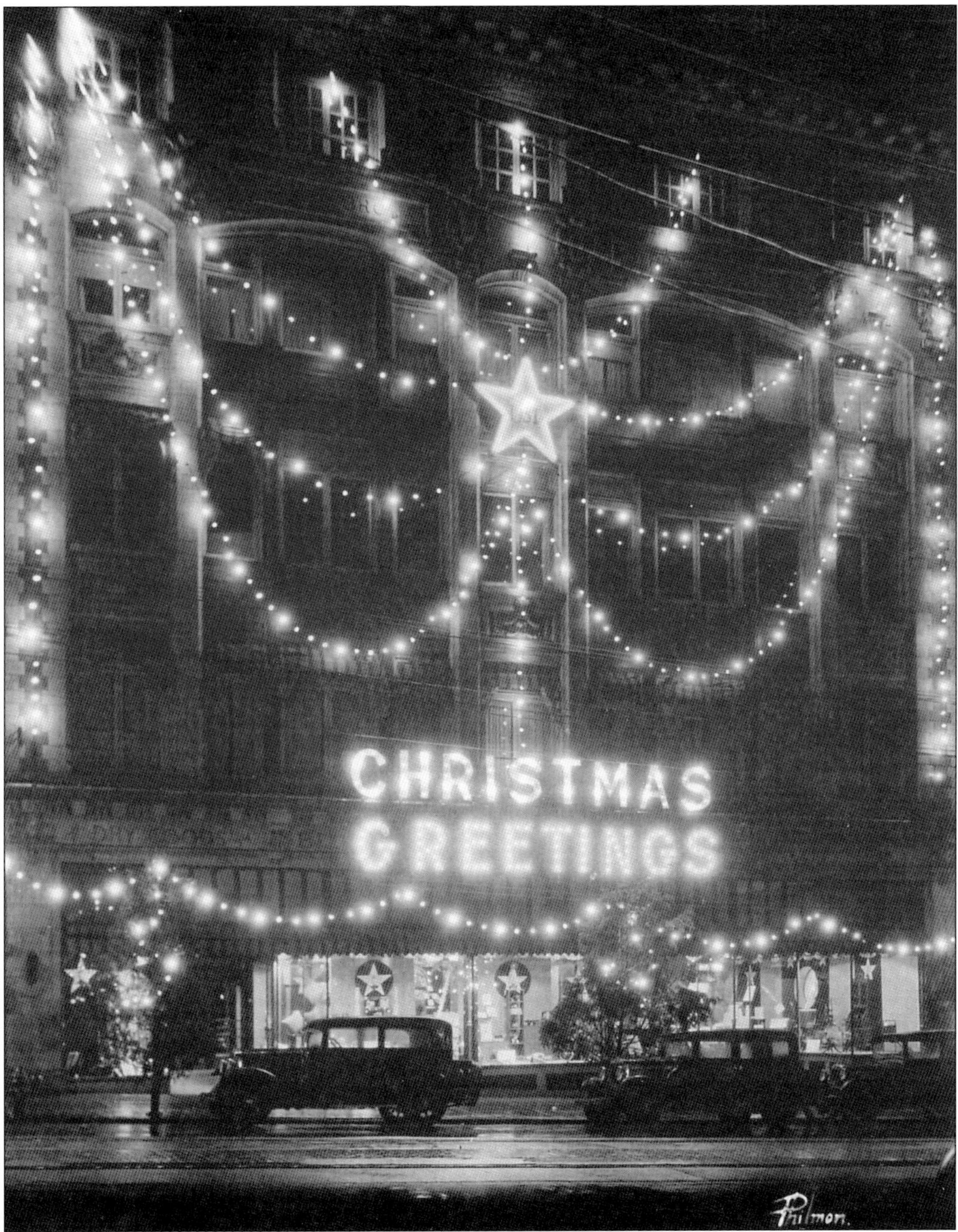

In its heyday as Charlotte's business and retail center, Tryon Street was decked out for the holidays. "Christmas Greetings" flashed the festooned lights of this Belk Brothers department store display that also brightly proclaimed the year—1931—in a star at the center. (Duke Power Archives.)

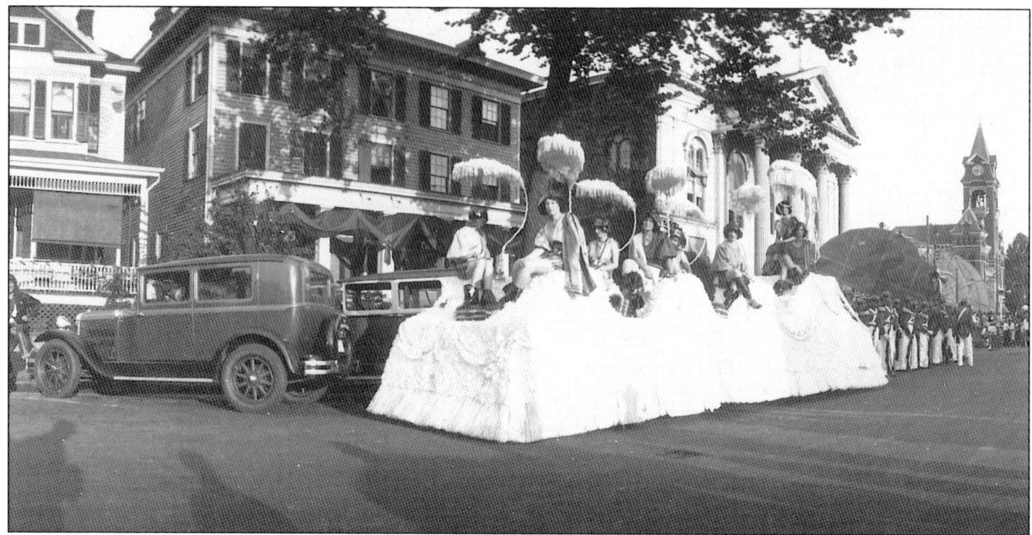

Houses just north of the city hall formed a no-nonsense background to this 1928 photograph of the Feast of Pirates parade, taken by Louis T. Moore. On the left, a Buccaneer lurks in front of the residence of J.J. Joyner. The house on the right served as headquarters for the North Carolina Sorosis. (New Hanover County Public Library.)

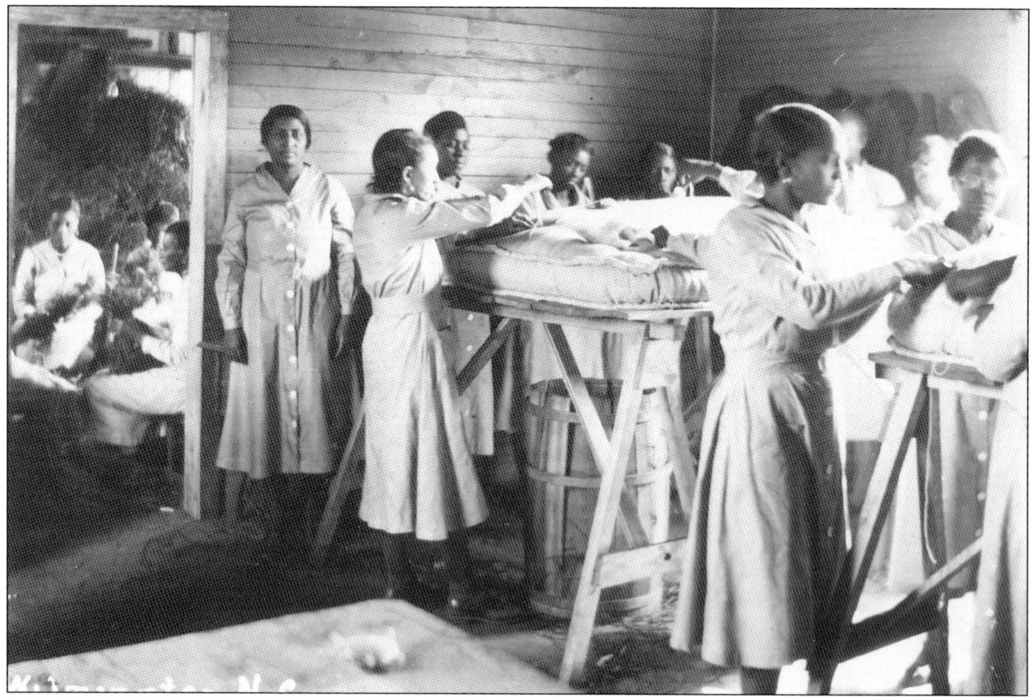

During the 1930s, the Emergency Relief Administration operated a mattress factory in Levi McKoy Moseley's building at 615 Nixon Street. Sixteen women—including Mr. Moseley's daughter Margaret Williams—assembled mattresses for the needy. Levi Moseley's sister, Augusta Moseley Cooper, was a noted Wilmington leader and historic preservationist. (IA2988.)

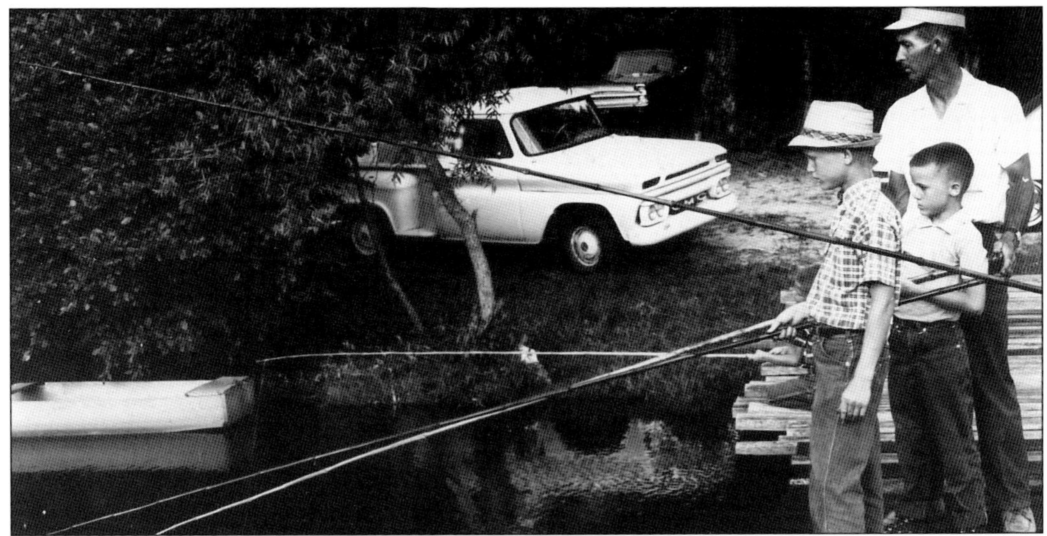

Next to baseball, hunting and fishing were the most popular sports. Fishing occurred at the many creeks that flowed into the Tar River. The usual catch was perch, shad rock, or an occasional catfish. (BBH.)

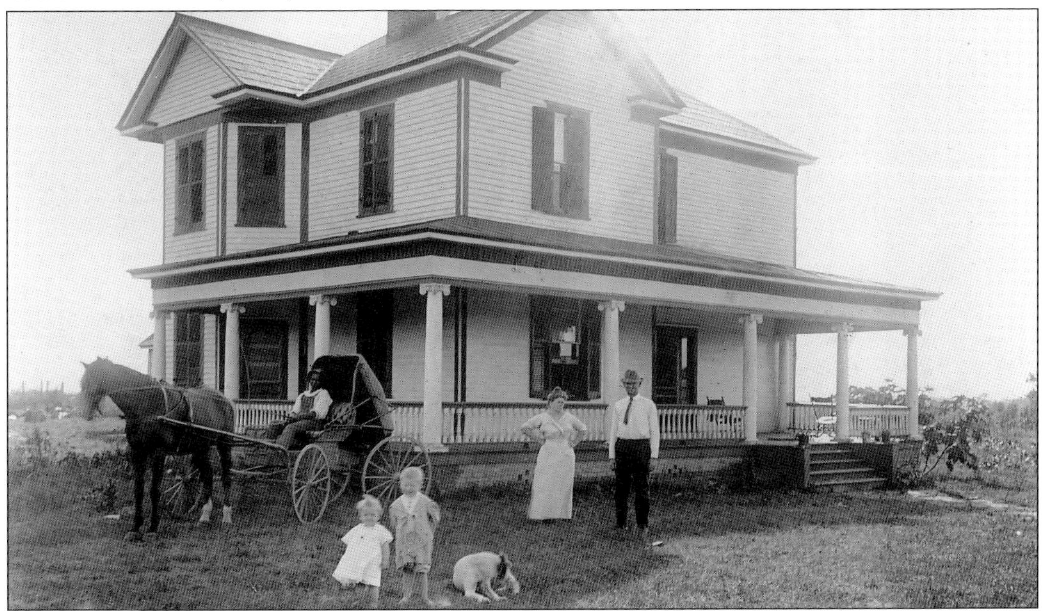

Around 1910, John Robert Pitt Sr. and his family were living in this farmhouse in the Davistown community near Wiggins Crossroads. Along with Pitt are his wife Elizabeth Wiggins, son John Robert Jr., and daughter Elizabeth Wiggins. The little boy on the carriage was not identified. Carriages were used to take the families to town once a month. Davistown boasted one of the three new post offices located along the new East Carolina Railway. The Pitts could travel to the county seat of Tarboro about ten miles away, or to the new community of Pinetops, about five miles to the south. A shopping trip to Tarboro and back would take the better part of the day. (PC-Dew.)

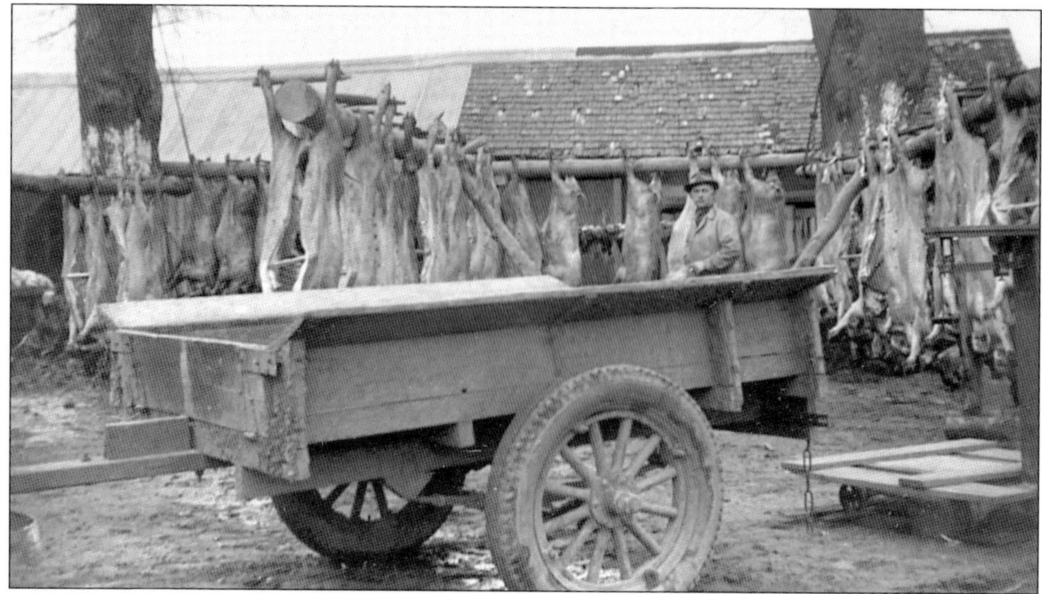

An Old-Fashioned Hog Killing in Martin County, *c.* 1940s. In the days before refrigeration was the norm, hog killings were often social events in farming communities. Families would assist each other in the butchering and preparation of meat for curing and storage in the smokehouse (Courtesy of the Francis Manning Room.)

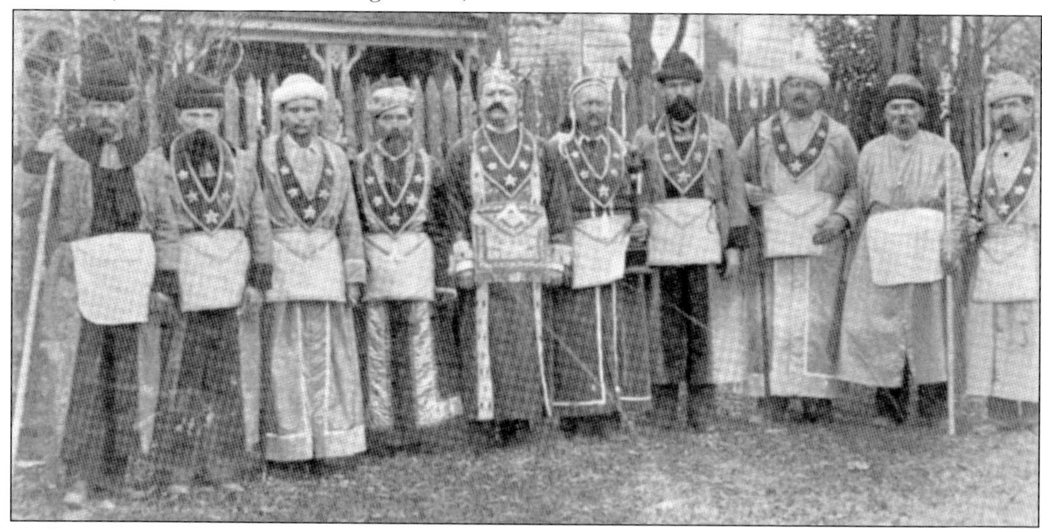

Williamston Masons, *c.* 1893 are pictured from left to right (and followed by each individual's professional occupation and position within the Masons) are as follows: Alec H. Smith (lawyer, steward), Samuel R. Biggs (county treasurer, secretary), James A. Teel (register of deeds, senior deacon), John H. Hatton (blacksmith, senior warden), Harry W. Stubbs (state legislator, master), Eli Gurganus (merchant and peanut broker, junior warden), Dr. W.H. Harrell (physician, treasurer), James D. Leggett (merchant and farmer, junior deacon), Richard Clary (police officer, steward), and William H. Bennett (register of deeds, tyler). (Courtesy of the Francis Manning Room.)

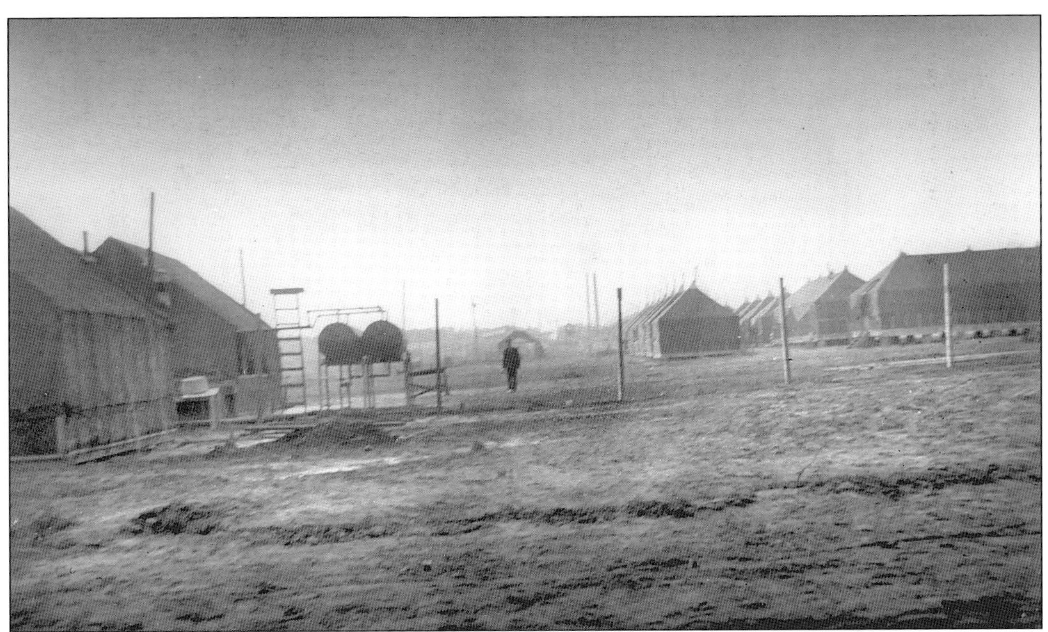

A View of the Williamston Prisoner of War Camp, c. 1944. This temporary stockade held both German and Italian prisoners of war during World War II. Prison labor from the camp was used at the nearby Standard Fertilizer Company and on farms throughout the county. (Courtesy of the Francis Manning Room.)

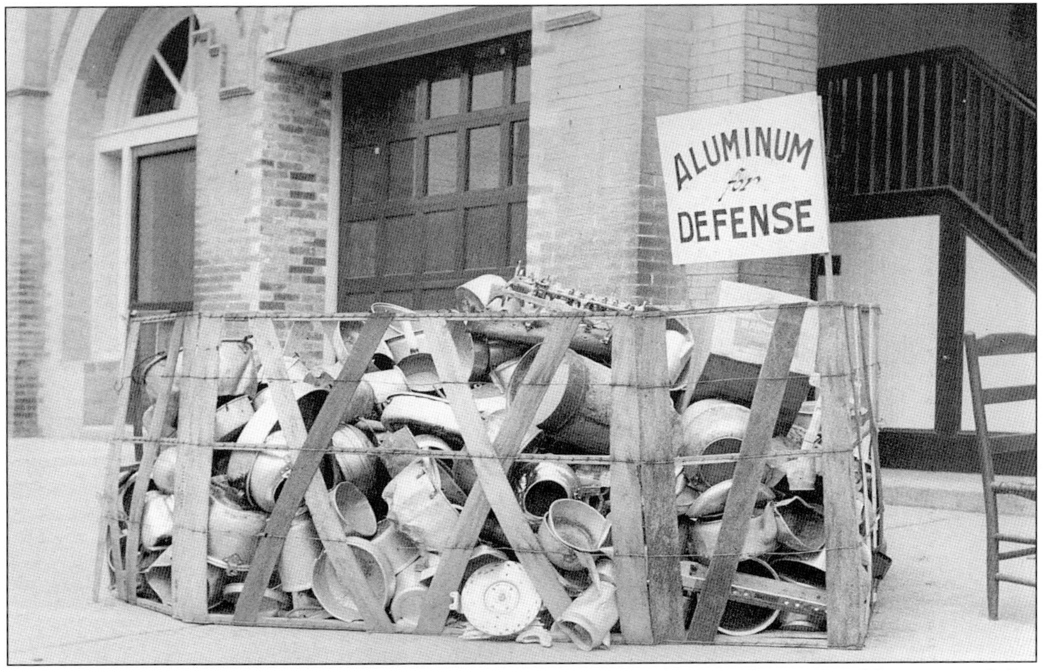

An Aluminum Drive Collection Point in Front of City Hall, c. early 1940s. (Courtesy of the Francis Manning Room.)

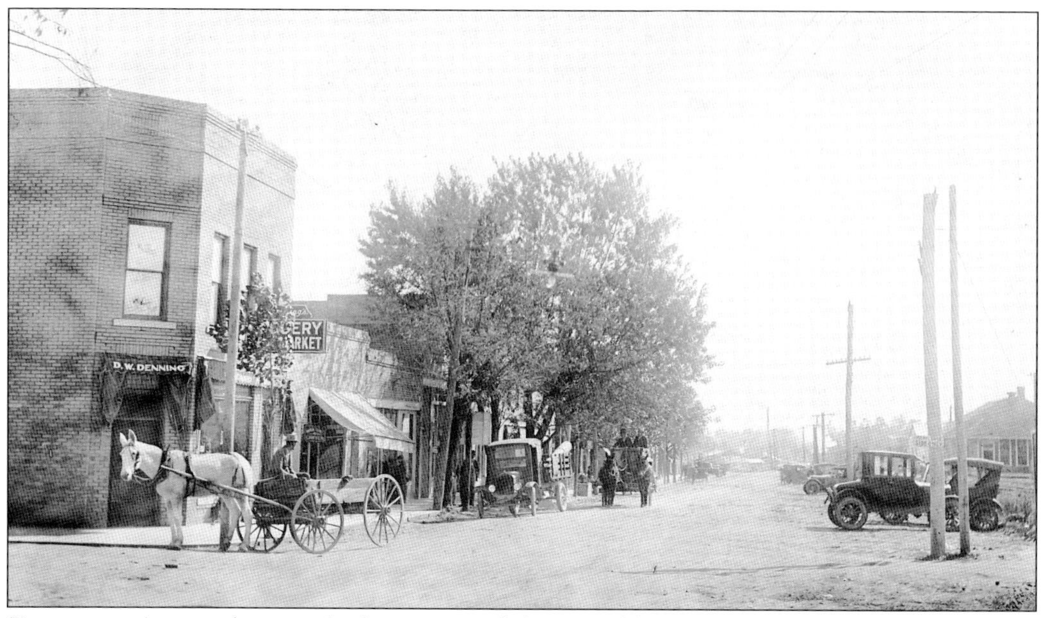

Downtown Angier photographed in 1920 with horse and buggy in the foreground.

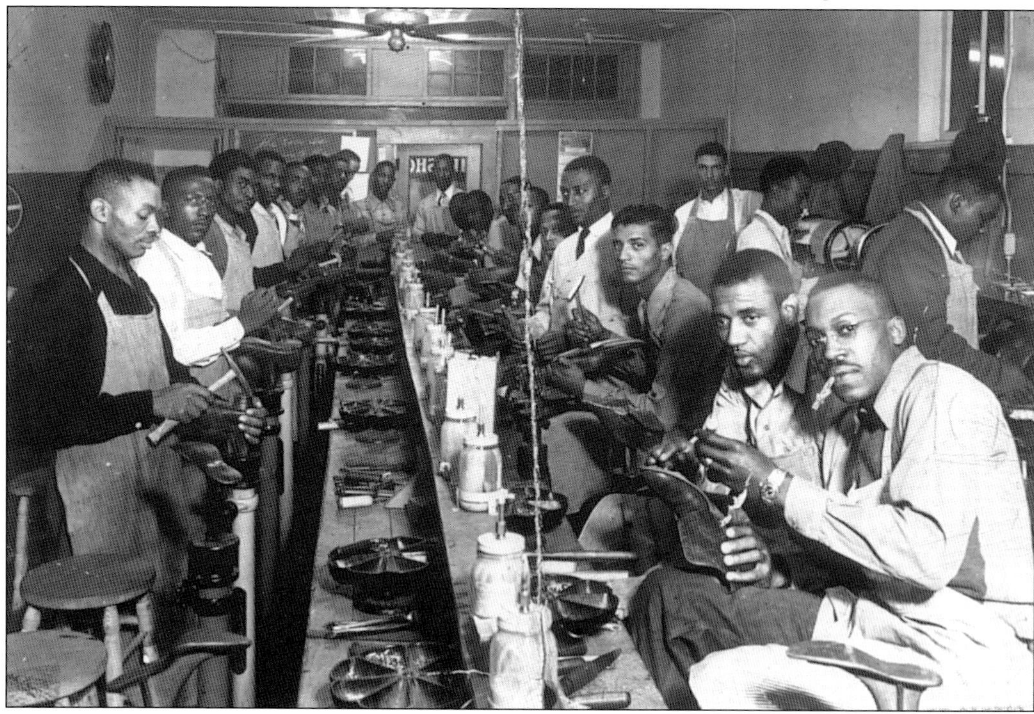

This 1940 photograph shows apprentices working along a workbench equipped with a shoe repair apparatus at Shelly's Modern Shoe Shop and Shoe School, located at 520 Pettigrew Street. The blackboard in the back to the left states, "The race is given to the swift." (Courtesy of Durham County Public Library.)

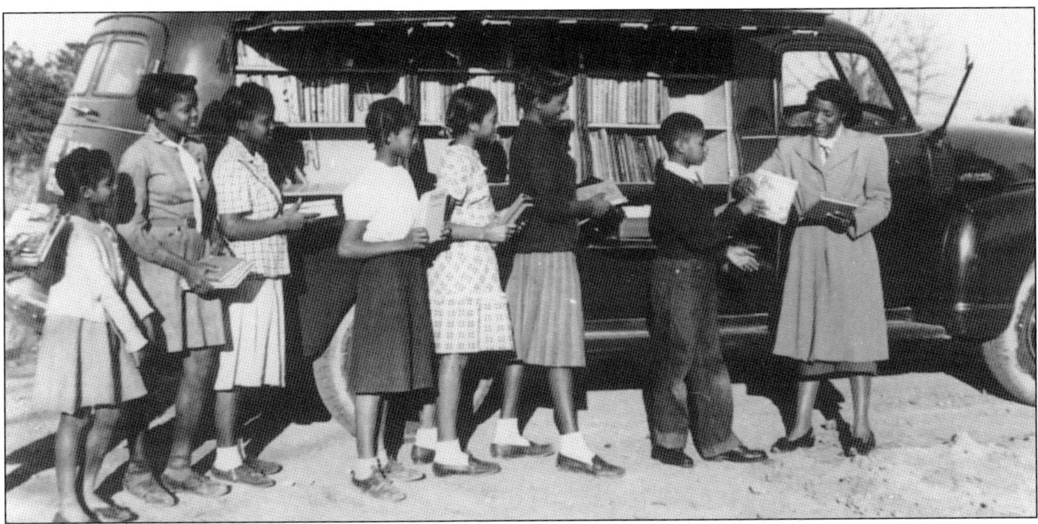

Annie Mae Tucker, circulation librarian at the Stanford L. Warren Library in Durham, is captured in this mid-1940s photograph with a group of patrons choosing books from the Bookmobile on a stop in the Rougemont area. In 1942 the Bookmobile services went to such areas as Union, Lower Fayetteville Road, Hickstown, Rocky Knoll, Bragtown, Rougemont, South Lowell, and Barbee's Chapel. (Courtesy of Dr. Beverly W. Jones.)

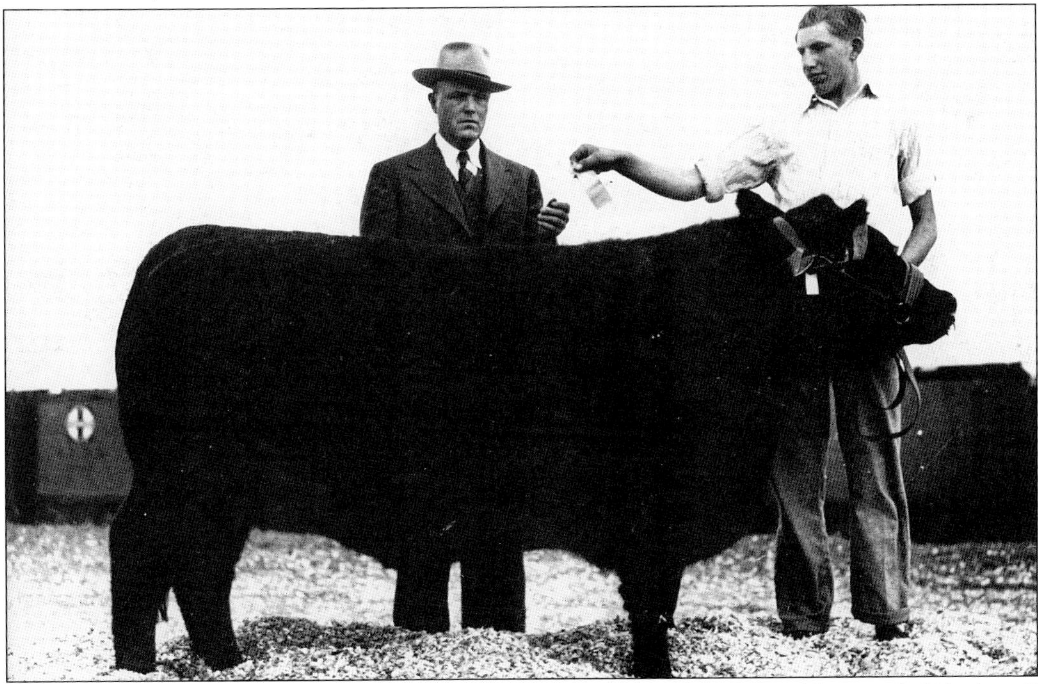

Pictured here is Sullivan Fisher (right) winning the Grand Champion ribbon with "Blackout" at the 4-H Meat Animal Show and Sale in 1943. The show was held at the Eastern Carolina Livestock Arena on Highway 97. Mr. Fisher was known for 50 years as the leading breeder of steers in Nash County. (Courtesy Fisher.)

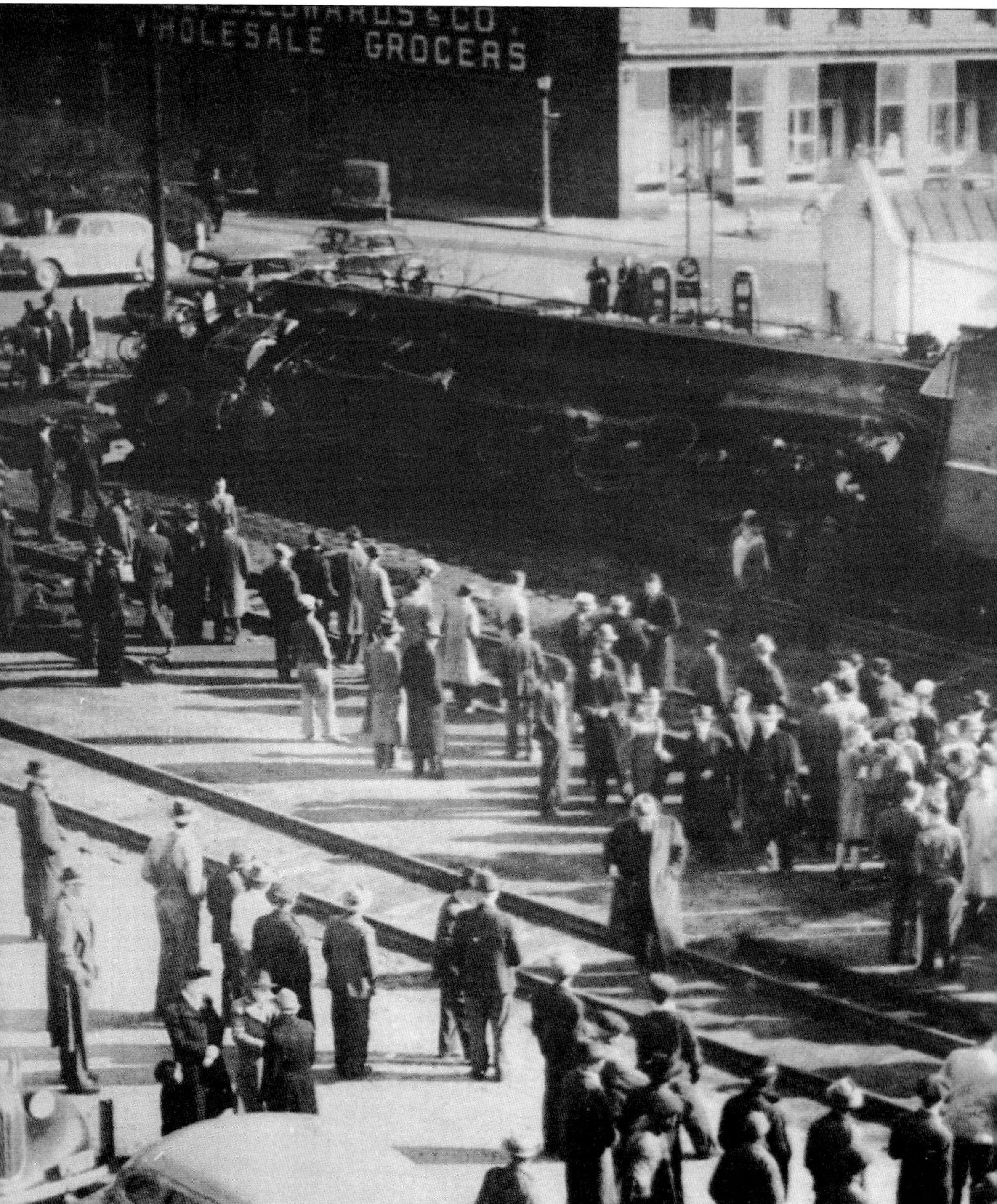

In 1942, this ACL engine derailed on Main Street and attracted sightseeers from many miles

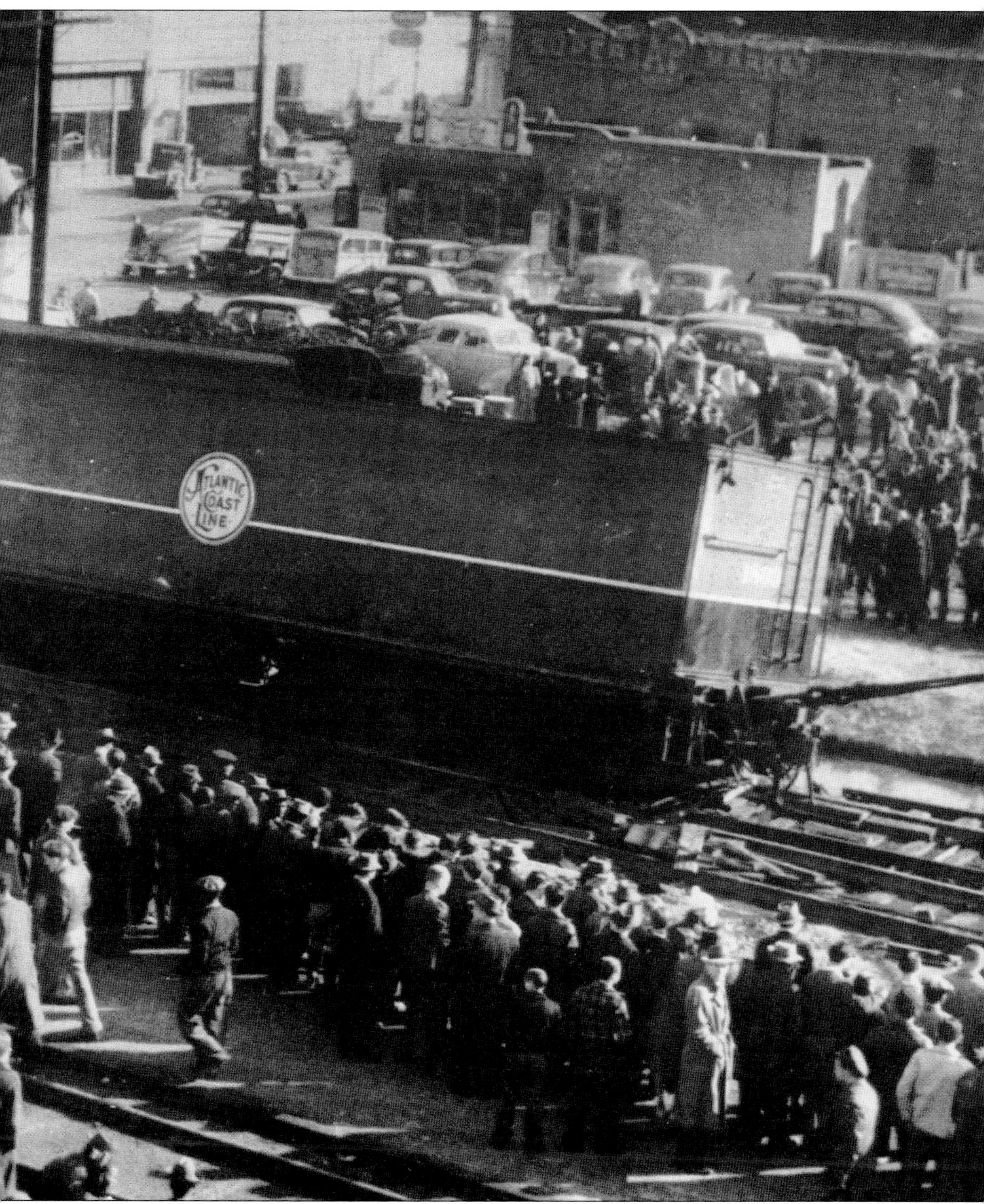

around. (Courtesy Barringer.)

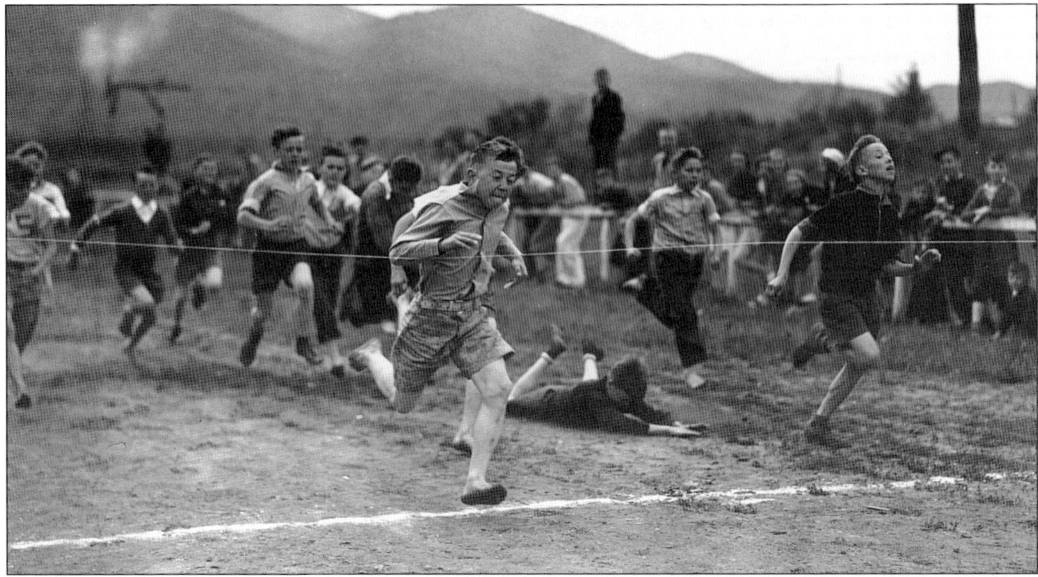

This photograph, taken at the Roanoke County school races in 1937, is one of the earliest existing photojournalistic images by Carol W. Martin. (© Carol W. Martin/Greensboro Historical Museum Collection.)

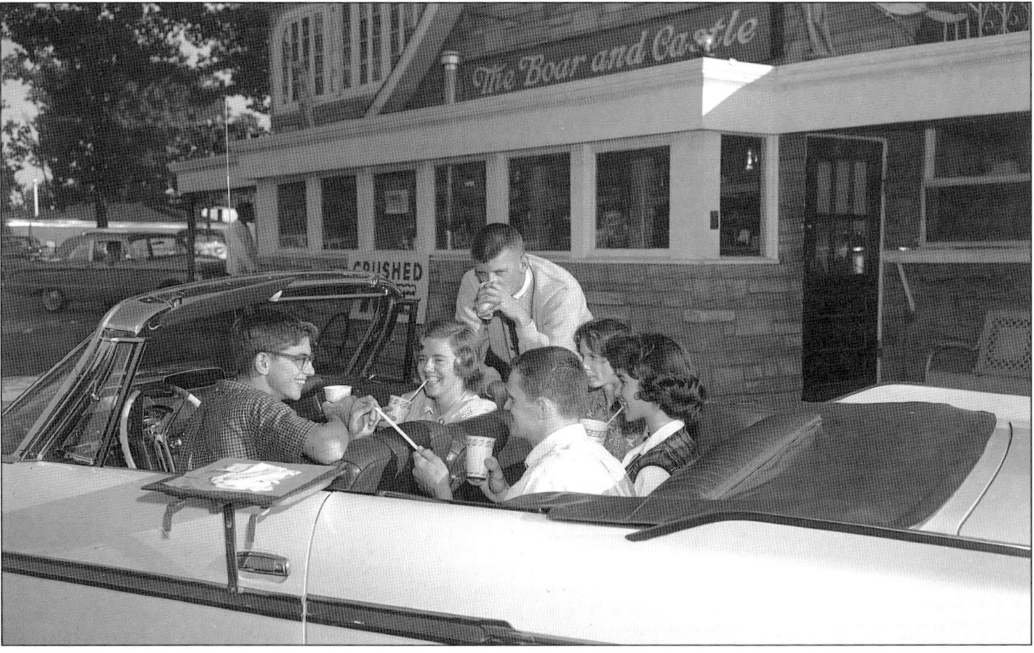

Greensboro (Grimsley) High School students relax at The Boar & Castle on October 6, 1961. The Castle opened on West Market Street in 1937 and soon became a popular eating establishment, especially for young, mobile, "cruising" teenagers and college students. Most people have long forgotten that the Castle, which closed around 1980, was the site of a golf driving range from 1938 to 1942. (© Carol W. Martin/Greensboro Historical Museum Collection.)

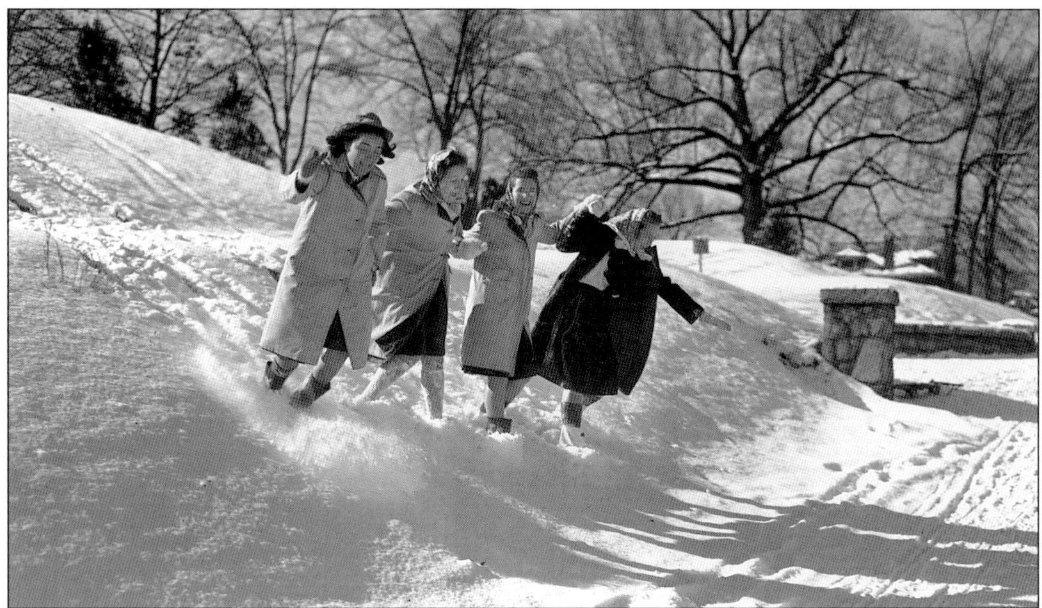

These young women from Greensboro College are finding safety in numbers as they enjoy the snow on the front lawn along West Market Street around 1942. Greensboro College was an all-female college when it was founded by the Methodist Church in 1838 and became co-educational in 1954. (© Carol W. Martin/Greensboro Historical Museum Collection.)

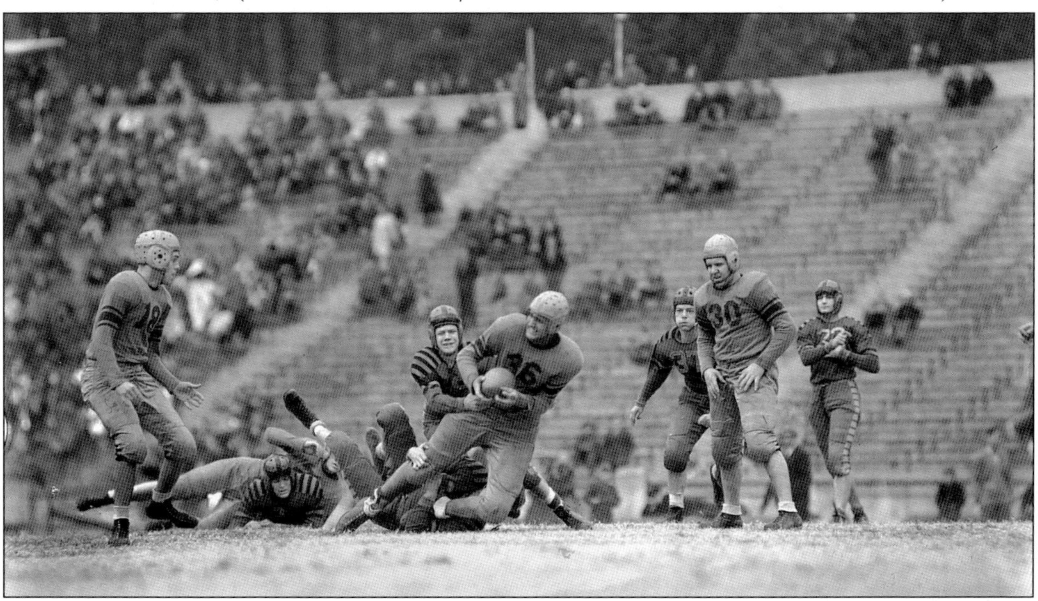

Greensboro (Grimsley) High School (GHS) played Durham to a 6-6 tie in the 1938 state championship game in Chapel Hill. The solid uniforms belonged to GHS, and pictured, from left to right, are #18 Warren Johnson, #36 Herman Smith, and #30 Ray Sawyer. GHS won state championships in 1942 and 1954, tied in 1956, and won its last state crown in 1960. (© Carol W. Martin/Greensboro Historical Museum Collection.)

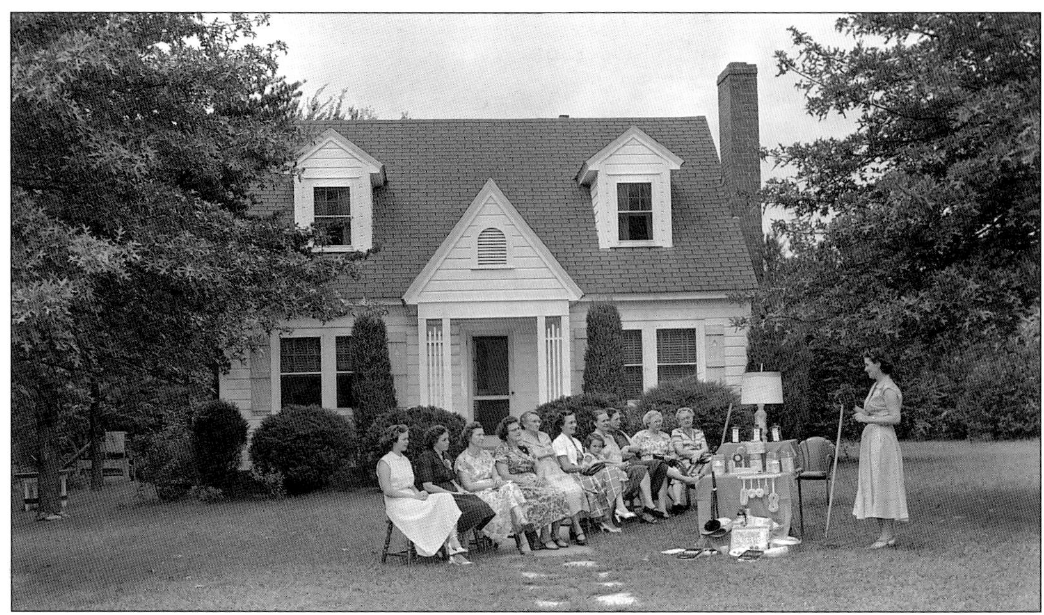

"What Stanley products would you ladies like to buy today?" Selling to housewives at home during the day, in this case at H.S. Covington's on Westridge Road on September 15, 1952, was a common occurrence after World War II and before women began to enter the workplace in greater numbers in the 1960s. Founded in 1931, Stanley Home Products is still in business today as a division of the Fuller Brush Company. (© Carol W. Martin/Greensboro Historical Museum Collection.)

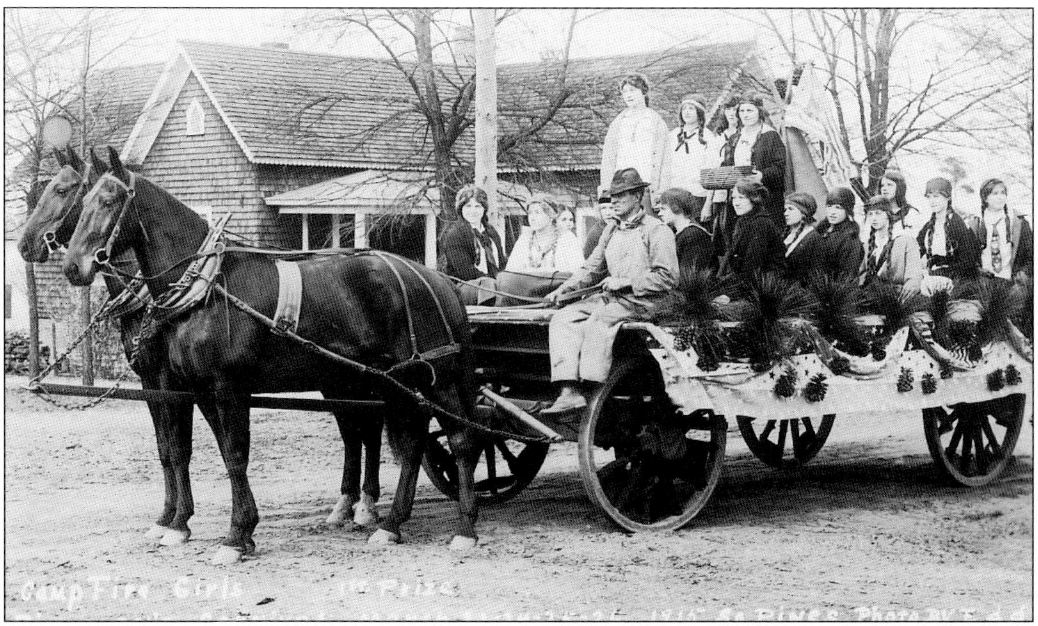

The Firemen's Carnival was an annual four-day event celebrated by residents and tourists alike. Pictured is a crowd of onlookers gathered around a young girl trying to climb the May Pole.

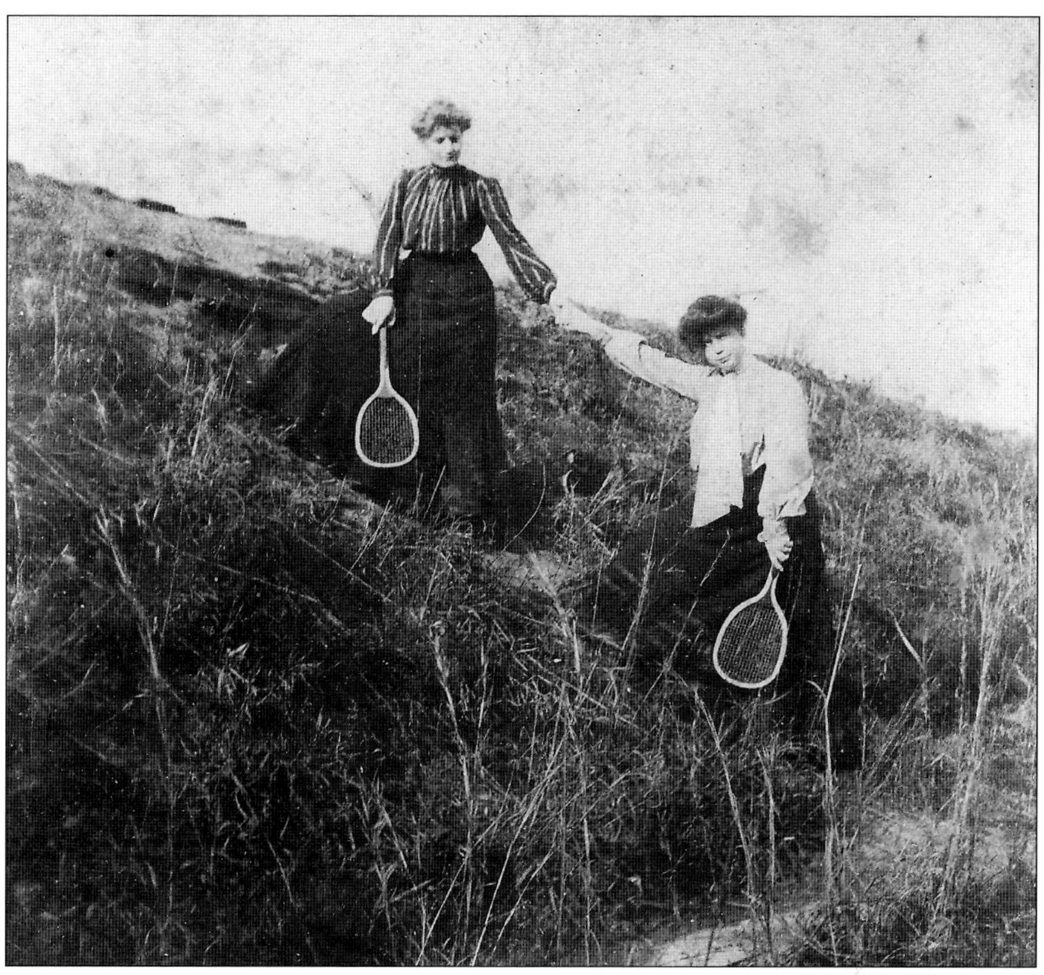

Two young women frolic in the countryside near the Jackson Springs Hotel after a game of tennis. Pictured in the lower right is Ila Blue, of Aberdeen.

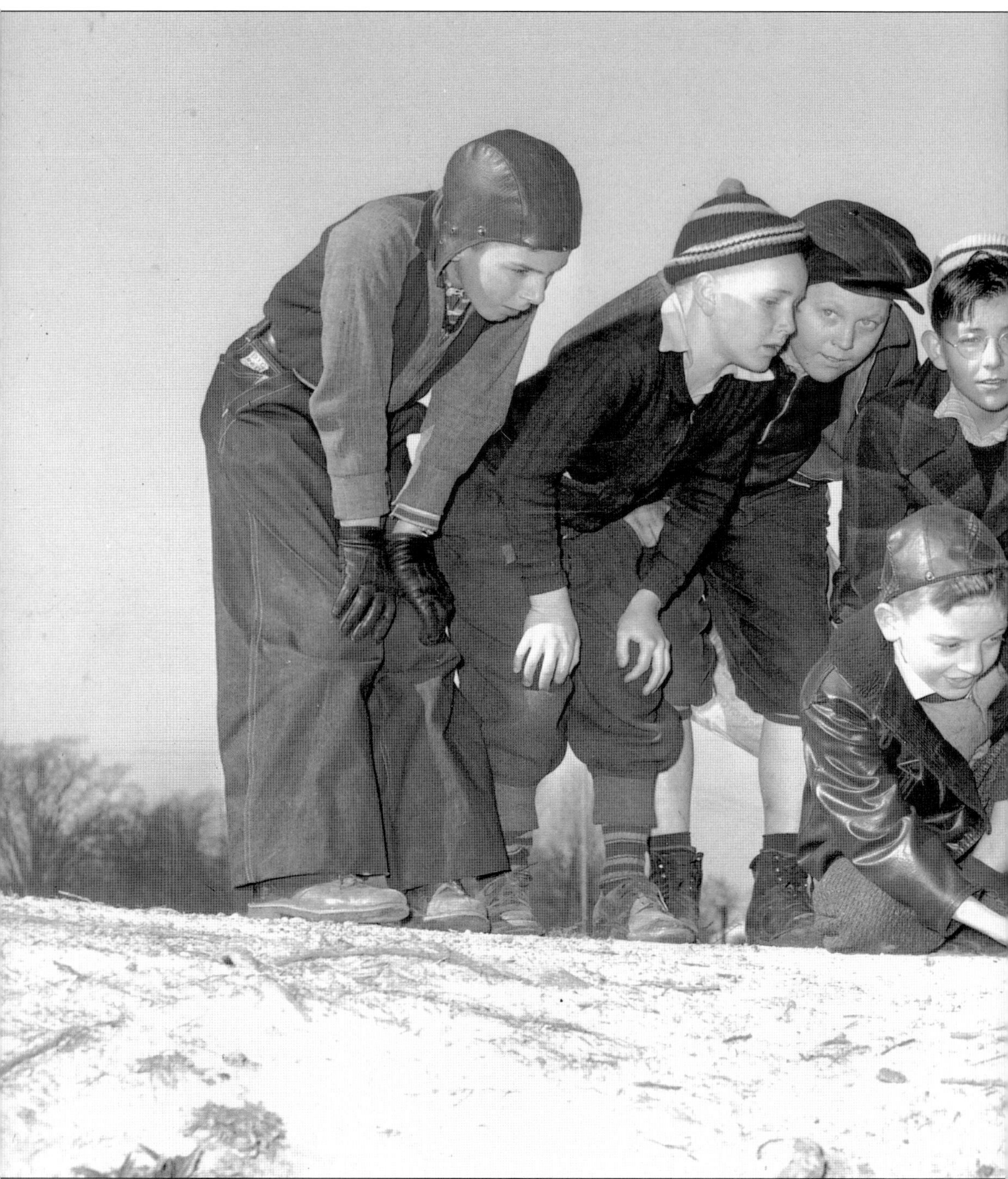

Martin captured these boys "Knuckling Down" in a game of marbles sometime during the 1940s. Unbeknownst to them, they were playing an extremely ancient sport. Terms such as aggie, glassie, mib, and slag are rooted in 16th-century England and more contemporary American

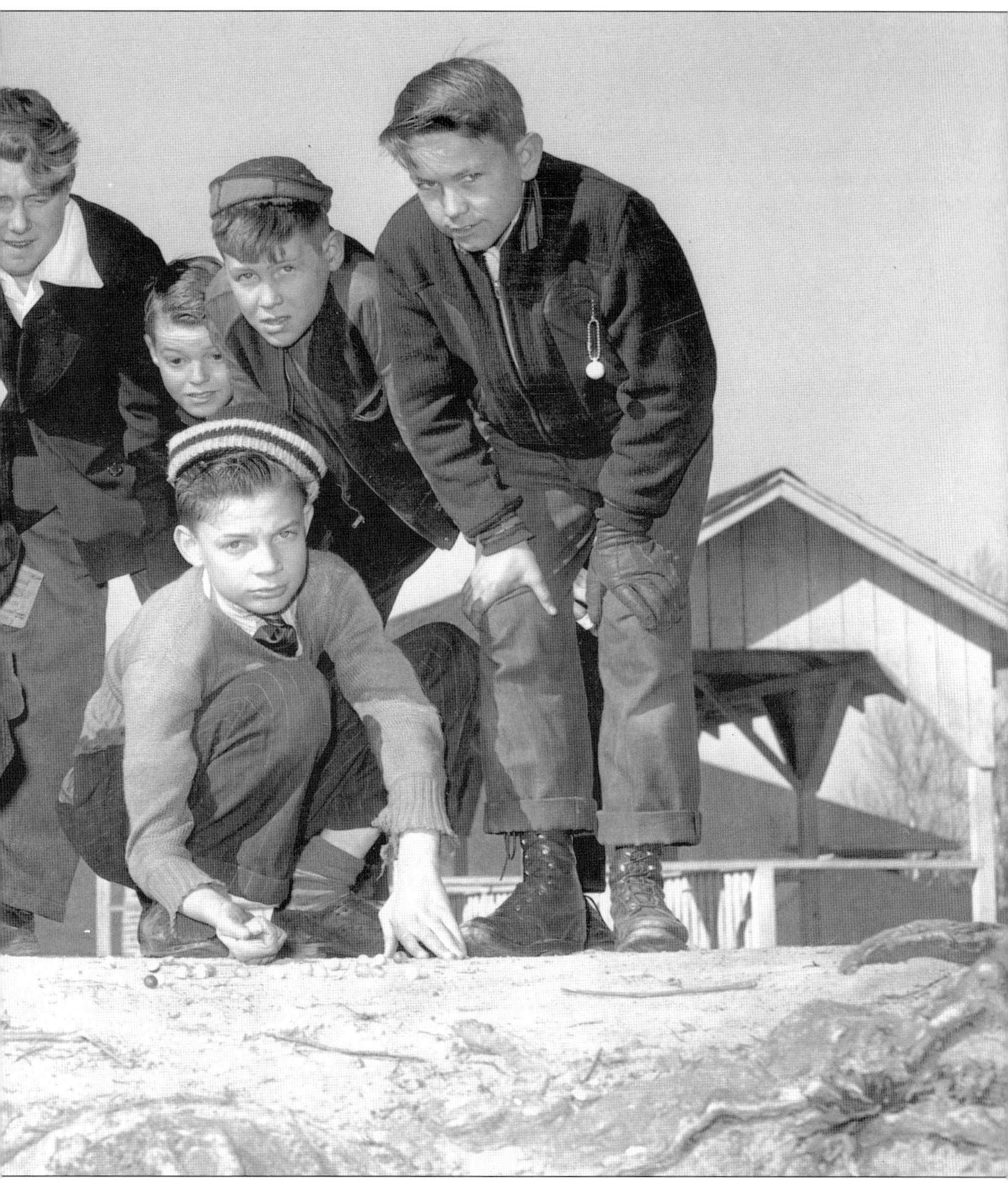

street language. A verse from the 1771 poem "Marbles" suggests that little has changed: "Knuckle down to your taw / Aim well, shoot away / Keeping out of the Ring / You'll soon learn to Play." (© Carol W. Martin/Greensboro Historical Museum Collection.)

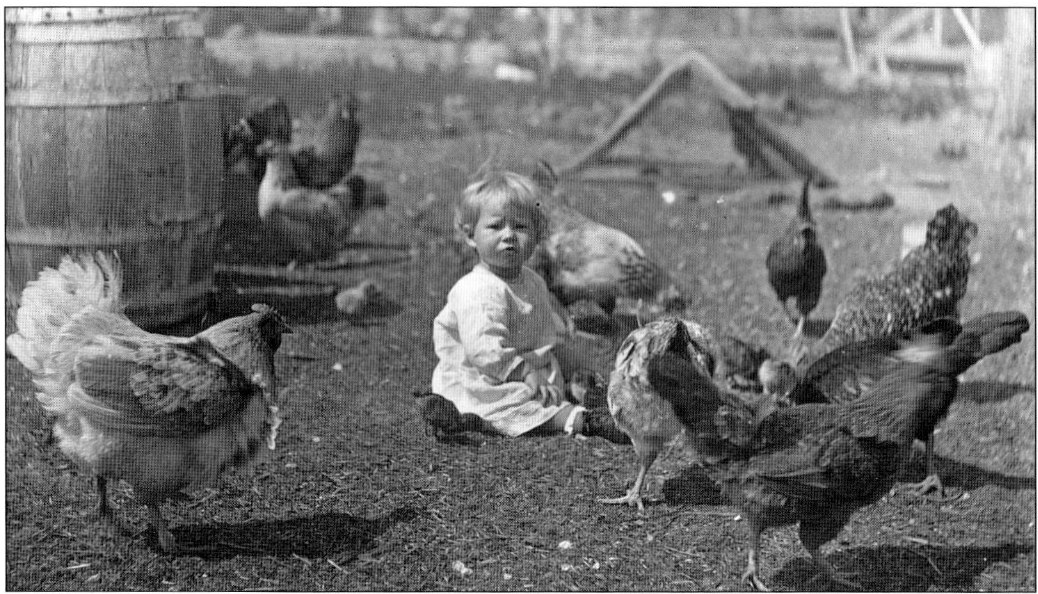

Not too long ago, you did not have to be a farmer to have livestock in your yard. Backyard chicken coops provided many a Wilmingtonian with fresh eggs and Sunday dinner roasters. In this 1912 scene, Jane MacMillan sits with feathered friends at the corner of Wrightsville and MacMillan Avenues in Winter Park.

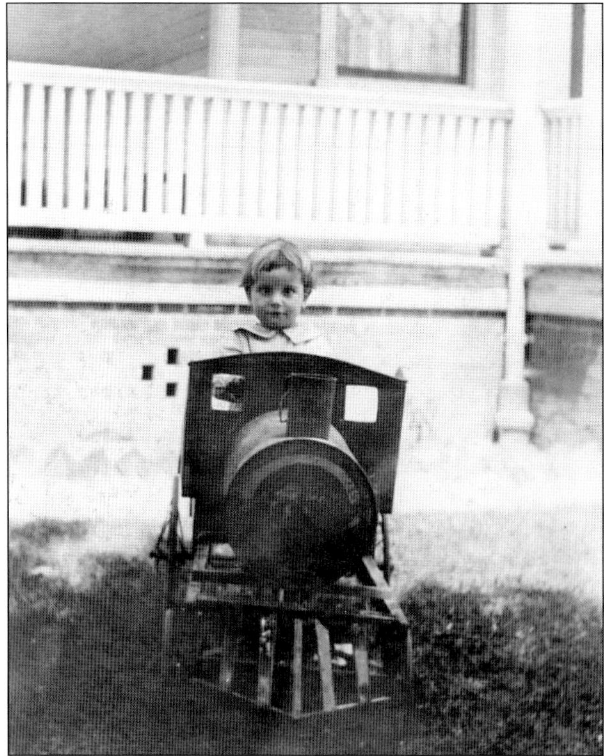

The creativity and ingenuity of an unidentified toy maker are captured in this photograph of a miniature locomotive of the 1910s. The child is also unidentified, but is thought to have been photographed in the vicinity of South Third and Woodall Streets in Smithfield. (Courtesy of Gordon Hudson.)